The LIFE

of a

NEW JERSEY

ROAD TROOPER

Sal Maggio

SUNBURY
PRESS®

Mechanicsburg, PA USA

Published by Sunbury Press, Inc.
Mechanicsburg, Pennsylvania

SUNBURY
P R E S S ®
www.sunburypress.com

Copyright © 2023 by Sal Maggio.
Cover Copyright © 2023 by Sunbury Press, Inc.

For information about special discounts for bulk purchases, please contact Sunbury Press Orders Dept. at (855) 338-8359 or orders@sunburypress.com.

To request one of our authors for speaking engagements or book signings, please contact Sunbury Press Publicity Dept. at publicity@sunburypress.com.

FIRST SUNBURY PRESS EDITION: February 2023

Set in Adobe Garamond | Interior design by Crystal Devine | Cover by Lawrence Knorr | Edited by Lawrence Knorr.

Publisher's Cataloging-in-Publication Data
Names: Maggio, Sal, author.
Title: The life of a New Jersey Road Trooper / Sal Maggio.
Description: First trade paperback edition. | Mechanicsburg, PA : Sunbury Press, 2023.
Summary: The autobiography of New Jersey State Trooper Sal Maggio, who served from 1967 until retirement in 2000.
Identifiers: ISBN : 979-8-88819-059-3 (softcover) | ISBN : 979-8-88819-060-9 (ePub).
Subjects: BIOGRAPHY & AUTOBIOGRAPHY / Law Enforcement | POLITICAL SCIENCE / Law Enforcement | POLITICAL SCIENCE / American Government / State.

Product of the United States of America
0 1 1 2 3 5 8 13 21 34 55

Continue the Enlightenment!

CONTENTS

ACKNOWLEDGMENTS

I would not be here if it were not for my parents, Michael Maggio and Jennie Maggio. They both immigrated from Italy (Sicily) through Ellis Island in the early part of the 20th century. About half of my uncles and aunts ended up here in the United States and about half immigrated to Canada. My father was very hardworking first working for Botany Mills in Passaic, N. J. for many years. When Botany Mills moved to North Carolina he stayed here in New Jersey working for Nevins Printing Company in Clifton, N. J. My parents taught me and my two sisters right from wrong and to do well in school. When I got my N. J. driver's license I was asked to join a gang at the other end of the block, called "Midnight Auto Sales." They stole cars and sold the parts to mechanics or body shops. I did not join. My friends and I played sports which kept us out of trouble. We played flag football, stickball, baseball, and basketball all year round. Even though my parents are both deceased, I thank them both for bringing me up the right way.

I would also like to thank my high school basketball coach (and English teacher) Mr. Richard Tarrant. He taught us the meaning of discipline on the high school basketball team. I believe he was a Marine before becoming a teacher and coach. We had a great basketball team in my senior year. We ended up with 22 wins and 2 defeats. We lost in overtime to Newark Central in the North Jersey Group 4 finals at Upsala College. Newark Central went on to beat Cherry Hill High School by 20 points in Atlantic City, N. J. to be Group 4 champs. Early in the season Coach, Tarrant used to bring his young son to practice if we practiced on a Saturday morning. He was about 4 or 5 years old. When I was a seasoned trooper in the late 1970's I stopped a car with Virginia license plates for speeding on I-78 Eastbound in Hunterdon County. The driver gave me his license and his name was Richard Tarrant Jr. (He looked like his Dad). I asked him if he remembered me from the Saturday morning basketball practices at Passaic High School. He just smiled. I told him to say hello to his Dad for me. What are the odds of that stop? I don't know, maybe 1000 to 1. Coach Tarrant went on to coach Richmond University and one year ended up in the final 4 NCAA College basketball tournament.

I would also like to thank my lovely wife Susan Maggio. When she found out I was thinking of writing an autobiography on my life within the NJ State Police, she encouraged me to do it. Thank you, Susan.

In the NJ State Police, I worked for some excellent supervisors as well as some poor supervisors as in any government organization or even a private company.

I would first like to thank (retired) Lieutenant Colonel (LTC) Lanny Roberson who helped me through the years. I first met Lanny Roberson on the phone when he was a Captain in charge of Internal Affairs and I was a Lieutenant and Deputy Troop "D" Commander on the NJ Turnpike. We discussed internal investigations in Troop "D." I liked his style compared to the previous Internal Affairs Captain. He would listen to me if I made a suggestion on an investigation. Finally, Captain Roberson was promoted to Major and took over the Field Operations Section which controlled all of the 1800 troopers on the road. When the Troop "B" Commander was being transferred, Major Roberson wanted me to take over that Command, and it was looking like it was not going to happen. Some Division Captain wanted that spot and as you know how Division Headquarters works, usually Division gets its way. But Major Roberson continued to push for me with the Superintendant, COL Carl Williams, and I got the assignment as Troop "B" Commander. Thank you (ret.) LTC Lanny Roberson.

While at Troop "D" Headquarters on the Turnpike, I worked for two different Troop Commanders, Captain Alexander Tezsla and Captain Robert Palentchar. Though I worked for Captain Tezsla the longest I learned a lot from both of them on how to run a Troop Command. (Captain Tezsla retired as a Major). Thank you (ret.) Major Al Tezsla and (ret.) Captain Bob Palentchar.

While on the road during the middle to late 1970's I was stationed at the Washington Station in Troop "B." I rode a lot of midnight shifts with Tpr. Joe Fucci and we became close friends. We still see each other socially when he comes up from down South to see his daughter here in New Jersey. Joe retired in 1998 as one of my Lieutenants and Station Commander of Perryville Station. Thanks (ret.) Lt. Joe Fucci for the good times we had at Washington Station.

After the State Police, I worked as a private detective for a large security firm in Newark, N. J. There is where I met Vincent Guarneri, the firms' bookkeeper. Vincent was very computer-literate and I was not. In the State Police, my secretary did all my typing and I did not know how to "surf the internet." Vincent Guarneri taught me all that I now know about computers and surfing the internet for information. Though Vincent lives in New York City, we still see each other occasionally for lunch. Thank you, Vincent.

Finally last but not least I have to thank (ret.) Detective Lieutenant Frederick Martens, a published author, for pushing me to write this book. As we have lunch and smoke cigars at a cigar shop once or twice a month, Fred continued to convince me to write a book on my life as a NJ Road Trooper and rising to the top as a Troop Commander. Thank you Fred for your persistence in having me write this autobiography of my life in the NJ State Police. You're the best.

I would also like to thank my publisher Lawrence Knorr of Sunbury Press for publishing this book and all the work that went into it. Thank you, Mr. Knorr and Crystal Devine.

Preface

THE BEGINNING

I was born and raised in Passaic and went to Passaic High School, graduating in 1963. I played football (for two years), basketball, and baseball for four years. Passaic High School was rated one of the top ten high schools in New Jersey. The troopers that I knew that graduated Passaic High School were; (ret.) Lt. Colonel Roy Bloom, (ret.) Captain Ed O'Rourke, (ret.) Lieutenant Patsy Dragotto, (ret.) SFC Al Kasanowsky (ret.) Detective Sergeant Al Geene (ret.) Lieutenant Porfiro Ayala, (ret.) Lieutenant Hector Ayala and active Lieutenant Ellecer Ayala. (The Ayalas are all brothers).

I knew nothing about the New Jersey State Police in high school or when I attended Fairleigh Dickinson University for one year. I received a full academic scholarship from the UNICO Foundation, the most prominent Italian American service foundation in the United States, and I commuted to the Rutherford Campus by car.

My favorite police TV show was *The FBI*, starring Efrem Zimbalist Jr. I thought it would be interesting to be an FBI agent. I also knew you needed a Bachelor's Degree to apply to the FBI. The UNICO scholarship that I received was only good for one year. I was a walk-on for the freshman basketball team and played pretty well. I was not happy with my college courses but would have stayed if I had been given a basketball scholarship. The athletic director denied me a scholarship. He stated all scholarships were given out to incoming first-year students. He said I would be back since I had excellent grades. I had two sisters in high school who wanted to go to college (which they did), and my father could not afford the three of us to go to college simultaneously. I then went to work at the Nevins Printing Company on NJ-3 in Clifton, New Jersey.

I was down by the park where we hung out and played ball, and I noticed that a friend, Patsy Dragotto, hadn't been around for a while. On a Sunday morning in the spring, I finally saw Patsy by the corner candy store with a short haircut. I asked him where he had been. He told me he was in the New Jersey State Police Academy in West Trenton and was training to become a Jersey Trooper. At the time, I didn't know what a Jersey Trooper was. He explained where they worked on the New Jersey Turnpike and Parkway and in the States rural areas that did not have local police departments. I was interested.

I looked into the local police and found out you had to live in the town where you applied. I knew I did not want to be a police officer in Passaic, maybe Clifton or Wayne, but I would have to move.

We would play basketball in 2nd Ward Park until the lights went out at 10 P.M. Then we would get a coke from the candy store and chat on the park benches. The cops would come by and chase us off the benches saying the park was closed at 10 P.M., which it was not. We would sneak back. Once when we were there, four police cars came and surrounded us and started chasing us. There were about ten of us, and three got caught, not me. They were taken to the police station, and their parents had to pick them up. I was not happy with the Passaic Police.

As the months passed, I started working for Serv All Motor Freight in Passaic. My route was lower Manhattan and Brooklyn, New York. I liked driving a truck and deciding how to make my deliveries. I only saw the boss or dispatcher when I showed up for work at 8 A.M. and 5 P.M. when I returned.

I started noticing the New York City Police, but again, you had to live in New York City, Long Island, or lower New York State to be a police officer in New York City. I even checked with the US Border Patrol on the phone. They explained you would have to live in Texas, Arizona, or New Mexico when you started. I asked how long it would take to get assigned to the Canadian border. I was told about fifteen to twenty years. (I have a lot of relatives in Toronto, Canada). So that was out.

In 1965 I conversed with two of my older friends, Ed Agnello (who became an attorney) and Bruce Miller (who became a medical doctor). They were surprised that I had dropped out of college. They advised me I would get drafted soon and possibly go to Viet Nam, which was starting to heat up. I was OK with that. The draft was only two years. They advised me to join the Army reserves or the New Jersey Army National Guard. (At the time, there was a National Guard Armory on River Road in Passaic, New Jersey). I then stopped in the Passaic Armory and spoke with Staff Sergeant Milko, a full-time New Jersey National Guard employee. I advised him that I was a truck driver. He offered they could use some more truck drivers. I signed up for six years and was sworn in the following administrative night by the Company Commander. I started doing weekend drills immediately, but my six-month active duty training was postponed due to Fort Dix being overcrowded with basic training.

In early 1966 I talked to a good friend, Al Kasanowsky (Al became one of my State Police classmates in 1967), and he said that the State Police was scheduling a written test in a couple of weeks at East Orange Catholic High School. It was a walk-in test for which you didn't have to have an appointment. We took the test, got letters that we passed, and then were scheduled for a medical, physical, and oral interview. Both Al and I both passed the physical and medical exams. We both knew what to expect because of our friendship with Patsy Dragotto, who was already a trooper.

Al and I drove to the oral interview together since our times were close. I went in first. Three officers in suits were facing me, one younger man, a psychologist, and me. The officers asked about my previous employment and why I quit specific jobs. One of the officers asked, "Why are you sweating?"

I replied, "I am nervous."

That didn't go over too well. Then the psychologist asked, "Are you married?"

I said, "No."

He then asked, "Do you have a steady girlfriend?"

Again, I said, "No."

"Do you like boys, then?" he asked.

The way I looked at him told him I was about to come over and hit him.

One of the officers intervened, "That's enough. You're dismissed."

I told my friend Al that I didn't get this job. Al went in next.

A couple of weeks later, we both got letters to report to the New Jersey State Police Academy in September 1966. (The previous Class #71 would graduate in August 1966.) Sometime during the summer of 1966, we both got another letter from the State Police Superintendent, Colonel D. B. Kelly, that, due to financial reasons, our class was being postponed to sometime in 1967.

I was still in the New Jersey Army National Guard doing monthly drills but had not gone away for active duty for six months. In early December 1966, Al and I got letters to report to the New Jersey State Police Academy on January 5, 1967. A week later, I was advised by the New Jersey National Guard that my orders were coming and that I was going to Fort Dix for six months, sometime in January 1967. I wanted to go to the New Jersey State Police Academy first, and I felt that the New Jersey Guard had postponed my orders since 1965 and they could do it again.

There were two military units in the Passaic National Guard Armory, the Infantry Company I was assigned to and the Military Police Company, which trained on different weekends. The Commander of the Military Police Company was Captain Martin Donohue, a lieutenant in the New Jersey State Police. I checked with my friend Patsy Dragotto, who was stationed in Troop C, and Patsy told me that Lieutenant Donohue was a Troop C Officer and worked at Troop C headquarters located on US-1 Southbound in Princeton. I decided to go and see him.

I drove down to Troop C headquarters on US-1 in Princeton unannounced, and I told the dispatcher that I was in the National Guard and would like to see Lieutenant Donohue about National Guard business. Lieutenant Donohue came out and ushered me into his office. I advised him of the problem with the date for the State Police Academy and military training coming in the same month. Lieutenant Donohue said it might be better to do my military training and then go into the State Police Academy. I advised him that the National Guard had put off my military training for two years since 1965, and going to the State Police Academy was more important to me. Lieutenant Donohue called National Guard headquarters in Trenton and spoke to Major Wilson. He told me through Lieutenant Donohue to report back to my Company Commander on the next administrative night, and my Captain would let me know. I reported to my Company Commander the next administrative night and was advised that my military orders had been postponed until after graduating from the New Jersey State Police Academy.

I gave notice to my bosses, Joe and Red, who were brothers and owned Serv-All Motor Freight. Joe asked, "you too?" Joe's nephew Roy Bloom also worked there and left to join the New Jersey State Police. (At one point, Roy Bloom was my Senior Man when we worked together on a Troop B Tactical Patrol Unit assigned to US-1 & US-9 in Newark, Elizabeth, Linden, and Rahway.

I was on my way to the New Jersey State Police Academy.

1

THE NEW JERSEY STATE POLICE ACADEMY

I arrived at the New State Police Academy with my classmates on January 3, 1967. Our class started with about forty-five recruits. I made a mistake driving up in my 1966 Chevrolet Corvette, which I purchased brand new in 1966. I made good money driving for Serv-All Motor Freight. I was single and still lived with my parents. It had a 327 cubic inch engine with 300 horsepower and a 4-speed manual transmission. It was white with a black convertible top. (Back then, it cost $4,400). I only had one car. We all wore our tan khakis with our name tags sewn above our left shirt pockets. We were first addressed by the Academy Commandant, Captain Martin Wallace. He said we would be thrown out of the academy if we didn't listen to the instructors or fell behind in our work.

Next to speak was SFC (Sergeant First Class) John Buhan. He was the academy's first sergeant and the only SFC assigned there. He was built like a fireplug, short and stout but very muscular. He spoke for a while like Captain Wallace and then stopped and started to look around at all the recruits. Then he asked, "Who owns that white Corvette convertible out there?"

I raised my hand.

He looked at me and said, "Do you think you will get a license to speed, Maggio? Well, you haven't graduated yet."

I knew I was in trouble.

The instructors then marched us into the bunkhouse, where we were going to sleep. Sgt (Sergeant) Raymond Workman was going to show us how our bunk should be made. After he finished, one of the recruits raised his hand and asked, "Do we have to make our beds?"

Sgt Workman asked who made his bed at home, and the recruit said his mom. Sgt Workman took him out of the bunk area, and we never saw him again. We were only there a few hours, and already one recruit was gone. I hope I will not be next because of my car.

Because of my military training and having attended two summer camps in Fort Drum with the National Guard, I knew how to make a bunk and make a quarter bounce off of it. But every morning after class, my bunk was ripped up, and my clothes were pulled out of the open locker and thrown on the floor. I knew what they were doing, but I wouldn't let them get my goat. Patsy Dragotto, already a trooper, told me what to expect.

We didn't go home the first weekend. Tpr (Trooper) Ralph Meade was the duty instructor, and on Sunday morning, he asked the class if anyone wanted to go to church. About eight of us said yes and drove to a Catholic Church in West Trenton. After the 11 A.M. mass, Tpr Meade asked us if we wanted something to eat before returning to the Academy. Of course, we said yes. We went to a tavern and had pizza and beer. Boy, were my other classmates upset that they didn't go to church.

After two weeks of hell, we finally went home for the weekend. We left on Saturday at around 4 P.M. and had to be back by 10 P.M. on Sunday. On Sunday, about five or six of us used to meet at a tavern on Olden Avenue in Trenton around 7 P.M. and have some fast food and beer. We had to be careful that the duty instructor didn't smell our breath on Sunday night. Of course, we went right to bed.

In the third week, they were still breaking my chops, but I was surviving. We were off and home after the second week, and I got a call from my classmate, John Giuliani, that he was having car trouble and asked if I would pick him up on Sunday to head back to the academy, which I did. The following weekend we stayed up late on Friday studying for a big test, we took on Saturday morning. After cleaning most of the division headquarters and washing troop cars, we were let go late Saturday afternoon. I told John I was exhausted and not to fall asleep on the way home. We traveled north on US-1 to the Parkway and then to our homes. I was tired, and John was sleeping. We were just past the New Brunswick State Police Station on US-1 North when I started dozing and ran off the right side of the road. I hit the grass berm, which was snow-covered. I missed the telephone pole but hit the guidewire, which tore the right front fender off the car.

A few minutes passed, and I saw a marked State Police vehicle approaching and stopping behind my car. Two troopers came out of the vehicle, Tpr Archie Roberts and Tpr Bill Yodice. I had to think quickly when Tpr Roberts asked me what had happened. I told him a dog ran out in front of me, and I turned right to avoid the dog and hit the guidewire. I don't think he believed me and asked me what color the dog was. I said black. I then told Tpr Roberts that we were State Police recruits heading home from the academy. The troopers took us back to New Brunswick Station, and my car had to be towed. In the station, I saw an older trooper sewing five stars onto his winter blouse, so I called him sergeant. He yelled he was not a sergeant; he was a trooper. (I later learned that he was a sergeant and was demoted for drinking on the job). Tpr Roberts told me he would complete the report and send a copy to the academy. He told me to report the accident to an instructor when I returned on Sunday night. Then he arranged with the State Police on the Parkway to relay us home. John and I made other arrangements to return Sunday with other recruits. I rode back with my classmate Al Kazanowsky whom I grew up with in Passaic. Sunday night, I reported the accident to the instructor who had the duty, and I made my first special report explaining the accident.

On Monday, SFC Buhan saw my special report and asked if I was speeding. I told him no and that the dog had caused the accident. I know he didn't believe me. The instructors still were ripping my bunk apart and throwing my clothes on the floor.

The week after I had the accident, we went to the gym to box. I held my own boxing since I had to fight when growing up in an inner city neighborhood. I had just finished knocking down a classmate, and we were told to exit the ring. As I started to leave, Sgt Rich Malanga, one of the physical instructors, told me to get back in the ring, which I did. He sent in a fresh classmate. We fought for three or four minutes, but I didn't go down.

As we started to leave the ring, Sgt Malanga told me to get back in. He put another fresh classmate in with me. I now knew what they were doing. They wanted me to quit. I persevered and blocked most punches and did not go down. Sgt Malanga then let me out of the ring.

A week later, the instructors advised our class that Channel 3 *CBS News* out of Philadelphia would be doing a story on our academy this week. A couple of days later, CBS filmed us in class and interviewed some of my classmates (not me). We then went to the gym to box. Sgt Malanga then said he would pick two recruits to box on camera for the news station. He first picked recruit Mike Risi. Mike was a weightlifter and could bench press five hundred pounds. The instructors knew that Mike and I worked out together at the Passaic YMCA. I figured they would not pick me. I was wrong. Sgt Malanga picked me and said he wanted to see blood! Mike and I went at it, and we both had bloody noses when we were stopped. The program aired the next night on the six o'clock news on Philadelphia Channel three. The instructors would not let us watch it, but some of my classmate's relatives and friends in South Jersey saw it and said it was terrific, especially me and Mike fighting in the ring.

We were in our eighth week of a 16-week course, and the instructors were still picking on me and other recruits. I kept getting demerits and shining the instructor's gear. They also kept ripping apart my bunk but not every day. Most recruits left on their own, and the class kept getting smaller. I knew the badge could not be reissued once you graduated and earned it. If I were going to quit, it would be because I didn't like the job, but I would hold that badge number for life so I would not leave the Academy.

Right about the eighth week, I was shining some instructor's gear in the evening, and the duty instructor, Tpr Charles Purgavie shoved me against the wall, and nose to nose, he asked what he must do to make me quit.

I said, "A pine box, sir. The only way I'm going down the road was in a pine box, or I'm not going, sir."

Trooper Purgative just shook his head and walked away. He must have told the other instructors the next day, I don't know, but they either felt I would make a good Trooper or picked on someone else. They didn't bother me after that exchange with Trooper Purgative.

Another classmate had been a local police officer and had already graduated from the local State Police Academy in Seagirt. He was small and fought smaller recruits in the ring. In the beginning, he was knocking the hell out of the other recruits, but as time passed and they learned how to defend themselves, he started getting knocked around himself. He then left the academy on his own to go back to his local police department. (Not trooper material).

During our boxing class, a contest developed on who was the best boxer. Two classmates, Doug Osborne and Doug Van Sant, both middleweights, were mentioned as the best all-around in-shape classmates. The instructors found out and arranged a match between Osborne and Van Sant. We couldn't wait to see the match. Unfortunately, when it came to pass, the instructors made the whole class face away from the ring and not let us watch the bout—just another way to bust our chops.

Another classmate was having a hard time both physically and with the tests. We all thought he should have been dismissed. He was a nice guy but very weak. He graduated, and at the graduation, he, his father, and the superintendent, COL (Colonel) David B. Kelly, had their picture taken together. I guess it pays to have friends in high places.

We had periodic inspections before the commandant, Captain Wallace. The captain, during an inspection, would stand in front of each recruit and state "hands," after which you put your hands out so he could inspect your fingernails. At one of these inspections, I finished polishing my shoes and got a piece of black polish stuck under one of my fingernails. When I put my hands out, Captain Wallace saw the polish under one of my nails, and he yelled at me, calling me a dirty pig and not fit for the academy. I got a couple of demerits for that one.

On another occasion, my classmate, Mike Risi, who I fought in the ring on TV, was ordered by Sgt Phil Berman, another physical instructor, not to lift any weights since he was overdeveloped. Well, Mike got caught lifting weights by Sgt Berman, and Mike was put out on the grinder (roads between buildings) and was told by Sgt Berman to keep running until told to stop. Mike started running at about 4:30 P.M. Sgt

Berman forgot to tell the duty instructor, Tpr Purgavie, about Mike running around the grinder. After dinner (which Mike missed), it was going on 7:30 P.M., and Mike still wasn't back. I advised Tpr Purgative about Mike; he said he knew and gave me a demerit for questioning him. Tpr Purgative went out and got Mike. Mike came in and was totally exhausted. He took a shower and went right to bed. I don't recall Mike ever lifting weights again.

Another item I recall well was our class on driving a troop car. Tpr Ralph Meade taught the course. When it was my turn, I got behind the wheel of Tpr Meade's unmarked troop car. Tpr Meade sat right front. We drove out the back gate and down to the main road, made a right, then another right onto NJ-29 North, then back in via the front entrance. That was the extent of being taught how to drive a troop car. I was lucky that I drove a large box truck in New York City for over two years and had good driving experiences. Now the State Police give a very detailed and extensive driving course that you must pass to graduate.

The training I thought was relevant to the job was investigating a mock motor vehicle accident (and doing the report) and testifying in a court setting with an instructor acting as the judge. Also, a simulated family dispute trained you for the real thing. The firearms training was over the top, with all my classmates doing well with this training. The head firearms instructor was Sgt Joseph Pagnillo, who was assisted by Tpr Clifford Chippendale. Back then, we carried a Colt .38 caliber revolver with a six-inch barrel that held six rounds. We also trained with a 12-gauge pump shotgun and a .45 caliber riser semi-automatic rifle. We practiced at least three times a week. The firearms training was excellent.

The swimming instructor was Sgt Arnold Kleeberg, a Navy Seal, while he was in the service. We all had to swim the length of the pool underwater to graduate. One of my classmates had a problem staying underwater for the whole length of the pool. Sgt Kleeberg tirelessly worked with him, and he finally made it. Sgt Kleeberg was an outstanding instructor.

Sgt Malanga gave us a class on how to take a motorist out of a vehicle if they were resisting. Of course, he picked me to demonstrate. He had me sit in the driver's seat of his troop car and told me to hold on tight to the steering wheel. I was holding on as tight as I could, and he grabbed me by the lips, pulled me out of the car, and slammed me down on the street. I got back in the car and curled my lips into my mouth to avoid being ejected from the vehicle. This time Sgt Malanga pulled my hair on top of my head, and out of the vehicle, I came and was thrown onto the street again. He had me get into the car again and threatened he would not pull my lips or hair but hang on again. I was hanging on as tight as I could, and he grabbed my left thumb from the steering wheel and yanked it so hard that I again came out of the vehicle, landing on the street. I never forgot this class and occasionally used these techniques while on the road. Sometimes I thought Sgt Malanga was a sadist, but he was an excellent instructor, as was Sgt Phil Berman, the head physical instructor.

Just before graduation, I was speaking to my classmate Daniel Nelson (Nelson was a teacher before entering the academy). He asked me what I would do if I didn't like being a trooper, I told him I would go back to driving a truck, but I would give the job a chance for at least six months to a year. (Daniel Nelson resigned from his position with the State Police on February 23, 1968.)

Every morning one of the recruits was given the detail to raise the American flag by division headquarters. One day the detail was given to a recruit. He put it upside down. No one noticed until troopers assigned to division headquarters came to work, and someone notified the academy staff. Well, the recruit, after putting the flag upright and after morning classes, spent the rest of the morning running on the grinder.

Another thing the instructors would do if they were not happy with the training the previous day was waking us up around 2 or 3 A.M. and take us out for a run.

The food at the academy was not very good—some eggs for breakfast but mostly cereal. Lunch was mainly baloney sandwiches. I lived on peanut butter sandwiches. Dinner was also weak, with a lot of starches. The instructor's used to march us to our meals, and we would stand behind our seats at attention until the instructor yelled "seats." Then we could sit. Now the recruits get a more balanced meal. Most of my classmates lost some weight. I stayed at the same weight, 205 lbs. when I started and graduated. Thanks to peanut butter sandwiches.

We had mainly classes in the morning, and after lunch, we had our physical classes like boxing, self-defense, and of course, running up to five miles a day when we got to the eighth week. We usually had only about five minutes for a short shower before dinner. After dinner, we sometimes had a class and then free time from 8 P.M. until lights out at 10 P.M. Of course, if you had some demerits to work off, it was done between 8 P.M. and 10 P.M. (shining the instructor's leather gear or some other detail).

Our class (the 72nd) continued to graduation. Twenty-seven out of the forty-five that started got their badges and diplomas from the superintendent, COL David B. Kelly. We graduated at the new state rotunda just built behind the State House. We put on a marching demonstration for family and friends. After graduation, my dad had to drive me to a body shop on US-130 to pick up my Corvette that was finished being fixed (I had $1,500 in cash when I graduated to pay for the repairs). Before graduation, my classmate Al Kazanowsky and I were advised by the academy staff that we were being assigned to Troop C in central Jersey, even though we lived in north Jersey. We were both assigned to the Tennant Station in Manalapan Township near Englishtown.

The total length of the academy for our class was sixteen weeks, and returning for two weeks after the 60-day Trooper-Coach program. Now and for at least the past ten years, the training was twenty-six weeks. The most important training you learn is discipline. The instructors beat it into you. I learned discipline by playing high school sports and semi-pro baseball and basketball. I'm sure the classes today get plenty of discipline training. To me, the trooper-coach program was the best training until you are on your own. Hopefully, you have a good coach. Even with all the training troopers get, even more today, you learn this job on the job and the road, gaining experience as you go along. At about the two-year mark, I would consider myself completely trained, but training continues with experience and periodic in-service training sessions. The academy dropout rate runs between 35 and 50 percent. The classes now start at around 200, with an anticipated graduation of 100 to 120. This was possible at the Seagirt New Jersey Training site but not at the West Trenton site. The State Police have been running at least one class per year but are just keeping up with retirements with a force of just under 3,000 troopers. (There are also about 1,000 civilian employees that work for the State Police).

For many years at least, since I took the written test, after the written test, an applicant took the physical test, then the medical in which a medical doctor examines them. Then you were scheduled for an oral examination. Recently many applicants who had passed the written test failed the physical test. Apparently, they were not in good physical condition. Now, the physical test was given before the written exam to eliminate this problem.

Recently, the state purchased the Divine Swim Club outside the division headquarters' rear gate. This was where a new New Jersey State Police Academy would be built when it was fiscally possible. The current site in Seagirt was also used by the New Jersey Army National Guard (which owns the facility), New Jersey State Correctional Officers training, and the Division of Criminal Justice Training. The State Police needs its own training facility, and it should be at division headquarters like it was years ago.

Though the training has changed over the years, the basic training remains about the same. The dropout rate is still high. The discipline training was still firm. The New Jersey State Police Academy training was probably one of the country's most intense and complete training academies, the best of the best. It was very intense and thorough, as I remember most of what happened as if it happened a short time ago, not over fifty years ago.

Troop C Posts, here I come.

2

TROOP C POSTS

Before reporting to Troop C headquarters in Princeton on May 8, 1967, I bought a Hargrove *Map of Monmouth County*, and on Sunday, May 7, 1967, my classmate Al Kazanowsky and I took a ride to see where the Tennant State Police Station was. The hamlet of Tennant was in Manalapan Township, and the building was built by the township to be used by the State Police until the township had its own police department. The building was less than a year old.

All my classmates assigned to Troop C reported to the troop commander, Captain Theodore Schmidt, at 9 A.M. (No one was late). Captain Schmidt spoke to us for about twenty minutes, telling us to do what the station commander and our coaches said. He then told us to report to our respective stations in our POVs (Privately owned vehicles). Al followed me to the Tennant Station.

At the Tennant Station, we first met with the station commander, SFC Sam Ferreri. I then met my coach, Tpr Gino Garibaldi, who had over four years on the job. Al and I brought our clothes in and were assigned a bedroom. We were told to change from our suits to our khakis and wash all the troop cars in the parking lot, which we did. My coach then gave me instructions on what was to be done by recruits; emptying garbage cans, cleaning dirty dishes in the kitchen, and cutting and filing teletypes (teletypes were information on stolen cars, wanted persons, and other crimes, filed on hooks in the report room).

I then suited up in uniform and went on patrol with my coach. He told me to call him by his first name unless we were in the station. He asked me how old I was, and I told him I had just turned twenty-two in the academy. He did some quick figuring and surmised I had a job until 2000. (The pension plan was changed back with the 69th Class in that you could not retire early at fifty, you had to stay until fifty-five and receive a 50 percent pension). I was unaware of any pension information and didn't even know if I would like this job.

Since we lived in the station working a primary two days on and two days off schedule, Tpr Garibaldi's schedule and mine were the same. During a thrity-one-day month, you might work three days, but usually, the station commander would throw in a night pass, meaning you were off at 5 P.M. on the third day.

At my first station, I was introduced to my first troop car. It was a marked 1966 full-size Ford Galaxie. It had a three-speed standard transmission on the column, no power brakes or steering, and you opened the window for "fresh air." Most troopers used a transistorized radio taped to a 6-volt battery for an AM radio, which worked pretty well. Things changed over the years, and all troop cars had power brakes, power steering, air conditioning, and an AM radio. Of course, this wasn't for us but for resale value for the state.

After a week on the job at the Tennant Station, a couple of troopers brought in a suspect in a stabbing at a migrant labor camp. The sergeant brought out a plywood box with a strap and a light bulb on the top. The sergeant hid behind the corner with the cord to the box. The trooper said that the box was a lie detector and was asked routine questions at first. When asked if he stabbed the victim, the suspect said, "no." The sergeant turned on the light bulb, and the trooper slapped the subject in the head and called him a liar. The suspect then admitted to the crime—Jersey justice at its best.

Another thing that I witnessed at Tennant Station was when a migrant couple came in and asked either for a divorce or to be married. The sergeant or senior trooper would take out a Bible and say, "By the powers invested to me by the State of New Jersey, you are now man and wife" (or divorced if applicable). Coming from Passaic, I never knew this form of policing was going on.

I started driving the troop car during the first week and wrote some traffic summonses. Late in my first week, I investigated a two-car motor vehicle accident in Manalapan Township at an intersection. A lone male driver attempted to make a left turn in front of an Asian couple, and they struck almost head-on. The cars had some damage, but there were no injuries. I issued a summons to the driver making the left turn for failing to yield to an oncoming vehicle. He was furious and suggested the other car must have been speeding. He said he would see me in court. When I returned to the troop car, my coach was laughing. He mentioned that I just gave a summons to the most hated lawyer in Monmouth County, hated by the troopers from Tennant, Howell, and Keyport Stations. He suggested he would contest the charge and that I should subpoena the other driver (which I did). About a month later, I went to court in Manalapan Township. Municipal Court.

At the hearing, numerous troopers were in uniform, some in civilian clothes. Also, the defendant had hired a court stenographer at his own expense. I presented the case myself, and there was no municipal prosecutor. The judge was an old lay magistrate, not a lawyer, which was in my favor. After hearing all testimony, the judge found the lawyer guilty of an improper left turn and imposed a fine of $20 and $5 court costs. All the troopers clapped and cheered. My coach told me I had just made my "bones" in Troop C.

Another incident I remember vividly was at the Freehold Diner. My coach and I were working the midnight shift. We stopped at the diner for a cup of coffee and sat at the counter. It was about 3 A.M. on a Friday. Sitting in a booth behind us were four young white males who had been drinking. One of the males started making loud derogatory comments about the State Police. He even growled that the "yellow strip down our legs should be down our backs." My coach got up and told me to watch his back. He motioned to the individual who made the comments to get up and said he wanted to talk to him. He took the individual about six or seven feet away and, nose to nose, said something to him. The subject asked what the coach said and raised his right hand. Gino hit him in the chin with an uppercut, and he went right down. I jumped up, faced the other three individuals in the booth, and told them to sit tight. Coach cuffed the individual, and we dragged him out of the diner and put him in the Monmouth County Jail in Freehold under a hold. In those days, you could put a prisoner in any county jail for twenty-four hours until you got bail set and brought the paperwork to the jail. We then went back to the station, and Coach typed up the complaint for drunk and disorderly, and on the phone, the court clerk set bail at $100. This amount of bail was a lot of money back then. After we finished this arrest, I asked Coach what he said to the individual we arrested, and he only said, "Something derogatory about his family."

In the Tennant Station, there were a lot of migrants who lived temporally on the local farms picking fruit and vegetables and then moving to the next farm or another state. The migrants were Hispanics from Mexico, Puerto Rican, or African Americans from down South. Some had work visas, and some did not. Coach and I were on patrol one evening. It was dark. I was driving, and we got behind an old vehicle speeding down a county road. We put the red light and siren on, but the car refused to stop (back then, the troop cars only had one red light on the roof). Coach told me to drive close to the vehicle and force it to go faster, which I did. Going around a curve, the car lost control, ran off the right side of the road, and turned over onto its right side. Two young Hispanic males climbed out of the vehicle. They did not appear hurt. My Coach had me cuff the passenger so he wouldn't run away. The driver handed Gino his expired Puerto Rican driver's license and expired registration. He did not have an insurance card. Coach wrote the driver a slew of summonses, expired license, expired registration, reckless driving, and driving without insurance. Coach then told the driver he had two hours to get his vehicle off the road or we would come looking for him at the migrant camp. I asked Coach, "What type of report do we fill out?"

He said, "None. They will remove the car themselves, they have no insurance, and the driver will probably throw away the summons I wrote him when they move to the next camp. But I will get credit for the summons I wrote."

Back then, one of the rules was that you had to wear your hat all the time, even in the troop car. My coach was spotted in his troop car without his hat, and a Troop C lieutenant wrote him up. The complaint went to the Troop C commander, Captain Theodore Schmidt. Back then, there was no appeal if you got a written reprimand (commonly called a blue ticket because it was typed on light blue paper) for a rules violation. We didn't have a strong union or bargaining agent to protect us at the time. Coach made a lengthy special report to Captain Schmidt, including his height of six feet four inches, the size of his hat, and the height of the distance from the seat to the roof of the troop car. His report declared there was no way that he could wear his hat in the troop car. Later that week, Coach was summoned to see the troop commander at Troop C headquarters in Princeton. When he came back, I asked him what had happened. Coach said he got a blue ticket, and Captain Schmidt told him to "slouch" when in a troop car (this rule of wearing a hat in the car was eliminated sometime in the early seventies).

Once I was riding with my assistant coach; we got a call from the local hospital to notify a woman that her husband had passed away. They did not have a working phone (every recruit had an assistant coach to fill in when court or vacations interfered with the schedule). As we pulled into the driveway of a single-family house, a woman came out the front door, looked at us, and started screaming. The Coach was driving. He then backed out of the driveway, and we left. I asked, "Aren't we going to tell her that her husband passed away?"

He just said, "She knows."

I would not have handled this notification this way, but it did get the job done. I will be commenting on this type of call later on.

Another call I went on with my assistant coach was a raid set up by a detective from Troop C headquarters. Apparently, a party at a hall was being set up and included some go-go girls and porn movies. Some of the wives found out and made the complaint. This was a significant violation back in the sixties and seventies. The hall was in Howell Township., and troopers from Howell, Tennant, and Keyport Stations were assigned. I was placed at the rear door with three other troopers, and we were told not to let anyone out or hit them with our batons. When the front door was breached, three male subjects attempted to flee out the back door but were stopped by me and the other troopers. After a discussion between the troop lieutenant and the Howell Station detective, the dancing girls, the bartender, and the hall manager were the only people arrested.

While on the trooper-coach program and off duty, I was with my parents having Sunday dinner at my Uncle Kramer and Aunt Lucille's home in Newark. They lived off South Orange Avenue in the Vailsburg section. My uncle Kramer owned a barbershop in Newark. After dinner, my uncle Kramer and I went for a walk. He wanted to show me the Italian American Club, where he was a member. The club was on South Orange Avenue in the Vailsburg section. We walked in and sat at the bar. I saw men playing cards at two tables in a back room through an open door. There was also a pool table in the bar with men playing pool. About forty men at the club looked like Italian Americans. Then my uncle Kramer introduced me to the bartender stating, "this is my nephew Sal; he's a state trooper."

You could have heard a pin drop.

The bartender asked me, "Where do you work?"

I said, "Down in Monmouth County—I just graduated from the State Police Academy last month."

Then conversations picked up. After we finished one drink, I left the club with my uncle.

I told him, "This club looks like a hangout for the mob!"

Uncle Kramer explained, "All I know is the Campisi brothers run the club, and all they do is handle numbers." (The Campisi's were an organized crime family taken down by the New Jersey State Police in the mid-1970s, and they went to jail for long periods. They were involved in armed robberies, homicides, and any criminal activities that carried a profit.)

Not long after, my Uncle Kramer sold his barber shop and moved to Union.

While at the Tennant Station, there was a call of a car running into the Freehold Circle. I was sent to check it. I found the car sitting in the middle of the circle. The driver was drunk and half asleep. Further checking found that the vehicle was an unmarked troop car, and the driver was an SFC stationed at Troop C headquarters. The car had no visible damage, just two flat front tires from hitting the curb around the circle. I called for a tow truck and drove the SFC back to Tennant Station. The duty Sgt told me to put the SFC in the station commander's bedroom since SFC Ferreri doesn't sleep at the station. At around 8 A.M., the station commander, SFC Sam Ferreri, came in and went nuts when he saw this SFC sleeping in his bed. SFC Ferreri had another trooper drive the SFC home. Of course, there was no accident report on the troop car, the tires were replaced at the local garage, and no charges were lodged against the SFC. Today it might have been a different story on any charges against the SFC. Today a police officer (or a trooper) could forfeit his job and even his pension if he tries to cover up a charge against a person because he was a police officer on or off duty.

Another detail that I had and learned the hard way was the traffic detail at the Freehold circle by the Freehold Racetrack. The detail was to empty the parking lot as fast as possible so the race track crowd could make it to the Monmouth Track to catch the last couple of races. My coach told me to hold up the traffic on NJ-33 until the parking lot was empty. I was doing this, and the motorists on NJ-33 were blowing their horns because of the wait. I felt the motorists on NJ-33 were right, and I stopped the traffic coming out of the parking lot. This caused two rear-end accidents in the parking lot, which I had to investigate. Back then, all accidents had to be typed, and I couldn't even issue a summons for careless driving because the accidents happened on private property. After that, when I had the race track detail, I let the parking empty before allowing NJ-33 traffic to proceed. "The racetrack driver's won."

I was impressed by the station commander, SFC Sam Ferreri. He ran the station and worked 8 A.M. to 4 P.M. Monday to Friday, with weekends and holidays off (unless there was an emergency). He did not sleep at the station and made about $10,000 yearly (I started making approximately $7,200 yearly). He also drove a nice new unmarked troop car. I hoped then that I could rise to be a station commander. I was starting to enjoy this job of being a trooper and learning the ins and outs of police work. I was also enjoying the camaraderie amongst the troopers at the Tennant Station.

After being cut loose from the trooper-coach program, I was advised by my cousin John Klinger that I should carry a backup weapon since we rode alone up until the midnight patrol. My cousin John was a canine patrolman for the Metropolitan Police in Washington, DC. I purchased a .25-cal Beretta automatic, and even though carrying it was against the State Police rules, I would rather be judged by twelve than carried by six. I carried this weapon for many years while a road trooper and a road sergeant. The State Police now allows troopers to carry a second weapon, but you must qualify with the firearm.

After being on my own for a couple of weeks, my military orders sent me to Fort Dix for six months. I had to turn in all my uniforms, gun badge, and ID card to the supply sergeant at Troop C headquarters in Princeton. All I had to show that I was a trooper was a State Police blood type card with my name and badge number. When I arrived at Fort Dix, I discovered that trainees were not allowed to park their POVs on the post. Most parked them in Wrightstown, just outside the base. It would cost me $30 a month to park at a lot. There was a State Police Station in Wrightstown on the north side of town. I stopped at the State Police Station called Fort Dix Station. I was dressed in my military summer khaki uniform. I spoke to the State Police desk sergeant and showed him my State Police blood type card. I asked him if I could park my car at the station for the next six months and that I would use it on the weekends if I were off duty. The sergeant told me to wait and that he would get the station commander. The station commander, SFC Joseph Rogalski, came out of his office to meet me. He asked me where I was stationed, and I told him Tennant Station. He asked me what type of car I had. I told him a 1966 Chevrolet Corvette. He said something like, "it's nice to have money," and told me to park my vehicle on the left side of the garbage dumpster.

Back at Fort Dix and the reception center, I was assigned to a training platoon with SFC Dubois as our DI (Drill Instructor). When we arrived at our barracks, SFC Dubois handed out an information card for our names, addresses, home units, and civilian occupations. I put down New Jersey State Police for my profession. After reviewing all the cards, SFC Dubois called me into his office. He asked me if I was affiliated with the State Police at the Fort Dix Station, and I told him I was stationed at the Tennant Station north of Fort Dix. He gave me sergeant stripes and told me to pin them on, and I was his platoon guide. I was allowed to pick four squad leaders. Being the platoon guide allowed me to assign all details to the training platoon. After completing basic training and Heavy Duty Vehicle Driving School, I was discharged early after five months. I then went to Troop C headquarters, picked up my gear, and reported back to Tennant Station. I then did my two additional weeks of academy training with the 73rd Class since I missed it with my class. I was starting to like the schedule of two on and then two days off schedule. It gave you a lot of time off, but you worked hard and long hours.

One day on patrol, I received a call for a severe car-truck accident. I pulled up at the scene along with my classmate Tpr Al Kazanowsky. A migrant family: husband and wife in the front, and two kids in the back, had run a stop sign and were run over by a loaded dump truck. A senior trooper pulled up. He had about six or seven years on. He told Al and me to put out flares and watch what he does. He handled the fatal accident, but he made sure Al and I read the report and learned from it. This was one of the things I liked about Tennant Station. The older troopers helped the junior troopers learn the job.

I also noticed the older married troopers had trouble living on their salaries. There was no paid overtime, and the married troopers had to shop while working to get discounts on whatever they needed. I didn't have a problem since I was still single. I could see the bargaining agent or union we had for the State Police getting more assertive in the future, like most local police departments have the PBAs (Police Benevolent Association) to bargain for benefits and raises.

While still at Tennant Station, I met with Tpr Valcocean Littles, who came from the class after me (73rd Class). Tpr Littles had the same coach as I had. Tpr Littles was only the third African American trooper in the State Police. The first was Tpr Paul Mc Lamore, and the second was Tpr Leon Adams. I heard other troopers use the N-word in front of Tpr Littles. He said it didn't bother him because they meant the black migrants were always getting in trouble in the migrant camps. Tpr Littles had spunk and knew the racial problems in the State Police, especially with the older troopers. Tpr Littles accepted these racial problems and helped correct them as he rose through the ranks. Tpr Littles and I always stayed friendly even though I remained on the road, and he went into narcotics and eventually retired as a lieutenant colonel in 1997.

Manalapan Township Police Department was formed in 1970, and the Tennant State Police Station was closed in 1975. Finally, by the end of October, my class was transferred, and I went to Keyport Station, located on NJ-35 North, in an old house. The owner lived upstairs, and downstairs was the station (this Station closed sometime in the mid-1970s due to having no local area or interstate highways to patrol and the local police growing and taking over the state highways).

I reported to the station commander, SFC Thomas Olkowski. We had one Sgt, one DSG (detective sergeant), and the senior man. Keyport Station did not have any local areas to patrol that did not have a local police department, and Keyport Station was a traffic station. We did investigate all the motor vehicle accidents on NJ-35 and NJ-36 in Hazlet Township, Keyport Borough, and Union Beach Borough. We also assisted the local police with bar fights on the weekend, especially in Union Beach Borough. Additionally, we had truck details at the state scale on US-1 in Woodbridge Township.

I liked Keyport Station because many high-ranking members of organized crime families lived in Monmouth County. Depending on manpower, the DSG would give us the addresses of alleged members in the evening, and we would stake out their houses in an unmarked car to see who was visiting who. Lookups were obtained on the license plates, and the DSG would forward the information to the State Police Organized Crime Bureau in division headquarters.

One day I was sent to the state scale in Woodbridge Township by the Sgt to get some heavyweight violations (depending on the amount the truck was overweight, the fines could range anywhere from $100 to $800 or even more). I arrived at the station at about 4 P.M. with about five heavyweight violations. The Sgt was on the phone and was looking kind of stern, "A State Police major is on the phone and wants to talk to me about a summons you wrote today." (There were only two majors in the State Police, no lieutenant colonels, and about 15 captains).

The major asked, "Do you know where Cape May Station is?"

I stated, "Yes, in A Troop."

He knew I lived in Passaic County and said if I wrote a summons to one of his friends again, I would be stationed in Cape May Station. Then he hung up.

The Sgt asked, "Did you check the list of trucks not to write, which is behind the desk in the scale house?"

I said, "I was never told about any list. Please do not send me to the scale house again."

I didn't think it was right to let some companies go and only charge companies that didn't have "friends" in the State Police. Though I did not like letting some trucking companies slide on overweight violations, I now knew where the list was at the Woodbridge Scale, and since I didn't want to be transferred to Troop A in South Jersey, I honored the list (more on this when I was stationed at Hackensack Station in Troop B).

Another incident I remember while at Keyport Station was an arrest I made for possession of stolen property. I was alone and on patrol on NJ-36 South in the evening. I got a radio transmission that the Hazlet police were looking for an old white Cadillac with a New Jersey registration that did not match the vehicle. The driver was wanted for stealing a color TV from a motel on NJ-35 in Hazlet Township (When the subject checked into the motel, the clerk went out and got the plate number and car description of the vehicle in question. When the subject left, the clerk checked the room and found that the color TV was missing, and he called the Hazlet Township police.).

Suddenly I found myself behind the white Cadillac with the phony license plates. I put my overhead light on (only one light back then), and the subject pulled over to the shoulder. He was nervous when he produced his license and registration.

"Why did you stop me?" he asked.

I answered, "Your license plates don't match your vehicle." I took the keys out of the ignition, pulled him out of the car, and handcuffed him. "Do you have a color TV in the trunk?"

He said, "No."

I opened the trunk, and there was the stolen color TV.

"I don't know how it got there," he said.

The subject never admitted to stealing the TV and pleaded not guilty at the preliminary hearing. This case went to Monmouth County Superior Court for trial, which was heard months later, and he was convicted of receiving stolen property and sentenced to five years in state prison. I was shocked that his public defender could not get a better deal for him, but he refused to plead guilty.

When things were slow, one of my pet charges was littering. While driving, people would throw cigarettes, coffee cups, tissues, and other garbage out the car window. Sometimes I would park near a fast-food place on NJ-36 South in Keyport Borough. I would watch when three or four teenagers would pull up at the drive-in window for an order. I would then follow them south on NJ-36. Soon wrappers and soda containers went flying out the windows. I would stop the vehicle and advise the driver that he had two choices. Get one summons for littering if they picked up all the debris they threw out of the car, or I would give each person in the vehicle a summons for littering. I never had any subjects refuse to pick up the litter and only get one summons. To me, this was a learning experience for young people.

Another incident at Keyport Station was when I was riding along with another trooper who was senior to me by a couple of years. We both stood about six ft two inches. We were on US-1 and noticed a white male subject hitchhiking. The subject was only about five ft and two or three inches. He was in his early twenties. Charlie asked me if I wanted to issue a warning for hitchhiking. I said yes, and we stopped on the road and addressed the subject. The subject became unruly and grabbed my right arm. I wrestled him to the ground and cuffed him. He said he had no other way to travel since his driver's license was suspended. We arrested him for disorderly conduct and put him in the Middlesex County Jail. A couple of months later, we were summoned to the Woodbridge court since the subject pleaded not guilty. The subject was standing between me and the other trooper, and the judge stated, in effect, are you crazy? You could have ended up in the hospital messing around with these two big troopers. After hearing testimony, the judge fined the subject $100. The other trooper then asked the judge if he could suspend the fine, which he did. The subject apologized to us outside the courthouse, and we gave him a ride home. I never forgot this and knew that sometimes a person deserves a break if he is down on his luck. I thanked the other trooper for his foresight, and we became lifelong friends even though we never worked together again. He retired from the State Police as a captain in 1993 and eventually became the chief of detectives at the Ocean County prosecutor's office.

Another case I had at Keyport Station involved a two-car motor vehicle accident. I received a call from the station to investigate a two-car accident on NJ-36 where Hazlet Township meets Middletown Township. When I got there, a Hazlet Township patrolman was arguing with a Middletown Township patrolman about where the accident occurred. I met with them and said we knew the accident occurred in New Jersey and that I would handle it. They gave me the two licenses and registrations and left (I didn't need them for any traffic control.). Both vehicles had extensive damage, but there were no reported injuries. There were no witnesses to the accident, and both drivers said the other driver ran the red light. I could not tell by the damage who ran the red light.

I then returned to Keyport Station to complete and type the accident report. The senior man was in charge of the station. I told him what happened at the accident scene, and he advised me to write each driver a summons for running the red light and let the judge figure it out. Back then and for some time, the State Police wanted a summons written to whoever caused the accident. I then wrote each driver a summons and mailed it to their homes.

A month later, I received a subpoena to testify on the contested summonses. Now in Hazlet Municipal Court, I gave testimony on investigating the accident and issuing each driver a summons for going through a red light.

The judge asked, "Do you have any witnesses to the accident?"

I stated, "No, I do not."

The judge said, "If you don't know who ran the light, how would I know? Never issue a summons to someone if you don't have proof of the violation."

Both summonses were dismissed. I felt embarrassed and left the court.

Back at the station, I told the senior man what happened in court, and he just shrugged and said, "You will still get credit for two moving violations."

I learned the hard way never to issue a summons if I didn't have the evidence to get a conviction. I never did that again during my nineteen years on the road as a trooper and road sergeant. Not all, but many municipal courts did not like to hear accident cases unless it was drinking and driving, leaving the scene of an accident, or a non-moving violation. The judges would say that unless you had a witness or saw the accident, it was a civil matter to be handled by the insurance companies, even if the person who caused the accident admitted wrongdoing and his statement was on the accident report.

Another incident at Keyport Station was while I was assigned station record duty which meant I handled the front desk and radio for our patrols. The Sgt was taking a nap. I had two patrols out and heard the back screen door close. Back then, we didn't lock the station since it was open 24 hours a day. Naturally, I was in uniform and armed with my 2-inch .38-caliber revolver. I left my desk and walked back to see who was entering the station. In the report room, I saw a black male wearing civilian clothes, and I started drawing my gun. He put his hands up and offered he was Detective Leon Adams from the Narcotics Bureau.

After checking him out, I realized that he was a State Police detective and was stopping by to get gas. The gas pump was located behind the station. We had a quick cup of coffee, and he advised me that he was going to a bar in Keyport Borough to try and make a narcotics buy. He told me if he didn't call the station by 10 P.M., send troopers to the bar since he might be in trouble. He called at 9:30 P.M. and said he was OK and done at that location. Back then, narcotics detectives worked primarily alone. Years later, in Troop B, when I was a tactical patrol sergeant assigned to a narcotics raid, I would meet Lieutenant Adams, who would be handling the raid. He always remembered the incident at Keyport Station. He would point his finger at me and say, "bang, gotcha." Detective Leon Adams had a rewarding career in the State Police, retiring in 1990 as a captain.

I had a court case one day at the Holmdel Township Municipal Court. The judge went through his list of the rights for anyone who was there contesting a case or even pleading guilty to a charge. Then the judge asked, "Anyone contesting a case, please raise your hand."

Three individuals did not have a tie or jacket on. The judge looked at them and said, "Go home and change. If you address the bench in this court, you must wear a tie and jacket." He went on for a while about his dress code and the problem of people not dressing correctly for court and even going out to dinner.

One individual raised his hand and said, "But I live in Elizabeth."

The judge replied, "The court is open from 7 P.M. until midnight. You have plenty of time to go home and change."

As we all know, today, there was no dress code anymore. Most people dress like slobs, whether going to court, out to dinner or even church. I enjoyed the judge telling the people who had court business to go home and change. Today, it was a shame that people no longer dress appropriately for anything.

I was coming to the end of my time at my second Station. Back then, a new trooper was transferred twice, and his third Station was supposed to be his last, at least for a while, or when his class was transferred to the toll roads. All of my classmates got transferred except one. In chapter 1, I spoke about a classmate who didn't do well in the Academy and then, on graduation day, had his picture taken with his father and the superintendent, COL David B. Kelly. Well, this same classmate had bought a house in Toms River, New Jersey; his second station was Toms River Station, and he stayed there. I guess it's nice to have friends in high places. I was transferred to Howell Station, one of the busiest Stations in Troop C. I started to like being a trooper and learning as I went along.

As I walked into the Howell to report to the station commander, I was met by a man in a jacket and tie who I assumed was a detective. He asked me, "Are you a trooper? Are you armed?"

I replied, "Yes, and yes."

He then asked me, "Come with me. I need help investigating a stabbing complaint."

His name was Detective 1, Louis Taranto. We went to the hospital and interviewed the victim. The victim knew who stabbed him and advised Det 1 Taranto. Det 1 Taranto knew the perpetrator, said he would pick him up later, and drove me back to Howell Station so I could check in. Det 1 Taranto was one of the best station detectives I worked under while a road trooper. Det 1 Taranto had an outstanding career in the State Police, retiring as a lieutenant colonel in 1989. He then became the police director of the Lodi Police Department in Bergen County.

I then reported to SFC Thomas Lawson, the station commander. Since this was my third station, I now wanted to be a "shore guy," Along with some other troopers from north Jersey and some other friends, in early June of 1968, we rented a bungalow in Normandy Beach, which was a part of Brick Township. I figured I had the whole summer to find an apartment in the shore area since the bungalow was rented until Labor Day weekend. Also, the bungalow was only about eighteen miles from Howell Station.

I liked Howell Station, and we were much busier than Keyport Station and even busier than Tennant Station, my first station. Also, the camaraderie was great.

One night I was assigned to a late patrol with Tpr Matthew Conti. Tpr Conti was the oldest trooper at the Howell Station. We went out at midnight, and if it was quiet, we could return at around four or five A.M. and take a nap. Well, it was not quiet. We didn't get back to the station until 8:30 A.M. when the day patrols were out. We handled eighteen calls, including three motor vehicle accidents, a couple of burglaries and theft complaints, and suspicious vehicle and person complaints. It was the busiest late patrol I ever worked during my nineteen years as a road trooper and road sergeant. Also, to my astonishment, Tpr Conti handled half the calls and the paperwork. We even made one warrant arrest which he gave me. I was very impressed with the senior men in Troop C. They did their share of the work and were always teaching junior men like me how to handle different types of calls.

As a side note, on one weekend I had off, I was down at the bungalow in Normandy Beach with my classmates Al Kazanowsky and Mike Risi and a close friend Ed Agnello who had just graduated from Columbia Law School. We also had invited, as a guest, Osborne Davis, a black male from Passaic. Osborne was a friend that had never been down at the Jersey shore. We were on the beach enjoying the weather. Osborne looked at me and said, "This is the life!"

As it started to get dark, we went back to the bungalow and drank beer on the front stairs. Three white males came by and said, "We are from the beach association. Did you invite a black man to the beach?" (Osborne Davis was inside the bungalow then.).

Ed Agnello, the attorney, jumped up and replied, "We invited him (Osborne)." He then pointed to me, Al, and Mike and said, "And these guys are State Troopers. I will ask them to arrest you if you don't leave our property."

I was surprised that an association would show its prejudices in the open. We didn't have a racial problem back in Passaic, where I grew up.

Now at my third Station in Troop C, I was learning the job as I went along and learning from the senior men. I got in the habit of stopping a vehicle for a violation, not the driver. I didn't care if a driver was white, black, brown, male, or female. If a driver was polite and admitted they were wrong, I would often only issue them a warning. But if they were argumentative, I would probably issue a summons for the violation. I would give a break to a motorist who looked down on their luck and tended to provide no break for a person driving a fancy expensive car dressed to the hilt. I used this method of enforcement, and it did me well during my time on the road. Also, stopping many vehicles gave me more chances to find people wanted for crimes or for possessing drugs or illegal weapons.

One day while I was on patrol, I received a call from the station to Signal 30, which meant to return to the station. I was told to see the station commander, SFC Thomas Lawson, at the station. SFC Lawson told me I was transferred to Troop B (north Jersey). I told him I didn't want to leave Troop C or Howell Station, that this was my third Station, and that I was living in Normandy Beach for the summer and looking for an apartment down the shore area. SFC Lawson explained they need more troopers in Troop B because they are about to open some new interstate highways in north Jersey. SFC Lawson said you were picked because you live in Passaic. I then replied that my classmate Mike Risi, now stationed at Howell Station, lived in Garfield and wanted to go to Troop B. Mike had told me a little while ago that he wanted to eventually get to Bloomfield Station on the Parkway (Troop E), where they work an 8-hour day. SFC Lawson called Troop C headquarters in Princeton and explained my plight to the first sergeant. I heard the first sergeant say the teletype was cut and hung up. SFC Lawson said, " I guess you are going to Troop B."

Later SFC Lawson found out that I was being assigned to Newfound-land Station, located on NJ-23 on the borderline of Passaic and Sussex Counties. Newfoundland Station was seventy miles and about one and a half hours from where I lived in Normandy Beach. I guess now I will no longer be looking for an apartment down at the shore.

Troop B, here I come.

3

TROOP B POSTS

In the fall of 1968, I reported to Troop B headquarters to see the Troop B commander, Captain George Quinn. Troop B headquarters was located in an old house in Morristown, which had been so since 1929. He advised me that I was going to Newfoundland Station, a general police station that patrolled Hardyston Township, one-half of Vernon Township, and assisted the smaller local departments in the area. Captain Quinn advised me to report to the station commander of Newfoundland Station.

Newfoundland Station was located on NJ-23 South in West Milford Township, Passaic County, just south of the border with Sussex County. It was an old building with a one-car garage attached to a liquor store. The owners of the liquor store owned the Newfoundland Station. It was convenient at night before we went to bed to have a beer, and they also had pizza. The gas pump was right out in front of the station. The station commander advised me that including me, there were only eight troopers, one sergeant, and one detective stationed there. When you came to work, most times, only two troopers were working, so you had the calls for the next 48 hours. He also showed me a paper on the bulletin board with the number 90, stating that was the station number of traffic tickets to be issued that month.

On my first day, I also met the station senior man. When the station commander went home at 4 P.M., the station senior man showed me the actual station traffic summons number located on the back of the paper with the number 90 on it. The actual number was 80. He said each of the eight troopers wrote about ten or 11 summons a month. He added we are a general police-type station like I came from at Howell Station in Troop C. Every station in the State Police had a traffic summons number, usually based on what the station wrote during the same month the previous year.

This policy changed over the years. Troopers are now evaluated on the total job they do. Still, suppose you are assigned to a traffic station. In that case, you are expected to have a complete traffic program, especially if you are assigned to the New Jersey Turnpike, Garden State Parkway, or Atlantic City Expressway. When the STFA (State Troopers Fraternal Association) was formed in 1963 as the bargaining agent for State Troopers, they continually called keeping track of troopers' traffic activities a quota. But in reality, it's the volume of acceptable work depending on where the trooper was stationed. More on this in a later chapter.

That first day, I went out with a senior trooper. He was showing me Hardyston Township. When we pulled into a dirt road to a fence with a sign that identified the place as a nudist camp and private property, he had a key on the troop car key ring for the gate, which he opened. We drove through, and he locked the gate behind us. Then he looked at me with a straight face and said, "Take off your clothes and just put on your gun belt and hat."

I just stood there, and then he started laughing.

He then said, "I do this to all the new troopers stationed at Newfoundland, and one time a trooper started to take his clothes off, and I had to stop him."

We then drove around the lake, seeing males and females naked. They were all waving at us, and we waved back.

After having dinner at a local diner, I went out with another trooper who was going to show me the area we patrolled in, Vernon Township. As it was getting dark and we were riding around Greenwood Lake, I saw a sign noting we had just entered New York State. We drove to a large tavern with a slew of vehicles parked out front. The trooper drove around back to the kitchen door. The cook greeted us and asked, Do you want something to eat?"

The senior trooper replied, "No, just a couple of beers." (When I was in Troop C, I had a beer in the station before going to bed but never on the road while working.)

As we were drinking our beers, a go-go dancer came into the kitchen, looked at the senior trooper, and said, "Hello!" Then she kissed him.

"Who is this?" she asked, pointing at me.

"He's the new trooper stationed at Newfoundland and has to be initiated," said the senior trooper.

The young lady only wore a g-string and pasties on her nipples. She brought her left breast up to my mouth and ordered, "Bite off the pasty, baby!"

I did so with pleasure. You probably would be fired if you did that today and got caught. We then left the tavern and returned to New Jersey to resume patrol. Today while a trooper was working, he had to be very careful about doing anything against the rules. The public all have cell phone cameras and delight in taking pictures of police officers, especially while making an arrest and having to use physical force.

I started to like Newfoundland Station. With only eight troopers there, it had camaraderie. Living in the station and even eating in made the troopers tight.

While I was on patrol, the station senior man asked me to stop in. It was a weekend, and the station commander did not work on weekends or holidays. When I arrived back at the station, He asked me how many summonses I had written today. I stated two. He said that gave me 14 for the month, and we had already hit the monthly number, and there were two days left in the month. He told me not to write anymore. I complied. I liked the station and the area, and since it was my fourth station, it should be where I would be stationed, at least for a while. The senior man also told me that the station commander, SFC Harold Monsees, was being transferred, and we were getting a newly promoted station commander, SFC Joseph Delaney. I liked SFC Delaney. He was fair with the pass list and tried accommodating you if you needed a particular day off. SFC Delaney had a foot problem, and he only could wear white socks. So he was given the nickname "White Socks" when someone talked about him. When I bumped into him either at an in-service training or division headquarters, he always remembered my name and loved the days he was stationed at the Newfoundland Station. Years later, SFC Delaney retired as a State Police captain assigned to the State Police Lab.

The buck sergeant assigned to the Newfoundland Station was OK but seemed to keep to himself. One day on a Sunday night, after having a couple of beers, we hit the sack at about 1 A.M. The sergeant or the senior man would take the phone to bed, answer any calls, and send out troopers. A little after we went to bed, a car pulled up to the front of the station and started beeping its horn. The sergeant opened the front bedroom window and asked the motorist, "What do you want?"

The motorist replied, "I need some gas and saw your gas pump in front of the station."

The sergeant said, "That gas is for the State Police only. The Shell Station, one mile down the road, opens at 6 A.M." He then closed the window.

The motorist kept beeping his horn and yelling, "I need gas!"

The sergeant opened the window and said, "I will be right down."

He then went into the kitchen and filled a big pot with water and went up to the window as we were on the second floor and poured the water on top of the motorist, and then yelled, "If you don't leave, I will have a couple of troopers come down and take you to the county jail!"

The motorist then drove away. Of course, what we did in 1968 cannot be done today. I thought the sergeant did a fine job with that irate motorist, and I complimented him over coffee in the morning.

The station had one detective. In 1966 he did my State Police background investigation. I lived with my parents on Lucille Place in Passaic. Detective Clark told me now at Newfoundland Station that when he got out of his car by my house, a young man stepped out from behind a tree and yelled loudly. He started pulling his gun, but the young man ran away. I told the detective that the young man was from the neighborhood and was slightly mentally challenged and did that to most people getting out of their car, including me. He mentioned he was glad he didn't shoot him. So was I.

One day I went with the station detective to handle a suspicious person complaint at Lake Wawayanda State Park in Vernon Township. We met with a state park ranger at his office. The ranger watched two white males with his binoculars who had rented a rowboat but didn't have any fishing gear. Detective Clark and I could see through the binoculars that the subjects were smoking. Detective Clark and I put on the ranger's old green work clothes. We took some fishing rods the ranger had, got in a rowboat, and rowed out to the two subjects. When we got close, the detective stood up and said, "State Police."

The subjects threw their cigarettes in the water along with a floating plastic bag. I picked up the bag, which contained suspected marijuana. The subjects were placed under arrest at the ranger station. One of the subjects admitted that they came here from Union to smoke marijuana and still got caught. Back then, possession of marijuana was a misdemeanor and had to go before the Sussex County Grand Jury. We then took the two suspects before the judge of the Vernon Township Municipal Court. The judge was a lay magistrate and only had a high school diploma. He owned the Esso Gas Station next to the courthouse. The judge asked Detective Clark what bail should be, and as I remember, the answer was $500. Bail was later posted, and the subjects were released. About a month later, Detective Clark and I were asked to appear before the same judge on this case for a preliminary hearing, and that counsel represented the two subjects. Before the hearing, the judge asked Detective Clark what he should do. After the attorneys completed their case, the detective told the judge just to refer the matter to the Sussex County Grand Jury. Both attorneys claimed Detective Clark and I committed an illegal search and wanted the charges thrown out. The judge referred the matter to the Sussex County Grand Jury. Back then, this was called "Jersey Justice," and around 1970, all municipal judges had to be attorneys. No lay magistrates were allowed anymore.

Most of the court clerks in the area would like us to have an out-of-state residence post bond that many times, the violator would not pay the summons by mail. Of course, this wasn't possible all the time. One day I stopped a big Lincoln with New York plates for speeding with a lone male driver on NJ-94 near the gas station the judge owned. I had the violator follow me to the gas station. He saw me speaking to the judge, wearing work pants and a white t-shirt. The judge then got in his

Cadillac and drove to the courthouse across the street (The judge didn't like to walk.). The judge went into the court through the back door, and the violator and I went through the front door.

"Hello!" I said to the court clerk as we approached the judge, who was now wearing his black robe and sitting on the bench.

"Your honor, this is the violator I stopped," I explained and told the judge the charge.

The judge looked at the motorist and said, "You can pay the fine and costs now or post bail. The penalty is $10 plus $5 court costs, or you can post $20 bail and come back for a hearing."

The motorist elected, "I'll pay the $10 fine and $5 court cost."

As we left the court, the motorist said, "Boy, this is something else!"

I smirked and said only, "Jersey Justice."

He didn't have to come back and saved a six-cent stamp if he had to mail it in. He could not wait to leave the area.

The first time I almost used deadly force was at Newfoundland Station. Two State Police detectives were staked out at night in the Gingerbread Castle in Hamburg. This attraction had been broken into on the weekend, and the numerous vending machines were ripped open and all the money taken (The Gingerbread Castle has now been closed for many years.). The attraction was broken into by the thieves three times, almost exactly six months apart. Now the detectives were going to stake it out six months from the last break-in. Another trooper and I were on weekend late patrol, and we knew of the stakeout at the Gingerbread Castle. We received a call from the Sussex Station that there were shots fired at the location of the Gingerbread Castle.

The other trooper and I did not know if the perpetrators or the detectives were shot. All that was said on the radio was that one subject was down, a white male, and another, a black male with a green baseball cap and a white t-shirt, ran out and was heading south on NJ-23. I was driving, and we were headed north to the shooting on NJ-23. I spotted a black male with a green cap and a white shirt running south on NJ-23. I slammed on the brakes, coming to rest in the center of the road. I jumped out with the station shotgun and started chasing the suspect. I began to aim at the suspect and yelled, "Stop, or I'll shoot."

He stopped and pleaded, "Please don't shoot me like you shot my friend!"

I placed the subject under arrest, and we took him back to the Gingerbread Castle. The two detectives advised us that while they were hiding and watching the suspects, the white male started using a crowbar to break open a vending machine. When the detectives jumped up and identified themselves, the white male came at them with the crowbar, and they shot him twice. One detective hit him in one leg, and the other detective hit him in the other leg while the black male ran out the door. They both received lengthy prison terms. One of the reasons I did not shoot at the black male subject was I did not know where the pellets would go. I was a small game hunter at the time and familiar with shotguns. The State Police shotgun was a Remington 12-gauge pump loaded with .00 buckshot. Each shell carries between 8 and 12 pellets, and there was a house close to the shoulder of NJ-23 South, and I did not want to hit the house or, God forbid, anyone in it. When you shoot a firearm, you must know where the bullet or pellets are going if you miss your target. I first learned this when I went for my New Jersey hunting license. The state game wardens taught it, then in the military and, of course, in the New Jersey State Police Academy, where it was drilled into your head.

Also, at Newfoundland Station, I investigated my first fatal motor vehicle accident. It was a one-car accident in which the driver ran off NJ-94 in Vernon Township and hit a tree. The driver died, and there was no one else in the vehicle. The driver was a white male about twenty-one years old. Back at the station, I was told I would have to assist the medical examiner with the autopsy the next morning and then drive the organs to the State Police Lab in West Trenton, New Jersey (Now there are four State Police Labs: Little Falls in north Jersey, Seagirt in the shore area, West Trenton in central Jersey, and Hammonton in south Jersey.). The autopsy was held at the Sussex Hospital, a small hospital in Sussex Borough. The medical examiner worked alone, and I was his assistant. He had me put on rubber gloves and a face mask. He would hand me an organ (brain, liver, etc.), and I would put it in a round cardboard container and mark the top with what was inside. At the station, SFC

Delaney advised me it was too late to go to the division headquarters lab. I put the organs in the refrigerator until the next day.

The next morning a senior trooper came to work. He was a stout trooper who loved to eat and would eat just about anything in the refrigerator. The trooper looked into the fridge and asked, "What's in the containers?"

Another trooper answered, "Cow organs."

"Are they good to eat?" asked the senior trooper.

"Yeah, just fry it up a little," said another.

The senior man started to cut off a piece of brain and put it into a frying pan and was finally stopped by another trooper. I just looked on and was glad some of my evidence didn't get eaten.

Later, I watched that stout trooper take a large pizza, fold it in half, and eat it like a sandwich. I saw him do it once in Newfoundland Station and Netcong Station. Back then, troopers and local police officers would assist medical examiners, but later on, they had assistants, and troopers or police would watch, listen, and take notes.

While at Newfoundland Station, I investigated an airplane accident, the only one I investigated during my career. I received a call from the station that a small plane had landed on NJ-23 North in West Milford Township. The highway was a dual lane, two lanes in each direction. When I got there, I found that a small one-engine plane had lost power, and as it came down, it hit the top of an old pickup truck causing a significant dent in the roof, and then landed on the highway. There were no injuries. I advised the station and said that I had no airplane accident reports. I was advised to use a motor vehicle accident report, which I did. I interviewed the pilot, who explained that he had lost power and had no choice but to land on the highway. The old farmer, who was about eighty years old, and the pickup truck driver, was upset. He stated that he has been driving for over sixty years, never had an accident, and was now hit by an airplane. I took all the information I could from the truck driver and the pilot's license and plane information. Of course, my report was given to the FAA (Federal Aviation Authority), responsible for the accident investigation. The tow truck company that was called took the wings off the plane and towed it to their garage, and the pickup could drive away.

I was getting to like the Newfoundland Station. The troopers were good and pulled their weight like Troop "C." I was starting to make some criminal and warrant arrests but had to hold back on traffic summonses because of the antiquated numbers system. Of course, this all changed in the coming years. Regarding drinking driving arrests, the State Police used the old Drunkometer machine to test breath. This method used a mathematical equation to get a breath reading, and I was not an operator of this machine. Generally, if I brought a suspected drunk driver into the station, the sergeant or senior man told me to take him home. Other than that, I thought I had found a home at Newfoundland Station. After being at Newfoundland Station for about four or five months, I was told by the station commander, SFC Joe Delaney, that I was being transferred to Hackensack Station. I couldn't believe it. I asked SFC Delaney whether I did something wrong. He said no, I don't want to lose you, but something was wrong at Hackensack Station, and I advised the troop commander, Captain Quinn, that you can do the job there. I later found out that due to a police corruption case with the New York City Police which resulted in the Knapp Commission, division headquarters wanted the letting go of "friends" stopped at all the State Scales. I thought I was done with scale work, but now it was for real, as I was told.

Hackensack Station was a rental building located on US-17 North, just North of NJ-46. The station area was I-95 from the George Washington Bridge to I-80, then I-80 West to Paterson, where I-80 ended and was incomplete. The station also had the State Scale on US-17 South in Mahwah. We also helped the local police with US-17, NJ-46, and NJ-4. The station commander, assistant station commander, and about four senior troopers were also transferred. I replaced a senior trooper who went to Newfoundland Station. The new station commander was SFC Robert Delaney. After we all brought our gear in and were assigned a bedroom, we were advised the troop commander, Captain George Quinn, was en route to speak to all of us.

Captain Quinn stated the days of the "friends" were over, and he wanted to see the big company names on the overweight sheets, not just unsuspecting small companies. He added that he would check the overweight sheets to see if the job was being done. I was glad. Finally, I could go to the scale, write all overweight trucks, and not worry about being transferred to Cape May County.

I was at the scale house one day, and as I was about to write an overweight summons to a driver, the driver came in and asked me to stop and that his boss, the company's owner, was in the area and was going to stop in. I continued to write the summons as the "boss" came into the scale house. He identified himself as the owner of this large paper company from upstate New York. Then he showed me a State Police business card from a lieutenant from division headquarters with his signature on the back of the card. I just continued to write the summons. Also in the scale house was a State Police Weigh Team member.

A couple of days later, SFC Delaney advised me that a couple of detectives from Internal Affairs were coming up to interview me on an issue at the scale house. At the station, I met with two detectives from Internal Affairs. They asked, "Can you identify the person who gave me the lieutenant's business card?"

I said, "Yes." (Apparently, the trooper from the Weigh Team notified the Internal Affairs Bureau of the business card incident.) I then accompanied both detectives to upstate New York to attempt to identify the person who showed me the business card. We walked into the owner's office and sat down.

One of the detectives asked me, Is this the man?"

I said, "Yes!"

He then asked the owner, "Do you have a business card from a State Police lieutenant?"

He took out the card, showed it to the detectives, and said, "I met the lieutenant at a State Police softball game and tried to use it to get out of an expensive overweight summons."

I am sure that nothing came of this. The lieutenant retired in 1976 as a captain. It was nice to know that letting certain trucking companies go at the scales was over, and I was not going to Cape May County. Truck enforcement has changed drastically since then. Now the State Police has a Commercial Vehicle Inspection Unit that is highly trained and enforces state and federal safety laws and regulations.

Though I was happy that there were no longer "friends" in truck enforcement, I was very disappointed in the senior men at Hackensack Station. They were lazy and did not want to do any work, and this was a complete change from Troop C and even Newfoundland Station. They might have gone to the scale to weigh trucks, but they were never on patrol on I-80 or I-95, our primary responsibility. Very seldom did they ever investigate motor vehicle accidents.

One day I was on patrol early with my classmate, Tpr John Giuliani. We were assigned to patrol I-80 and I-95. I don't know where the senior men working were assigned, probably at the State Scale in Mahwah. We received a call from Hackensack Station that a serious accident occurred with a tractor-trailer and a couple of cars. The accident was near the bridge connecting Elmwood Park with Paterson. We both got there together and started to help the injured, and I called in for an ambulance, a heavy-duty wrecker, and a couple of car wreckers.

The trooper on the station record and radio was a senior trooper; he mentioned on the radio, "There is another accident in Leonia, near the George Washington Bridge."

I advised him, "We both are needed here on this serious accident."

He asked on the radio, "Can't you handle it?"

I advised him to get another patrol for the accident in Leonia.

Later on, when I returned to the station, I argued with him about what had happened today and that the senior men here should do their share of the work since they make more money than the junior men.

A few weeks later, the shoe was on the other foot. I was on the station record and radio, and that same senior trooper was on patrol with another patrol on I-80 and I-95. I gave the other patrol an accident call in Hackensack on I-80. The senior trooper said he would assist. The other patrol had arrived at the scene and said it was a minor accident with no injuries. I got another call for a one-car accident on the I-80 ramp to the Parkway in Saddle Brook. I gave the call to the senior trooper, but he said, "I am tied up with the other patrol."

Naturally, I asked him, "Can't you handle it?"

When the senior trooper came into the station, he was hot.

Before he could beret me, I leaned into him and told him what I thought of the senior men at this Station.

He later apologized to me for starting this mess.

Another time after a significant snowstorm, I was on patrol of the interstates, and I ran into multiple accidents at the entrance to the express lanes of I-80 Eastbound. The DOT (Department of Transportation) had closed off the express lanes with wooden barriers, and they had been plowing snow into those lanes. I flared out the area to avoid more accidents and spotted another troop car heading west. The senior man did pull over onto his left shoulder and asked if I needed help, and I said I could use some help. He mentioned that he was going home to eat and I should call the station for help. No help was available, and I investigated all four accidents. I started hating Hackensack Station.

Once I was on reserve time watching TV. It was about 4 P.M. The sergeant asked one of my classmates to hold the book down so he could go home for dinner. My classmate had to write any entries on a pad and not sign onto the station record so the sergeant could have a long dinner. He lived about a half hour from the station. At about 6:45 P.M., a troop lieutenant stopped in for inspection. He questioned my classmate about why he wasn't signed on the station record. What I loved about my classmate was that he didn't lie. He told the truth to the lieutenant, who immediately called the sergeant and ordered him to return to the station. When the sergeant arrived, the lieutenant chewed him out, ordered him not to leave the station again without signing out, and not go home for dinner anymore. I never saw the sergeant leave the station for the rest of my time at Hackensack Station.

While at Hackensack Station, I investigated my second fatal accident. This happened at about 2:30 A.M. I reported to work at 8 A.M. The sergeant advised me to dress quickly and that I had to investigate a fatal accident that had happened overnight. The late patrol went to the scene, and the "senior man" told the junior trooper to handle the accident even though the junior trooper was being transferred in a couple of days. The senior trooper would not take the accident. The accident was a one-car accident on I-80 East in Paterson, where the highway ended.

Young people would enter the road and race eastbound to the exit for NJ-20. The vehicle was an old Ford sedan driven by a young male who was alive and in serious condition at the hospital. The driver's brother, who was sitting right front, was killed. It was a couple of days before I could interview the driver. When I did, the driver stated he was not racing, was cut off by another vehicle, lost control, and hit the bridge abutment. I could see that he was distraught by the death of his brother. There were no witnesses to the accident. I discussed the case with Passaic County's prosecutor's office, and, based on the circumstances, they would not prosecute the driver. I agreed with their decision. This was the only fatal accident I investigated when I was home sleeping. Later the station commander, SFC Robert Delaney, discussed this incident with me and apologized to me for the sergeant's decision and the senior man who should have investigated the fatal accident.

On another note, when I was on patrol of I-80 and I-95 in the evening, I got a call from the station to stop in. A trooper, not a senior trooper, was on the station record and radio. He was three years senior to me but a good trooper who was also transferred to Hackensack to eliminate the overweight truck problem. When I stopped at the station, he stated that I was very productive in stopping many vehicles and requesting lookups on driver's licenses. I didn't know what he was getting at. He continued that the only other patrol was a senior man who loved boats and hung out at the boat docks on the Hudson River. In other words, I had no backup while on patrol with this trooper. I thanked the trooper for his information which I digested. This was just another bad mark against the senior men at this station.

Another problem at this station involved the court system. Bergen County has a "District Court" which handles all traffic cases from the State Police, the Bergen County Police, and the Bergen County Sheriff's Office. That made it pleasant because you didn't have to use all the Municipal Courts that line I-80 and I-95 in Bergen County. The only other court we used was the Paterson Municipal Court in Passaic County. The troop commander, Captain George Quinn, had a policy that if a violation was committed in an accident, he wanted a summons issued, usually for careless driving. The problem was in the Bergen Court District

Court; if you did not see the accident or didn't have a witness, the judge threw the case out without any testimony. Most insurance companies back then did not want their insured to plead guilty because by pleading not guilty, it could not be used against them in a civil action, even if they were found guilty. So, if you didn't issue a summons for the cause of the accident, you had to write a special report to Captain Quinn about why you didn't. So, most troopers issued the summons, including me, rather than having to explain it on a special report.

Once I saw a rear-end accident happen on I-80 in Hackensack City. I investigated the accident and issued the second vehicle driver a summons for careless driving. I went to the district court, and the judge asked me, "Do you have a witness to the accident?"

I said, "Yes, I witnessed it."

The judge was surprised.

The clerk swore me in, and after I testified along with the driver who got the summons, the judge found him guilty of careless driving. I could never understand the logic of this. In Troop C and west Jersey, judges heard the accident cases. Later, I learned that Bergen County was called "The State of Bergen."

Finally, in the spring of 1969, my class (72nd Class) was transferred to the toll roads. I was finally out of Hackensack Station and its senior man problem. I was transferred to Bloomfield Station, Troop E, on the Garden State Parkway.

As a side note, Hackensack Station was closed to uniform patrols around 1982, opening a new Troop B headquarters and Sub-Station in Totowa. Totowa Sub Station took over the responsibilities of Hackensack Station. Hackensack Station was used for a while by State Police Detectives but eventually closed for good when the lease ran out. There are two municipalities in Bergen County, Teterboro Borough and Rockleigh Borough, that do not have police departments. Teterboro laid off its police officers and was patrolled by the Bergen County Police. Rockleigh never had a police department and was patrolled by the Bergen County Police. Because of the high cost of the Bergen County Police, Teterboro is now patrolled by contract with the Moonachie Police, and the Northvale Police patrol Rockleigh Borough by contract. The Bergen County Police went out of business in 2021, and any responsibilities were taken over by the Bergen County Sheriff's Department. The State Police could have patrolled these two municipalities for free but were never asked. As I said, "The State of Bergen" does not want State Police in their county if possible. Later in this book, more will come on "The State of Bergen."

Troop E Post Bloomfield Station, here I come.

4

TROOP E POST

In early 1969 I reported to the Troop E Commander, Captain Karl K. Kloo, at Troop E headquarters attached to the Garden State Parkway Administration building in Woodbridge. Captain Kloo didn't have much to say. He told me I would be stationed at Bloomfield Station, which I already knew. He told me to head to Bloomfield and report to the station commander, SFC Richard Steinbruch. SFC Steinbruch said that he assigned me to Sgt Constant (Teddy) Kozel's squad and that I would be an early man since I lived close to the station. This was the first time I would work an eight-hour day shift. The stations on the Parkway and Turnpike worked an eight-hour shift schedule, six days on and two days off, and changed shifts every week. As an early man, my day shift was 6 A.M. to 2 P.M., the afternoon shift was 2 P.M. to 10 P.M., and the midnight shift was 10 P.M. to 6 A.M. Troopers rode alone on all shifts, but there were plenty of back-ups; ten troopers, including the sergeant on each squad.

The station area was divided into four areas. The first was Union County from the Union Toll Plaza South to MP-135, the county line for Middlesex County. The second area was Essex County from Union Toll Plaza North to Essex Toll Plaza. The third area starting at the Essex Toll Plaza was mostly in Passaic County and ended at the Bergen Toll Plaza. The fourth area started at the Bergen Toll Plaza and went through the Hillsborough Toll Plaza to the New York State line. Areas one, two, and three had three lanes in each direction. Area four had only two lanes in each direction and was called "the country patrol" because it was quiet, with fewer accidents or calls. Most of my squad was made up of junior men, but we had three senior men also.

You were assigned a specific area or an overlap patrol of two areas. I noticed right away that the junior men seemed to usually be assigned to the busiest areas, which were areas one and two, and the senior men areas three or four. I didn't mind this; I'd rather stay busy so the shift would go fast. I did get an overlap patrol of two areas once in a while, even areas three and four. Back then, we had to type accident reports. There were a lot of accidents at the toll plazas. Motorists would throw the quarter into the automatic lane, and some would stop until the red light said "Toll Paid." Then the next car would hit the first car in the rear. I got good at typing accident reports and started typing them at the toll plaza offices since they had good typewriters.

One day, Sgt Kozel, my shift supervisor, called me back to the station from area one. He told me I owed him three accident reports. I went out to my car and came back and gave him the completed reports. I told him I typed the reports at the toll plaza offices, either Union Toll or the new East Orange Toll Plaza. Sgt Kozel then asked if I didn't like him, and I said it's easier to type the reports below at the toll plazas than to return to the station. He understood and told me to keep doing it if I wanted to.

SFC Steinbruch must have checked the accident sheets and saw that the junior men were investigating 80 percent of the accidents. He put a stop to it. He ordered all his squad sergeants to assign the areas equally so the senior men would have areas one and two where most of the accidents were (shades of Hackensack Station). Bloomfield Station personnel come from Troop B. SFC Steinbruch's order, though not perfect, seemed to equalize the workload somewhat.

I didn't like Bloomfield Station because you were always being told to stay on Parkway property while on patrol. I thought the shoulder patch I wore said New Jersey State Police, not Garden State Parkway Police. I had to think of something else to generate some criminal activities. I had to spend eighteen months at Bloomfield before requesting a transfer back to Troop B.

I had a cousin, Victor Di Blasi, a Newark detective assigned to CSI (Crime Scene Investigations). Victor gave me a unique phone number to the Newark Police computer room for local criminal lookups. I started using the number right away. When I stopped someone with a Newark or East Orange address, I would call the station and have the sergeant call the number and see if Newark Police wanted the person. This turned out to be a great check and gave me the right to legally search the vehicle for any contraband. If the subject was only wanted for an outstanding warrant, I would take him to the closest Newark police precinct and turn him over to them. Fortunately or unfortunately, depending on how you look at it, other troopers at Bloomfield got the number and started doing the same thing that I was. This worked great until Newark Police got tired of us and changed the number. I couldn't ask my cousin Victor Di Blasi for the new number because he had quit the Newark Police Department and opened up an Italian American delicatessen in Dallas, Texas. Go figure.

Making a death notification was part of the responsibilities of a law enforcement officer. In chapter one, I was with my assistant coach, and we made a death notification by driving up the driveway to the house, and when the woman came out screaming, we left. He said she now knows and will contact the hospital. I thought that was wrong, and we should have ensured the woman was alright before leaving. I was detailed to investigate a serious accident on the Parkway Southbound in Bloomfield Township. It was raining very hard, and it was about 6:30 A.M. on a Sunday. It was the third fatal accident I have investigated so far. The car had hit the guide rail and flipped over several times. The driver was alone. The driver was dead. He wasn't wearing a seat belt, and his head was cracked wide open. I knew the ambulance personnel would not take the body if they saw his head, and I didn't want to wait a couple of hours for the medical examiner. As the ambulance pulled up, I bandaged the driver's head the best I could with gauze. The ambulance personnel looked at the driver and declared that he was dead and that they would not take him to the hospital. I told them that since you pronounced him dead (which they could not do), I would tell the family that he might have been alive and that you wouldn't take him to the hospital. You guys will get sued, not me. They took him to the hospital, and he was pronounced DOA (dead on arrival).

After clearing the scene, I returned to Bloomfield Station to notify the next of kin. The subject lived in Brooklyn. After several phone calls, I reached the New York police precinct that handled his residence. I told the desk sergeant, "I think you should make the death notification."

He replied, "My precinct does not handle the even numbers of the street. The next precinct does."

I called the next precinct, and that desk sergeant told me the first sergeant was wrong.

I went back and forth several times and finally called the dead subject's phone number. A male subject answered, "I am twenty-three, and the brother." The deceased driver was twenty-one years old.

I told him, "Your brother was killed in an accident on the Parkway."

I gave him directions to Bloomfield Station and said, "I will wait there for you."

He arrived in about an hour, and I gave him all the needed information. I also told him what happened with his New York City police precinct and advised him that these notifications should not be done on the phone. I advised him to see the precinct commander and explain what happened.

In another case, I assisted another trooper with a one-car fatality on the Parkway North in East Orange. It was a Friday night at about midnight. Two males in the car had hit the center overpass divider. Both subjects were taken to East Orange Hospital. One subject was pronounced DOA, and the other, though hurt, was going to live. Both subjects resided in Little Falls, so I notified the Little Falls police to make a death notification on the dead subject. The patrolmen assigned the detail decided to get a parish priest to accompany them to the deceased person's house. While waiting for the priest to get dressed, the hospital called the injured person's home and advised his wife that her husband was in the hospital due to an auto accident. She called the other wife, picked her up, and proceeded to the hospital, thinking they were both injured. When the Little Falls Police and the priest arrived, they were already gone. The dead man's wife became hysterical when they arrived at the hospital. The head nurse started yelling at me, "Why didn't you tell her?"

I advised her what I did and gave her the phone number of the Little Falls Police. "Go yell at them!"

I don't understand why some police officers and troopers have a problem with death notifications.

I was off duty and deer hunting in Holland Township, Hunterdon County, with my good Army National Guard friends, SGM (Sergeant Major) Brian Roseberry and SGM Jim Blazakus. As we walked into the woods from our cars, SGM Roseberry had to sit down and then keeled over. He had a heart attack. I called for an ambulance, and it came quickly, along with a troop car from the old Flemington State Police Station. I advised the trooper who I was and gave him information for his report. Then SGM Blazakus and I followed the ambulance to the Flemington Medical Center. SGM Roseberry was pronounced dead at the hospital. I advised the trooper doing the unattended death investigation that I would make the death notification and get the information to him. It was a weekday, and I knew that SGM Roseberry's wife worked as a legal secretary in Washington. I called the Washington Police and spoke to the patrolman in charge.

I knew the chief of police, who was not available. I carefully explained where Nancy Roseberry worked in the building next to the fire station. I explained that her husband had a heart attack and passed away and that we were all at the hospital. The patrolman I spoke with advised Nancy Roseberry that we were all at the medical center in Flemington and that "someone" got hurt. Nancy Roseberry arrived with her boss, who drove her. She entered the emergency room area and asked me what had happened. Thinking that she already knew her husband was dead, I said it looked like a heart attack had killed him. She became hysterical and then told me what the Washington patrolman told her. I couldn't believe this was happening again with notifications. I later notified the chief of police of Washington Borough, advised him of what happened, and told him I was very disappointed in how the patrolman attempted to do the notification. I told the chief that he should not be in law enforcement!

The chief said to me that he would take care of this. Of course, when I called the trooper at Flemington Station, I told him that I had notified Brian's wife at the hospital.

One of my favorite violations on the Parkway was a toll violator. The toll plazas were on the same radio frequency as our troop cars. They would call out a toll violator, and if I were close, I would attempt to stop the violator. The best way to catch a violator was to stop at the plaza office and see if they had an extra toll collector available to catch a toll violator. The toll collector would hide in an automatic cash toll lane and call out a violator who did not pay the twenty-five-cent toll. I would hide behind the toll office area, and if a violator was called out, I would chase them down and write them a summons for not paying the toll. It reminded me of when I got my driver's license in 1962, and in the summer, I would drive down to the shore with some friends and go to Seaside Heights for the day. There were five toll plazas between Clifton, where we got on, and the Toms River Toll Plaza. We avoided the tolls by getting off and going around the five toll plazas. By saving the ten tolls at twenty-five cents each, we used the money for gas which was thirty cents a gallon. It was no longer feasible in the coming years when the Parkway started to build ramp toll plazas, making it impossible to avoid the tolls.

While I was working, SFC Steinbruch gave me a detail. A constant toll violator who was mailed forty summonses for toll violations from Troop E headquarters would not accept the certified mail. So the summonses were returned to Troop E headquarters. He went through three barrier tolls heading south from his home and three more heading north to his house. He only violated one toll south and one toll north. I set up that morning early at the Essex Plaza South. Sure enough, he violated the Essex toll, and I pulled him over. I gave him a summons for the toll he ran and served him with the forty summonses he refused to accept by mail. I advised him that a court appearance was required. A month later, we went to the Bloomfield Municipal Court, and the subject pleaded guilty and was fined $820 for the forty-one summons. He told me after court that he only ran one toll each way to work and home because he felt the trip was only worth fifty cents each way, so he only ran one toll each way. He added that even with the fine of $820, he was about even in what he saved in running tolls and the fine. I asked him if he would continue running tolls, and he said no, it was not worth it anymore since the troopers were looking for him now.

I worked a midnight shift and was assigned area three (Passaic County). Another trooper had the overlap of areas three and four (Passaic County and Bergen County). The other trooper was about two years senior to me but still considered a junior man. A senior man had area four which was considered the "country patrol," with a lot fewer accidents happening there, and it only had two lanes in each direction. A call came from the station about a serious accident on the southbound exit ramp to NJ-17 South. The trooper who had the overlap patrol was given the call, and I was sent to assist him. When I got to the scene, I saw it was only a one-car accident with the driver dead and no other people in the vehicle. A relatively easy accident to investigate. I asked the trooper where the senior man was. He mentioned he had to go someplace. I never found out where the senior man went, but it reminded me of Hackensack Station when I investigated a fatal accident while I was still home sleeping. But things got better with the senior men since the station commander, SFC Steinbruch, put the "fear of God" into the senior men.

On another fatal accident early on the day shift, the call was given to a new trooper with area three. I had area two and was asked to assist. The accident happened on a Parkway entrance ramp from NJ-19. The car had four males, left the road off the ramp, and rolled over numerous times. There were three dead, and one survived. When I arrived at the scene, the new trooper tried handing me the driver's and passenger's information. He said, "Boy, you got a bad one, Sal."

I said, "No, you got a bad one, but I will help you."

He had only been stationed at Bloomfield Station for a couple of weeks and was only one class senior to me. He learned fast and was an excellent trooper while I worked with him at Bloomfield Station. He did a great job on this fatal accident even though the driver was deceased and there were no criminal charges.

The problem arose much later on with this accident. The Parkway competed with other toll roads in the country to be the safest that year.

The Parkway Authority sent its engineers to survey where this triple fatality occurred. They decided it was not a Parkway accident but an NJ-19 accident. They changed the accident location to the NJ-19 exit ramp and transferred the report to Little Falls State Police Station. They were utterly wrong. The car ran off the roadway at least five hundred feet into the ramp and was on Parkway property. I advised SFC Steinbruch of this and that I would call the Indiana Turnpike about this since they were in completion for this award. SFC Steinbruch ordered me not to call any other toll roads because we are not responsible for where this accident happened. The Parkway Authority is. I never called another toll road authority, and later I was advised by SFC Steinbruch that the Parkway did not win anyway. I never found out who won, but I was glad it wasn't the Garden State Parkway since they cheated.

As a road trooper and road sergeant, I arrested approximately two hundred motorists for drinking and driving. I only lost one case, and it happened while I was stationed at Bloomfield Station. I was on patrol in area two (Essex County) in the evening, and it was dark. I was following a car driving slowly and erratically, and the driver was unable to keep the vehicle in one lane. I stopped the car in the northbound lanes of the Parkway in East Orange. The driver was a middle-aged white male in a business suit. He had a strong odor of an alcoholic beverage on his breath, bloodshot eyes, and was slurring his speech. I got him out of his vehicle, and he could not pass a balance test. I placed him under arrest for drinking and driving. I called it in, and fortunately, there was a trooper working that could administer the breath test. The state was changing to the new breathalyzer machine, and troopers were starting to be trained on the new device. When I arrived at the station, I was advised by the station that Tpr Gary Knight was going to run the Drunkometer test. Tpr Knight was working with our squad that afternoon for some reason. I knew that if I had to ask the sergeant to run the test, he would just tell me to drive the motorist home. I was glad Tpr Knight was working with our squad that afternoon. The motorist took the test with well over .20-blood alcohol in his system. I wrote the summons for drinking and driving, and someone picked up the subject and took him home. This case was contested, and about a month later, it was heard in the East Orange Municipal Court. An attorney represented the subject. Tpr Knight and I testified, and the defendant's attorney could not get the blood reading thrown out. The defendant then testified. He stated that he was weaving on the Parkway because his son was buried in the cemetery that butts up against the Parkway in East Orange, and he was feeling melancholy as he passed the cemetery. He added that he only had two drinks with dinner that night before being stopped. After hearing all testimony, the judge found the subject not guilty because he had known the subject for thirty years and would not take the results of a machine over this subject that he had known so long. The judge should have recused himself, but he didn't. I discovered that the subject was the head of the Democratic party in Essex County. I brought this to the attention of the station commander, and he gave me a DMV (Division of Motor Vehicle) report requesting a hearing on this matter. I filled the information out and sent it in. I waited a couple of months and didn't hear anything, so I called the DMV hearing office. They advised that they had my report and would notify me when the hearing would occur. Another couple of months went by, and I called again and was again advised that the hearing was still pending. I was then contacted by a troop lieutenant and told to stop calling the DMV on this matter. They will call you. Naturally, the call never came, and I never got my hearing. "Nice to have friends in high places."

In another case that involved the procedures of CSI, I learned another lesson. I was following a black Cadillac driving erratically on the Parkway South in Nutley. I was driving a marked troop car, and the driver must have spotted me and taken off. I had already called in the New York state license, and it came back "stolen." I chased the vehicle of exit 145 South into East Orange. He ran red traffic lights on South Orange Avenue until he crashed into another car. He exited the vehicle and ran into the city. I had to stop at the accident scene to check for injuries in the other vehicle he struck. I described the fleeing suspect to the station as a white male about thirty years old wearing a gray sports jacket. Then the East Orange Police showed up, and I gave them the suspect's description and where he ran. They asked me if I would investigate the accident, and I said I had to call it in first. The Bloomfield Station replied to have the

East Orange Police investigate the accident but have the stolen vehicle towed back to Bloomfield Station. It belongs to a VIP (very important person). The station stated that the CSI people would check the car for fingerprints. Again since this was my investigation, I think I should have investigated the accident. Again my shoulder patch says State Police, not Parkway Police.

I found out the stolen car was stolen out of New York City and was owned by Camilla Edge, the wife of former New Jersey Governor Walter Edge, who was governor from 1917 to 1919 and 1944 to 1947. Governor Edge passed away in 1956. Camilla Edge, his wife, living in New York City, passed away in 1972. The CSI detective got some excellent prints off the stolen car but said it would take some time to check them with the criminal files in the state (Now, all police use the AFIS (Automated Fingerprint Identification System), which was computerized, and if prints are in the system, the results return immediately.). I asked the CSI detective why his unit doesn't check for prints on all abandoned vehicles left on the road. He stated they do if the car was used in a serious crime or, in my case, I have a suspect whom I saw. (I also think the VIP owner had something to do with CSI being called in). In any event, it took about two weeks, and the prints came back to a subject, a white male with a criminal record who had spent time in a New Jersey State Prison. The subject lived in Bloomfield, not far from our station. So one day, late in the afternoon, the station detective sergeant and I went to his residence and placed him under arrest. I charged him with possession of stolen property, eluding a police officer, reckless driving, and leaving the scene of an accident. The East Orange Police let me make all the charges that led to the accident since it was a continual violation. While processing the subject at the station, he asked me how long I had been a trooper. I stated about three years. He said he was a criminal for over ten years and would beat me in court on all charges. Sure enough, he did plead not guilty and was assigned a public defender. We went to Essex County Superior Court a couple of months later, and the subject was found guilty of all charges and sentenced to five years in state prison. As court officers led him out, we made eye contact, and I held up four fingers and said to him, "four for four." He was not a happy camper.

During a couple of summers or more, a white male about twenty years old would come out of the woods naked, wave at traffic stark naked, and then run back into the woods. He usually did this late in the afternoon northbound when traffic from the shore was heavy. Of course, he was long gone without cell phones. By the time the motorist either got to the toll plaza or home and called it in. The call would usually be, check out Rudy the Nudy; he's at it again. The area in question was at mile marker 135 north, the dividing line for Bloomfield and Holmdel Stations. One afternoon a Holmdel trooper in an unmarked State Police vehicle was right there and saw "Rudy." The trooper chased him on foot and caught him in the woods. He was arrested for lewdness and eventually paid a hefty fine. I remember that "Rudy the Nudy" didn't do his trick again.

As a note of levity, we had an old-fashioned soda machine at the Bloomfield Station. The way it worked was the soda bottles were arranged in a maze so that after you put your money in, you would take the flavor you wanted and pull it through the maze to the exit point. The problem was that the bottles were right side up. At night when the station commander was off, troopers would pop off the cap and drink the soda through a straw, put the cap back on, and leave the empty bottle in the maze. When the station commander came to work and saw the empty soda bottles in the machine, he became enraged. He said he would have them transferred far away if he caught someone drinking free soda. Finally, he had the machine taken out, and a brand-new modern Coke machine was brought in. Unfortunately, a State Police detective from the Organized Crime Bureau had stopped at the station and noticed the new Coke machine. He checked it, and when he saw it was owned by one of the organized crime families of New Jersey, he told his boss in division headquarters. COL David Kelly personally called the troop commander to remove the Coke machine immediately, which he did. No soda machine was there when I was transferred back to Troop B.

I was coming to the end of my eighteen months at Bloomfield Station. Thanks to the station commander, things were much better than when I arrived with the senior man problem. I still liked the hours at a road station; two days on and two days off gave you more prime time off. In August 1970, I sent my transfer request to go back to Troop B. When the station commander saw my transfer request, he called me into his office and tried to talk me out of the request. I advised him I was still single and liked the road pass list better. He wished me luck with the transfer. The transfer teletype came out, transferring me to Troop B effective Tuesday, the day after Labor Day 1970.

The STFA (State Trooper Fraternal Association) was the bargaining agent for all the New Jersey troopers. We had worked without a contract since I entered the State Police. I had been attending union meetings at the Friendly Sons of the Shillelagh, a tavern with a large hall located off NJ-18 in Old Bridge. Our attorney was Thomas J. Savage III. Sometimes the meetings got a little loud and boisterous. I don't think it was because we were all drinking beer. What do you think? Finally, word got back to the troops that the STFA wanted to have a slowdown and not write any summonses over Labor Day weekend, 1970. I thought this was wrong since we do all the work and the detectives and specialists skate. On the Parkway, you had to be careful. If a toll supervisor had a toll violator stopped, and the station sent you there, you had to write the summons. The same on an accident where one party was dead wrong. We discussed this with our whole squad at Bloomfield Station. But we could keep it to a minimum.

Before transferring back to Troop B, I worked the three-shift (2 P.M. to 10 P.M.) on Saturday and Sunday on Labor Day weekend. I was off on Monday, Labor Day. I was lucky I didn't have to write any summonses, but I would have if I had been forced to. Information on the "slow down" was in the *Newark Star-Ledger*, and the brass in division headquarters was livid. The division still was not negotiating in good faith, so our attorney sent COL David B. Kelly a letter that we were thinking of joining the Teamsters Union. That did it, and the state started negotiating with the STFA, and we finally got a contract in a few months, giving us a much-needed raise. I guess the slowdown didn't hurt.

I enjoyed my time at this toll road station (Bloomfield) for the eighteen months I was out there. All current troopers should do a tour of a toll road station. The problem now was they worked a 12-hour shift, and if they lived far away in west Jersey, it would be too long of a commute.

As I said previously, I didn't like being told to stay on Parkway property. My patch said New Jersey State Police. The brass wanted us to stay on Parkway property because the Parkway and the New Jersey Turnpike reimbursed the state for our salaries, benefits, and pension payments. So, in reality, we were rented to the toll roads. In 2003 the McGreevy administration consolidated both roads into one authority. The headquarters for both roads was on the Turnpike in New Brunswick. This eliminated the Garden State Parkway Troop E headquarters. Now the three Parkway Stations are a part of Troop D, with their headquarters in Cranberry, on the Turnpike.

In another incident, there was a vehicle that I called in as abandoned and requested a wrecker. Before the wrecker arrived, the car was hit by a Volkswagen Beetle, and the driver's head went through the windshield. The driver of the Volkswagen sued the Parkway for leaving an abandoned vehicle on the roadway. SFC Steinbruch stated that I might be getting a written reprimand for not staying with the car until the wrecker arrived. I complained that we never stay with a vehicle until the wrecker comes unless it's in a dangerous position which this one wasn't. This reprimand stayed pending until I was transferred back to Troop B.

One thing I liked about Bloomfield Station was when I was working the midnight shift (10 P.M. to 6 A.M.), the sergeant would call me at about 5:30 A.M. and say, make a stop at toll 45 North. That meant picking up a six-pack of Pabst Blue Ribbon beer at the Pabst brewery in Newark. I would go in the back door, take a six-pack out of one of the many refrigerators, say hello to the workers, and leave. The sergeant and I would have "one for the road" before going home. Of course, the sergeant took the remaining beer home.

Oh well, all good things come to an end. I was on my way back to Troop B. Due to all the confusion on the slowdown, I was never advised which Troop B station I was assigned to. I was only advised to report to Troop B headquarters in Morristown the day after Labor Day at 9 A.M.

Troop B Posts, here I come again.

5

TROOP B POSTS:
SOMERVILLE STATION & TACTICAL PATROL UNIT

In September 1970, the day after Labor Day, I reported to Troop B headquarters in Morristown. I first spoke with the First Sergeant and told him who I was.

He informed me, "The troop commander is not in. Let me send you to the deputy, a lieutenant."

I gave the lieutenant a firm salute and sat down.

He started out being very cordial and discussed the general facts about Troop B. He asked me, "Did you work over the Labor Day weekend?"

I replied, "I worked the afternoon shift on Saturday and Sunday but was off on Monday, Labor Day."

He asked me, "Did you write any summons on Saturday or Sunday?"

I said, "No, I did not."

The lieutenant stood up and said, "Get the hell out of my office."

I hurriedly left and went out to the first sergeant. The first sergeant told me, "You are stationed at the Somerville Station. Go there and report to the station commander, SFC William Widgren."

I quickly left the headquarters, not happy with my introduction back to Troop B. I had no idea at the time where Somerville Station was since I was never there. I-287 was not finished yet, so I headed east on NJ-24 instead of taking US-202 South. I ended up in Union, about twenty miles east of Somerville. After asking for directions in a gas station, I started heading west on US-22. As I went under the US-202 overpass, I saw the Somerville Station on the eastbound side of US-22 and naturally passed it. After making a u-turn, I pulled into the front of the station.

I went into the station and stopped by the window in the vestibule. There was an older senior trooper on the station record. I identified myself and told him, "I am now stationed here."

He replied, "I don't know anything about you!" and continued his business.

I thought, *here we go again with a cranky senior man*. I now had more than three years on the force, and I wouldn't take his guff. I yelled at him, "Open the damn door," which he did with a buzzer switch.

The trooper sat me down in the station commander's office and said SFC Widgren would be in shortly; he had to go out for something. SFC Widgren came back to the station about a half hour later. He introduced himself, took me upstairs, and assigned me a bedroom. After bringing all my gear in, I met with SFC Widgren in his office. He advised me that he had spoken with my previous station commander, SFC Steinbruch, at Bloomfield Station and got an excellent report on my time there. We went over the pass list to see any discrepancies, and there weren't any. He told me to go home and report for two days of work tomorrow. He also told me he would be scheduling me and all the other troopers for Breathalyzer school to learn and be qualified on the new machine to check the breath of drinking drivers. SFC Widgren was a gentleman. His senior man was a little weak. I was hoping I wouldn't have a problem with senior men as I did at Hackensack Station. I was wrong; Somerville Station only had a few senior men, and most troopers were young like me.

The Somerville Station area of responsibility was I-287 from the Somerset County line with Middlesex County, north, to the Bernardsville exit, where the road stopped and was still under construction. Edison Station in Troop C patrolled the Middlesex County area of I-287 from Piscataway to the Outer Bridge Crossing into Staten Island, New York. Somerville also patrolled I-78 from the Hunterdon County line east to Berkeley Heights, where the road was still under construction. For the local area, Somerville handled the general police calls in Millstone Borough and Branchburg Township since they did not have a local police department. After riding with another trooper for a few days, I started patrolling alone. I liked the area and was going to start looking for an apartment close by since I figured I would be here for a while. I found an ad in the local paper for an attic apartment in a private home in Branchburg, Township.

While on patrol in Branchburg, Township, I stopped at the house that advertised the apartment. I rang the bell, and an elderly woman answered the door and stated, "Is there anything wrong, officer?"

I said, "No, I am answering your ad for an attic apartment."

She showed me the way. The apartment had its own entrance in the rear of the house and was completely furnished with a small stove, refrigerator, color TV, and an air conditioner. It also had a beautiful view of the countryside. She explained it would be $150 per month, which I thought was very cheap compared to rent in Passaic County, where I lived with my parents and sisters. Now my sisters could each have their own rooms with me gone. The only problem was that the Troop B commander, Captain Joseph Rogolski, had a policy that he didn't want troopers living in the station area where they patrolled. So I didn't change my address and left it at my parent's house in Passaic. I only told one trooper where I was living just in case he could come and get me if something happened. Fortunately, he never told anyone else at the station, or I would have been transferred. I got to like Somerville Station, and it didn't hurt that I lived only five miles away. I even joined the Somerville YMCA. After being qualified on the Breathalyzer machine, I started making drinking driver arrests. There was a push on to get drunk drivers off the road by the state and federal governments. I was also making criminal arrests as I did at Bloomfield Station, with 50 percent being warrant arrests utilizing the NCIC (National Crime Information Center) or the SCIC (State Crime Information Center).

Some of my favorite arrests were illegal aliens. When I stopped a Hispanic, and he was nervous and evasive, I would ask him for his green card. Many of them had a green card, but it was usually expired. I would arrest them and take them back to the Somerville Station. I would then notify the INS (Immigration and Naturalization Service) in Newark and turn the subjects over to them either at the station or the Scotch Plains

Station in Union County. I enjoyed Somerville Station and had about fifteen days off a month. I still had time to go home and visit with my old friends from the neighborhood (and do my wash at my Mom's since I didn't have a washer or dryer at my apartment).

One of my first calls at Somerville was for a stolen bicycle. I drove to a relatively new home in a development in Branchburg Township. I was driving a marked troop car. The car in the driveway had New York plates on it. I rang the bell, and a middle-aged man answered the bell. I mentioned he had called on a stolen bicycle complaint. He said yes, but he said he called the Branchburg Police. I told him there was no Branchburg Police and that the State Police from Somerville handled the police calls in Branchburg Township. He was upset that he had just bought a house in an area with no local police department. He gave me a good description of the stolen bike, and I advised him that I would see what I could do.

I was driving around the development and spotted the stolen bike up against a house. I checked it, and it was the stolen bicycle I was looking for. I checked with the resident of this house, and they allegedly knew nothing about the bike. I then returned the bike to the subject, who reported it stolen. He identified it, and I had him sign a property report. He wasn't worried about not having a local police force anymore. He said that where he just came from in Brooklyn, he once had a piece of property damaged overnight, and when he called the police, it took them two hours to answer the call. I advised him to leave expensive property locked in the garage and not left on the front lawn. He agreed. I think I made a friend of the State Police with a previous New York City resident.

I was a coach with a recruit when we got a call of a woman choking at a restaurant in Branchburg Township. We were close and arrived in about two minutes. We went in, and the woman was on the floor, choking. I got her up and tried giving her the Heimlich method, but nothing came out. The first aid squad came and forced a tube with oxygen down her throat and took her to the hospital. She was pronounced DOA. I felt bad. I attended the autopsy the next day and watched the doctor struggle with a piece of meat stuck in her throat. He stated that nothing would have dislodged the piece of beef short of surgery. I felt a little better because there was nothing anyone could have done to save her life.

On another night, I received a call to assist the Bridgewater Police with a serious motor vehicle accident on US-22 Westbound. When we got there, the Bridgewater officer was putting out flares. He came up to me and offered he had never seen such a terrible accident, and it looked like everyone was dead. I know how he felt as I did when at my first station (Tennant), my classmate and I pulled up on a fatal accident with four dead, a whole family. I told the patrolman to help the recruit put flares out, and I would handle the accident.

One car was traveling east in the left westbound lane, and the other was west in the left westbound lane. They hit headlight to headlight at the top of the overpass for NJ-28. The vehicle's driver going the wrong way was dead, as were the driver and right-front passenger of the car going the right way. The two passengers in the car going right were seriously injured. There were no passengers in the car going the wrong way. The driver going the wrong way had a valid Georgia driver's license, and the vehicle he was driving was registered to his wife, who lived in Toms River. The driver had a New Jersey license but was suspended for two years for a second drinking and driving offense. His blood reading was .22 BA. He paid the ultimate price but took two innocent people with him.

I had another one-car fatal on I-287, but it was simple. It was a one-car that ran off the road accident. The driver was the only occupant, and he had a .17 blood alcohol level. This was my fifth fatal accident investigation.

In another fatal accident, I was dispatched to a two-car accident on I-287 on the bridge over the Raritan River that divides Bridgewater Township and Franklyn Township. It was in the evening, and it was dark. I arrived with another trooper who was a little junior to me. He stated that he wanted to investigate this one since he had never had one, and I said OK and that I would assist him. It was a two-car accident where one car struck another car in the rear. Unfortunately, a man between the vehicles was dead and almost cut in half. The woman driver in the first car was hysterical and said that she had broken down, and a nice man stopped to help and push her vehicle off the bridge. The driver of the second car was under the influence and was placed under arrest. I then looked up the road and saw another vehicle parked on the shoulder with its lights on. I walked up to the car, and a woman was sitting in the right front seat. She told me her husband was back there helping a vehicle stuck on the bridge. I then notified her of her husband's death. It's strange the way some death notifications are done. She was then taken to Somerset Hospital by the local first aid squad.

The only time I used deadly force was on a dog. I was serving a bench warrant for a man not appearing in court on a shoplifting charge. It was raining, and fortunately, I had left my raincoat open. The house was located on a dirt road in the country. There was a white picket fence around the house. It was daylight. As I got up near the front steps, the front door flew open, and a large German Sheppard came running at me. I pulled my weapon, aimed, and fired one shot hitting the dog in the throat and killing him. He landed on the bottom of the steps. The woman standing by the door yelled, "You shot my dog!"

I said, "And I will shoot you, too, if you don't send your husband out!"

He came out, and I arrested him on a bench warrant. I took him to Somerville Station and told the sergeant what had happened.

The suspect said, "You killed my dog, and I want compensation for it."

The sergeant told the suspect, "If you try to make a claim on the dog, we will arrest your wife for aggravated assault on a police officer for sending the dog after the trooper, and she will spend at least five years in state prison."

The suspect then said, "Ok, forget about it." I took him to the Somerset County Jail.

When I returned, I asked the sergeant, "Should I make a special report for firing my weapon in the line of duty?" We even made one out if you had to shoot a wounded deer.

The sergeant replied, "No report is necessary. I will make an entry in the station record on the incident."

It would be the only time I used deadly force in the line of duty, and no report was necessary. Nothing like the old days. Today if this happened and you didn't report it, you would probably at least be brought up on administrative charges.

Remember I said I might get a written reprimand for leaving a car unattended on the Parkway when I was at Bloomfield Station? I got a call in early 1971 from the first sergeant at Troop E headquarters. He said, "I found a written reprimand for you from your time at Bloomfield Station. Captain Karl Kloo (the troop commander) just retired. Would you like to have the reprimand sent to Troop B headquarters in Morristown or put it in the 'round' file?"

Naturally, I told him, "Put it in the round file. I don't deserve it anyway."

The Somerville Station DSG (Detective Sergeant) was Edward Moose. My first run-in with him was when I investigated a minor burglary in Branchburg Township and put the completed report in his box to be checked. When I returned to work after being off for two days, I found the report in my box with numerous red correction marks. A note on it said, "See me," and it was signed "Moose."

I saw him in his office, and he explained the mistakes. He then gave me the investigation report, and I signed it for him. He had typed it up.

I told him, "At Bloomfield Station (where I had just come), when an arrest was made, you just made out a special report, and the detectives typed up the investigation and arrest reports, and then you signed them."

DSG Moose reminded me, "You have high-paid secretaries out there."

He also taught me that if you make an arrest for a small amount of drugs or a weapon and you have three or four suspects when you are back in the station, put them in a room alone and tell them to discuss the case alone and either all are charged or one if he gives a written statement to that effect.

I thanked him for the lesson. DSG Moose was one of the better station detectives I have worked with on the road.

In early 1971, I was asked by the station commander, SFC Widgren, if I wanted to work with the Troop B CIO (Criminal Investigation Office) on a wiretap operation. He said he picked me for my interest in criminal arrests and that I lived in Passaic, near the wiretap operation. Of course, he didn't know I lived in Branchburg Township. I jumped on the detail since I had no idea how a wiretap operation works. The process was in a room upstairs from the Bloomfield Station on the Parkway.

It took me about one hour to get there from my home. I met there with a couple of Troop B detectives, and they explained how the wiretap worked and that I'd be working twelve-hour shifts. The wiretap was on an Italian American Club in Belleville. One tap was under the card table, and one was in a pay phone in the club. You had to listen to the tap and type the information on special wiretap reports. It was interesting, and I was getting good at typing the reports. The tap was good for thirty days. To drum up conversations on the wire, they had me raid a house in Belleville for selling untaxed cigarettes. I went there with three uniformed troopers, and we entered the house with a warrant and arrested the owner for selling untaxed cigarettes. We also confiscated about 1,300 cartons. I also did a narcotics raid in North Newark, where we found marijuana and made two arrests.

I did all the reports, and none bounced, thanks to DSG Moose at Somerville Station. I was sent to do the raids because the permanent CIO detectives did not want to be recognized by any suspects. I also got a call from the CIO, Lt. Mike Gallagher, for doing an excellent job on the raids and reports. We still had about a week to go on the wiretap when I got another call from Lt. Gallagher stating I couldn't finish the wire because Somerville Station had a new station commander, and he wanted me back. I had to report back to Somerville Station the next day. Lt. Gallagher said he would request me if he needed another road trooper again. It was interesting and fun, especially the raids I ran.

I reported to Somerville Station and the new station commander, newly promoted SFC Ben Mele. SFC Mele said he called me back early because he needed me because the station was getting an additional township to patrol. The Scotch Plains Station on US-22 East was closing, and Somerville Station would be patrolling Warren Township (Somerset County) when it closed. Taking over the calls in Warren Township created a lot more work in that about ten thousand people lived in Warren Township. They didn't have a local police department. We did get a few more troopers from the Scotch Plains Station when it closed. Division headquarters estimated that when I-78 was finished to Newark Airport, a new station would be built in Union County in Springfield. Unfortunately, that never happened, and to this day, we do not have a State Police Station in Union County anymore. Somerville Station got much busier with the addition of Warren Township to patrol.

Around this time, the State Police began hiring civilian dispatchers under a federal program called CEDA (There are many definitions for CEDA, but I found the best was the Center for Educational Development and Assessment.). Apparently, the federal government would pay the first year's salary, and then the state would pick up the wages. This worked out well. Now the sergeant could work with a dispatcher there and check his troopers and assist them with calls. This project was for all the road troops (troops A, B, and C but not for the toll road troops D and E).

One of my first calls in Warren Township was a suicide. A young girl about thirty years old and mentally challenged had hung herself in her clothes closet with a belt. I arrived on the scene with a senior trooper who had about fifteen years on. I started to cut her down, and the senior trooper asked, "What are you doing?"

I told him, "We have to wait for the medical examiner, and I don't want her mother to see her hanging anymore."

I laid her on the floor and put a blanket over her.

I went downstairs and advised her mother, "Your daughter has passed away."

Her mother was in disbelief.

I asked the senior man, "Have you ever handled a suicide?"

He said, "No, you take it!"

I wanted to anyway.

While at Somerville Station, we had a new device to check speeding vehicles called VASCAR (Visual Average Speed Computer and Recorder). This device was put into most all marked cars. It was a stopwatch with a distance computer on it. You put a distance into the unit, like between two overpasses using the shadow of the overpass. As the speeding vehicle passed through, you hit the start button on the first overpass and the off button when the vehicle hit the second overpass. The unit would give you the average vehicle speed between the two overpasses. This device worked very well in catching speeders. One day I was calling out speeders on I-78 West, and another trooper was pulling them over and writing the summons (An old trick we used back then was I would sign about five to ten summonses in my book and let the other trooper write them for me.). The other trooper called me on the radio and stated that he had an irate motorist stopped who wanted to see the machine that clocked him. I then drove down to the other trooper. The motorist looked at the VASCAR machine that still recorded his speed. The motorist continued that he had already beaten two radar summons in Union County and would beat this new machine. I told him we would see him in court. Sure enough, the summons was contested in municipal court and was appealed to the Somerset County Superior Court. Before hearing the case, the superior court judge went out with another trooper to see how this new machine worked. I was told the judge was impressed. The case was appealed to the New Jersey State Supreme Court, where the driver was found guilty, setting a precedent in New Jersey that VASCAR was an acceptable device to clock speeding vehicles.

I received a call from Somerville Station about an armed robbery at a gas station on US-202 South. When I arrived, the young attendant stated that a black male had walked in, pointed a gun at him, and taken his money. The subject was seventeen years old and a suspect in numerous break and entries on houses in Branchburg Township. For just being robbed at gunpoint, this subject was very calm. I didn't believe him. I thought he made up the story and took the $300 or so for himself. I made the report and discussed it with one of our station detectives. The detective was pissed off. He said this kid was a one-man crime wave. Later in the week, the detective took another uniformed trooper to talk to this kid in front of his parents. They entered the kid's house, and an argument ensued with the parents. Both parents got arrested for simple assault and resisting arrest. Naturally, there was also an internal investigation of this incident.

A few months later, it was early New Year's Eve, and I received a call from the Bridgewater Police Department that they were investigating a fatal accident on US-202. Apparently, the subject we were looking at for numerous break-ins in Branchburg Township had an argument with his friends, got out of the car, and tried to run across US-202, a dual-lane highway. He didn't make it. I then called the detective at his home and told him the news. He said I made his day. For a long while after the death of this young man, there were no breaking and enterings in Branchburg Township.

I bring up this incident because of a complaint against me by someone I arrested. I was given a call from the Somerville Station to check on two disorderly persons at a company picnic at a tavern in Warren Township. When I got to the tavern, only one car was left in the parking lot, with another wedged in behind it. Apparently, two individuals tried to leave, and both were obviously drunk. The bartender drove his car behind theirs and called the station for help. When I arrived, one of the suspects yelled, "The bartender won't let me go home!"

The bartender growled, "They should not be driving. They're both drunk!"

This was a company picnic where people could pour their beer from a keg.

I advised the two individuals, "You should thank the bartender for stopping you from driving. I will take you back to the station, and you can call for a ride and have them bring someone to pick up your car at the tavern."

I put them in my troop car and proceeded back to the station. As we approached US-22, one subject started getting nasty and yelling obscenities at me. He then asked, "Am I under arrest?"

I said, "No."

He said, "I am going to charge you with false arrest."

I pulled over to the shoulder and placed them both under arrest for being drunk and disorderly. They were both cuffed and taken back to the station.

At the station, only one was still making a verbal commotion and would not stop. While processing them, a trooper brought me a sandwich I had previously ordered. As I cut the sandwich, the boisterous subject asked, "Are you going to stab me now?"

I just ignored him. Both subjects were taken to jail and bailed out.

We appeared in court about a month or two later. The quiet subject pleaded guilty and paid a $100 fine. The boisterous subject pleaded not guilty and had an attorney.

While I was testifying, their attorney asked me, "Did you threaten to stab my client?"

Before I could answer, the judge stopped the trial, admonished the defense attorney, found the subject guilty, and assessed a $200 fine.

My advice to present-day troopers and police officers was to be careful about handling prisoners in that they will say anything to try and get out of a charge or even a motor vehicle summons. Remember, cameras and audio equipment are all over. More on this issue later.

Around 1972 or 1973, the Edison State Police Station was closed to uniform troopers. The station was used for a while by State Police detectives. Now Somerville Station had to patrol I-287 to Staten Island, New York. While on late patrol of the station area, I and another trooper got a call to assist a Middlesex County assistant prosecutor with a drunk driver on the shoulder of I-287 North in Piscataway Township. When we arrived, we met with this assistant prosecutor who had a female in his vehicle. He said, "I want this driver arrested for drunk driving!"

The man, a black male about fifty years old, was standing by his vehicle, parked on the berm, and not running. The left rear passenger window was broken. The man pointed at the prosecutor and said, "He broke my window!"

The prosecutor admitted, "Yeah, but I did it to check on the sleeping driver. You must arrest him for drunk driving!"

I knew this was going to be trouble. I thought that this prosecutor was trying to impress his date.

I took the subject in, and he submitted to a breath test. Back then, you had to have at least a .10-BA for a case of drunk driving. (Now it's .08 BA). The subject's reading was .11 BA, just above the legal limit.

After I charged the subject with drunk driving, I took him home. I advised him, "Plead not guilty, and I will take care of it in court."

We went to court in Piscataway Township. I had sent a copy of my subpoena to the assistant prosecutor who started this mess. I told the judge, "The subject was standing next to his vehicle with a broken window when I arrived."

The judge asked, "Was the car running?"

I replied, "No!"

He then asked, "Were the keys in the ignition?"

"No," I answered, "The subject had them."

He then asked, "Where was the witness?"

I told him, "I sent him a copy of the subpoena. He should have appeared."

Fortunately, the judge could surmise what happened and found the subject not guilty. Sometimes you have to do something you don't want to, but you do it, so you don't have a complaint against you. It can usually be worked out, as it was in this case.

I had my most serious troop car accident and my first one while stationed at Somerville Station. I was on night patrol with another trooper, and we were on I-287 North in Piscataway Township. It was about 3 A.M. We stopped a car for speeding, and they stopped properly on the shoulder. There were two white males in the vehicle. As the driver was getting out his license for me, the passenger was looking for the registration in the glove box. My partner was standing right front, and I was standing in front of the driver. I bring this up because I learned it at Bloomfield Station on the Parkway. Never take your eye off traffic while addressing a driver standing left front.

As the two subjects dug for their paperwork, I noticed a lone vehicle approaching us. I was wondering why he was in his right lane. Traffic was very light, and he could have pulled into the middle lane when he passed us. He kept coming, and finally, I noticed he was on the shoulder, coming right for us. I yelled at my partner to watch out as I ran to the front of the vehicle we had stopped. The car slammed into the rear of the troop car, sending the troop car into the car we had stopped and then into me. I was able to keep my balance as I was struck by the stopped vehicle. I then ran to the car that hit us. The driver then put his vehicle into reverse and started backing down the road even though his radiator was on the road. The car was still running. I was able to catch up to him, reach in, and shut the car off. He started to resist me, and I pulled him out of the car, threw him onto the road, and handcuffed him. He was obviously under the influence of an alcoholic beverage. A sergeant came out to investigate the troop car accident. His statement to the sergeant was that we pulled past him and then slammed on our brakes, and he hit us. The sergeant charged him with drinking and driving with a blood alcohol reading over .20. High bail was posted because he was from London, England, and was in this country for business purposes. He was driving a rental car. Like I mentioned before, never take your eyes off the road. You can get killed by a bumper as well as a bullet.

I was investigating a two-car accident on I-287 in Edison Township. I had the drivers and a passenger sitting in my troop car, and we were parked on the grass median. I had placed my briefcase on the roof of my car. After completing the accident investigation, the people left since their vehicles were drivable. After I finished my report, I pulled off the median and entered the roadway when I heard a loud bang. I looked in the rear-view mirror and saw my briefcase bounce off my trunk lid and onto the highway. I immediately pulled back on the median, but before I could retrieve my briefcase, a tractor-trailer ran over it, and it exploded. I had blank reports, spare handcuffs, and an entire book with ten summonses. I was able to retrieve my extra handcuffs. I returned to the station and explained what had happened to the station commander, SFC Ben Mele.

He said, "You will receive ten written reprimands, one for each lost summons. Now get back there and find at least one copy of each summons. You can make copies of them, and as long as you got all ten, you'll be OK."

Well, believe it or not, I found at least one copy of each summons. I made copies and issued the summonses from this book as fast as possible.

I asked SFC Mele, "Would I really have received ten written reprimands?"

He smirked and said, "No, just one. I wanted to put the fear of God in you, so you would try to find the necessary items to make copies."

That's the second blue ticket (written reprimand) I avoided.

We had a state senator who lived in our area of responsibility (Raymond Bateman was President of the Senate and, at this time, was acting governor since the governor was out of state.). The station commander gave me a detail to drive the senator to Asbury Park Convention Hall to give a speech. He gave me a brand-new unmarked Plymouth Fury to use for the detail. I picked up the senator at his house, and the trip to Asbury Park was uneventful. When we arrived, the manager wanted me to sit in the rear. I was in uniform. Senator Bateman said no and that I would sit near the head table, which I did.

As we left to go home, the senator asked me how his speech was, and I said it was excellent, which it was. He then asked me if we could get home quickly because he had someplace to go. It took about one and a half hours to get to Asbury Park from his home. Since I was driving a new Plymouth with a 440 engine, we made it back to his house in one hour flat. He thanked me as he quickly left my vehicle. When I arrived back at the station, I told the station commander that the senator was happy, and I even got a free lunch. He told me he picked me because he knew I used to be a truck driver and knew how to drive.

He gave me another similar detail a month later with the present governor of New Jersey, Governor William Cahill. I had to pick him up at a local airport where he was flying in and take him to a restaurant in Basking Ridge where he was giving a speech. Back then, the governor did not have a special State Police detail, he just flew somewhere, and the closest State Police station provided ground transportation. I made sure the unmarked car was extra clean. When the governor and his aide got in the back seat, and as I was driving them to the restaurant, the governor mentioned that there was a cigarette butt in the rear ashtray. I commented back to him, that's where it should be. He didn't say anything, but he told me to wait outside for him at the restaurant. No free lunch that day.

One of the programs the superintendent, COL David B. Kelly, had was on either Christmas or New Year's; he would send troopers from division headquarters to ride with road troopers. They ranged in rank from sergeant to lieutenant. no captains and they were all stationed at division headquarters. All they did was bitch with having to work a holiday or wanted to stop at a friend's house or a tavern to have a drink. The program lasted about two years and was canceled due to the complaints of the road troopers that had to put up with them. Maybe that's why I don't care for division headquarters to this day. Don't get me wrong, there are a lot of great troopers stationed there, but there are also many slouches that just want their weekends off and have a troop car assigned to them.

This following incident and arrest were quite comical or not, depending on how you look at it. I was on patrol of I-287 when I got a call from the Somerville Station that someone was chopping down a tree on the median of I-287 in Piscataway Township. The station advised me that it was called in by a passing motorist who got the license plate and exact mile marker of the incident. I checked the median, and sure enough, a Christmas-type tree was cut down. More evergreen trees were growing. The New Jersey DOT planted them for the beautification of the highway. The station radioed me the vehicle owner's address, who allegedly cut the tree down.

I went to the address, an apartment complex in Piscataway Township. I rang the bell, and a female opened the door, and I saw a male already decorating the tree and two children. I was let in, and I questioned the male, who stated he had cut the tree down for Christmas since plenty were growing on the median.

I advised him, "It is against the law; the tree belongs to the New Jersey DOT."

I used their phone to call the station. I informed the Sgt of the incident and that the tree was already up. The family was decorating it as it was a week before Christmas.

The Sgt said, "Bring the subject in and bring the tree."

When we arrived at the station, I put the tree behind the station and brought in the subject. The Sgt chewed him out for cutting down the tree but said, "Write a complaint summons with no bail and bring him home."

I asked the Sgt, "What about the tree?"

He replied, "Leave it behind at the station for now."

I drove the subject home, and when I returned to the station, I noticed the tree was gone. I entered the station and saw the tree on a stand in the report room and the Sgt putting some Christmas balls on it. The Sgt said, "I found some Christmas decorations in a closet and decided we should use the tree for Christmas."

I wouldn't have handled the call this way; I would have given the subject the complaint summons with no bail, but I would have let him keep the tree. Things were done differently years ago, and we did live in the station then, and now we even had a Christmas tree that year.

In March 1973, the Warren Township Police Department was started. The township had hired a police chief in 1972 who had been a captain in the Hillside Police Department. Chief Leonard Visotski had a new building built and had hired about fourteen police officers from other departments in the area. When the chief opened his doors in March of 1973, the State Police pulled out of Warren Township.

Around 1971 the State Police started the Tactical Patrol Units. The Federal Government purchased the vehicles to flood high accident rate areas, issue summonses for moving violations, and have the public see numerous marked cars. The only changes on the cars were a blue and a gold stripe under the State Police logo on the front doors. The troopers assigned also worked an eight-hour day and every other weekend at night for a drinking driving patrol. Unfortunately, one of the directives that road troopers did not like was when a tactical patrol trooper made a criminal arrest; he would turn it over to a road trooper, who had to do the paperwork, evidence preparation, and bail requirements. Then they would stop in and sign and take the completed reports back to their sergeant. Most all road troopers thought this was stupid. We surmised that the tactical patrol troopers thought they were better than us.

Well, now it was my turn. I was on reserve time watching TV, getting ready to go out at 8 P.M., when two tactical patrol troopers came in with four individuals under arrest for possession of marijuana (one small bag). One trooper stated he was taking credit for all four arrests and just dumped the four prisoners off in my lap to do the reports. As DSG Ed Moose trained me, I put all four subjects in the report room and advised them that either one of them gives me a statement that this marijuana was his, or all four of them would be charged. I gave them fifteen minutes, and one subject gave me a written statement that the marijuana was his. The other three subjects were released. I did all the reports, logged the evidence into the evidence locker, had bail set, and dropped off the subject at the county jail.

The next day the trooper who arrested the four subjects came in to sign and take the paperwork to his supervisor. When he discovered that I only charged one individual, he started screaming at me that I cost him an additional three arrests. I wasn't going to take his guff, and I invited him to the back of the station where I would have cleaned his clock. Of course, he declined and left the station with his reports. A little while later, the trooper's sergeant came in and started to chew me out. Apparently, DSG Moose heard the commotion, came downstairs, and started arguing with the tactical patrol sergeant. DSG Moose told the sergeant that he was wrong and that I was right, and if he didn't like it, to do his own reports. DSG Moose was so pissed off that he left and went to Troop B headquarters to see the troop commander. When DSG Moose returned, the directive was changed, tactical patrol troopers will do their own criminal reports. Thank God for detectives like DSG Ed Moose.

As a side note, when DSG Moose retired on December 1, 1988, the superintendent, COL Clinton Pagano, was the guest speaker at his retirement dinner. COL Pagano said that he had to increase the size of the Internal Affairs Unit to a bureau because of troopers like DSG Ed Moose. Everyone laughed.

Sometime around 1973, when I made a lot of arrests, the station commander SFC Ben Mele advised me that he was putting me in for a certificate of commendation since I had about seventy criminal arrests, including about ten drunk driving arrests. I thanked him but told him I didn't care about any awards; I just liked the road. I found out later from SFC Mele that the troop commander's cut-off for arrests was one hundred bodies. I did receive a letter of commendation from the troop commander. I want to add that most of my arrests were white males and some white females. There were not many minorities living in Somerset or Hunterdon Counties. Most of my minority arrests were illegal aliens and were Hispanic.

In late 1973 I got married. My wife wasn't pleased with me being away for two days when I went to work. We lived way out in west Jersey. So I put in for the TPU (Tactical Patrol Unit). Tactical patrol troopers took their assigned marked troop car home with them so that it would be a saving on gas. The job was usually a two to three-year assignment. I got the job right away. I was assigned to the unit working out of the old Newark Station on the New Jersey Turnpike. This unit patrolled US-1/US-9 from Jersey City South through Newark, Elizabeth, Linden, and Rahway. Two units were working here, so one would work a drinking-driving detail each weekend. Apparently, this area was virgin to police patrols, and both units made numerous drunk driving arrests. US-1/US-9 was the local road between the cities mentioned above, and the local people used it instead of the Turnpike, where you had to pay tolls.

I noticed a high concentration of minorities using US-1/US-9 for travel right away. I also noticed that most drivers were driving older vehicles, some in poor condition. This was for all drivers, whether white, black, or brown. When I stopped a vehicle for a motor vehicle violation, I started running their driver's license through the DMV (Division of Motor Vehicles) and found that many were on the suspension list. I usually would not tow their vehicle. I told the driver that I was going that way and would not be back for a while, and they could get someone to drive their car. Most appreciated the break. Many of the drivers I stopped had suspended licenses. I found that their license was suspended for insurance verification. Almost all stated that they didn't know that their license was suspended. I then would ask them if they had moved recently, and most stated that they had and did not notify DMV of the move. DMV mail was not forwarded. I would write the summons for driving while suspended and advise the driver to go to a DMV office to show proof of insurance and come to court with a DMV letter of their license restoration, and I will have the charge dismissed. I was amazed that so many people did what I said, and the Elizabeth judge also knew that DMV mail was not forwarded. The judge had no problem dismissing the charge if the subject did what I told them. With the two TPUs working in this area, the number of accidents went way down, and according to the Elizabeth and Linden police, the crimes along US-1/US-9 also dropped.

After about one year, the units were reassigned, and I was assigned to the unit working in west Jersey. We worked half the time out of Somerville Station and half out of the old Blairstown Station. Since we didn't have a home station, the Sgt kept all his paperwork in the trunk of his car. When we worked in the Blairstown Station area on I-80, we utilized the VASCAR machine all the time. We started to clock in the distance from an overpass to our vehicle parked on the right shoulder and opened the trunk. The trunk lid covered the red bar light on the roof. When the vehicle went by, the driver would slow down, but the average speed from the overpass to our vehicle, about two-tenths of a mile, was too much, and the speed usually was fifteen to twenty miles over the limit. Then I would slam on the accelerator hard, and as my vehicle jerked forward, the trunk would slam shut, and I would then chase the violator. Some troopers even took the spare tire out of the trunk and laid it on the back bumper to make it look like they had a flat. But when they clocked a violator, they had to get out of the vehicle, throw the spare back into the trunk, and then chase the violator. I didn't resort to the spare tire move; I was happy with just jumping on the accelerator to close the trunk.

One morning I got a call from one of the troopers I was working with on the TPU who lived about two miles from me. I stopped by his house and saw a significant dent in the driver's door of his troop car. He told me he had spent the night at his girlfriend's home, and when he got up to go to work, he saw the dent. Apparently, someone made a three-point turn in a driveway opposite his car, dented the door, and took off. I had him park his vehicle opposite his driveway to make it look like it happened here by his house. The rules state you can only drive the troop car to and from work and not use it for personal business. Then we called the Sgt, who was our supervisor. He pulled up, and the trooper told him, "Someone hit my car during the night and made a large dent in the door."

The Sgt then went to the troop car and slammed his hand on the dent. A lot of debris and dirt fell out onto the road. The Sgt looked at the trooper and stated, "This accident did not happen here, did it?"

I thought the trooper was going to cry. "Sergeant, I did it," he admitted, "It happened at my girlfriend's home."

The Sgt looked at me and asked, "Were you part of this fiasco?"

I stated, "Yes, I was."

The Sgt chewed us out for lying, but since it was the same type of damage as we had stated, he used the accident location by the trooper's house. I learned then that sometimes it's better not to lie and tell the truth; a supervisor will try to help you if he can.

In 1974 my father passed away from cancer. My mom, my two sisters, and I arrived at the funeral home at about 9 A.M. on the day of the funeral. The funeral director met us on the front steps and stated there was a tall man in the parlor waiting to see us. I had no idea who was there. I walked in with my mom and sisters and saw that it was the Troop B commander, Captain Joseph Rogalski. He paid his respects to my family and said if I needed anything to give him a call. I never forgot that, and when I became the Troop B commander, I followed in his footsteps and went to every wake for a trooper's father, mother, sister, or brother. I had the deputy Troop B commander attend if I was on vacation.

As far as making arrests of illegal aliens, things were going well while I was stationed in Somerville. When you ascertained that a subject was an illegal alien, the station would call the INS (Immigration and Naturalization Service) in Newark, and I would turn the illegal over to an INS agent either at Somerville or the Scotch Plains Station. Then during the Carter administration, the INS stopped taking illegal aliens, so we would have to let them go. It didn't matter what party was in charge. We stopped arresting illegal aliens. Under one previous administration, they stopped calling them illegal aliens and now referred to them as undocumented workers. Also, some significant cities call themselves sanctuary cities and do not cooperate with the INS or ICE (Immigration and Customs Enforcement Service). It's even worse today with the open southern border.

Another case that I was proud of went to the New Jersey State Supreme Court. My classmate and I already had a traffic case that went to the State Supreme Court involving the VASCAR, and we won that one. This was a criminal case. Our TPU was sent to Phillipsburg to assist their department with drinking, driving, and bar fights. At the time, the law in New Jersey to drink was eighteen, and it was still twenty-one in Pennsylvania. So the students from Lafayette University and other schools near Easton would come to New Jersey to drink and cause trouble. We worked there every other weekend on Friday and Saturday nights from 8 P.M. to 4 A.M. We even tried to keep a troop car by the free bridge from Main Street Phillipsburg to Northampton Street Easton, Pennsylvania.

Once on patrol, I chased a car into Pennsylvania onto Northampton Street before he stopped. I approached the vehicle, and all three young adults were laughing. The driver stated that they were in Pennsylvania and could not be arrested. He was only technically correct. I called for an Easton patrolman, who came and placed the driver under arrest for drunk driving. I was the patrolman's witness. I told the driver to have a nice night. He wasn't laughing anymore.

As far as the criminal case goes, I spotted four white males drinking beer out of the trunk of their car at the square by the free bridge. As I pulled up, one of the males slammed the trunk shut.

"It's too late," I said and opened the trunk.

The Town of Phillipsburg has an ordinance that you cannot consume an alcoholic beverage in public. I called for a Phillipsburg patrol since it was their city ordinance, and they could have the arrests. I asked them what do you do with the car? They answered we check it for valuables and tow it. I checked the vehicle for valuables and found a loaded twenty-five caliber automatic pistol in the glove box between the front seats. I asked them who owned this, and they all said they didn't know. They were taken back to Phillipsburg Police headquarters.

At the station, as instructed by DSG Moose of the Somerville Station, I said to the four subjects, "Either one of you gives me a statement on who owns this gun, or I will charge you all."

Finally, after they all spoke together, the vehicle owner admitted the gun was his and gave me a written statement. The other three were not charged with the gun charge.

A couple of weeks later, I was contacted by the Warren County Prosecutor's Office that there would be a probable cause hearing on my gun charge. Back then, for the first offense of carrying a pistol without a permit, the fine was $100 with no jail time. The problem was it took five years to apply to expunge the charge. I was also told that a large and prestigious law firm from Newark would handle the hearing. Apparently, the defendant's father was a big shot at Conrail and didn't want his son to have a criminal record. The attorney tried his best to suppress the search, but to no avail; the Superior Court Judge found the search legal. The case was appealed to the New Jersey State Supreme Court, where it was affirmed. There was no trial. The subject pleaded guilty after the Supreme Court hearing and paid a $100 fine.

Rumors were flying that the State Police was doing away with the "Barracks Life" and going to an eight-hour day like the Parkway and Turnpike. Apparently, it had to do with troopers living in the stations working more than forty hours a week as they did on the two toll roads. The STFA, the bargaining agent for the troopers, was negotiating a contract, and living in the stations came up. So in the spring of 1976, the State Police went to the eight-hour day for all. Because of manpower problems, two of the four TPUs were disbanded. I was transferred to Washington Station.

The problem was I was a union rep for the STFA for two tactical units, and Tpr Jim Pevonis was a union rep for the other two. So I called the vice president of the STFA and explained the problem to him. He stated that I had an excellent grievance and should put in a grievance for Tpr Pevonis and me. I put the grievance in against the tactical patrol lieutenant who transferred us. I got a call less than a week from the troop commander, Captain Thomas Lawson, who told me he found it in my favor, but only one of us could stay as a union rep since two TPUs had been eliminated. I told the captain that Tpr Pevonis should stay and that I would go to Washington Station as ordered. The opening was at Little Falls Station, and Tpr Pevonis lived much closer than me. Plus, I was already on for over two years and was ready to return to the road. So I won my first union grievance.

Washington Station, here I come.

6

TROOP B POST: WASHINGTON STATION

It was now the spring of 1976, and all road stations were working an eight-hour day, forty hours a week. We had a bustling area. We patrolled six towns or townships that didn't have a local police department and assisted with a few small departments. We patrolled I-78 from the Hunterdon-Somerset County line to the Phillipsburg exit. The last four miles toward Pennsylvania were not finished yet. I was assigned to a squad with a sergeant who I found out was a pain in the neck. I wasn't the senior man on the squad but the second senior man. The senior man had some mental problems, but he didn't bother me. He did bother the squad sergeant. The federal speed limit was changed to 55 MPH in 1974 and was not given back to the states until 1995. Of course, most troopers, if not all, would give a big break to speeders and not even stop them unless they were going at least 75 MPH, including me.

Toward the end of the first year at Washington, the division introduced the new K-55 radar machine to the road troopers, which sat on the middle of the dashboard. What a tool for clocking speeders. On a one-lane road, you could clock speeders coming at you from the opposite direction (called moving radar) or sit behind an overpass or bridge and clock vehicles. Talk about making the job easier to catch speeders. I was impressed. On I-78, I only had to wait one or two minutes, and a car would go by at over eighty miles per hour. After stopping the vehicle, if the driver were polite and had a valid license, I would write the summons

for 64 in a 55 zone. Most drivers mailed in the minimum fine for speeding, which was about $20, and $5 court costs. I only had one or two
motorists plead not guilty and used the defense that they were going well
over the speed limit of 55 MPH and that the summons marked 64 miles
per hour was wrong. When the judge would tell them that he would
amend the summons to the higher rate and take their license for thirty
days, they would change their plea to guilty.

My senior man would not enforce speeding with the new machine.
He said that it was clocking trees and buildings. When Troop B headquarters discovered that the senior man would not write radar summonses, they took action. Our sergeant was ordered to take the senior
man out and force him to write radar summonses. So they went out
with the senior man driving and the sergeant sitting right front. As they
left the station, they turned left on NJ-57 West. The senior man shut
off the radar machine as soon as they hit the road. The sergeant turned
it back on, and the senior man turned it off. The sergeant ordered the
senior man to return to the station, which they did. While the sergeant
called Troop B headquarters to tell them what happened, the senior man
changed into civilian clothes and signed out sick.

The senior man went straight to his physiologist (which no one knew
the senior man was seeing) and told him he was feeling much better, and
in the morning, he was going to work and "shoot" his sergeant. Naturally, the psychologist had to report this to the State Police. The Troop B
deputy troop commander ordered the Washington Station commander
to go to the senior man's residence and advise him to stay home on extended sick leave. I didn't know the station commander that well, but I
could surmise that he was the nervous type. The station commander told
headquarters that he couldn't do it and was going home sick. He then
left the station. Headquarters then sent a young SFC to go to the senior
man's residence and tell him he was on extended sick leave, which the
new SFC did. The new SFC then became the Washington Station commander. I never knew what happened to the original station commander,
but I am pretty sure he retired.

Eventually, the senior man retired on a mental disability that was
suitable for all. Two senior men were then asked to be the senior man on

my squad, but they didn't want to work for my sergeant. Even though I was only a Trooper II, I was then made senior man. Back then, it took twelve years to be promoted to Trooper I. Now it only takes nine years. The sergeant apparently knew that he would not get promoted to SFC and would probably retire as a sergeant. So he started to let me run the squad and do his paperwork. I didn't mind since it was good training before becoming a sergeant. Our sergeant was biding his time to retirement.

When we were working the day shift, the sergeant decided to go out, and he had to take a marked vehicle since no unmarked cars were available. He stopped in the center of Washington Borough, parks, and went into a hardware store to buy something. When he came out, he had a parking ticket on his troop car for overtime parking in a metered zone. The fine was $2, returnable to the Washington Borough Court. The sergeant then went to the Washington Borough police chief and complained to him. The chief took the parking ticket, and the sergeant left. I knew the chief, who told me he paid the $2 fine to get rid of the sergeant. I also asked the chief for a copy of the parking ticket, which he gave me. The sergeant later that day told all of us on his squad what happened and gave us the address of the meter maid who gave him the parking ticket and told us to get her and give her a summons for anything. I gave each squad member a couple of copies of the parking ticket the chief gave me. Each day either another squad member or I would put a copy of the parking ticket on the sergeant's vehicle. He was getting upset and said if he caught who was doing it, he would bring them up on charges. I finally told the squad to stop. But it was the sergeant's fault for telling us about the parking ticket.

We had very good civilian dispatchers at Washington Station. One, though a good dispatcher, was very nervous. One day on the 3 to 11 P.M. shift, this dispatcher was on duty with the station record and radio. The sergeant was home eating, and all the troopers were on patrol. One of our troopers stopped at a public phone in front of the National Guard Armory, next door to the station. The dispatcher was alone in the station. The trooper called the station and told the dispatcher that he hated the State Police and was coming to get him. The dispatcher tried to say he wasn't a trooper, but the trooper said he didn't care and was coming.

The dispatcher started screaming on the radio and calling for troopers to "signal 30" (come back to the station). I couldn't stop laughing.

The trooper who made the call went to the station's front door and yelled to let him in. The dispatcher refused, not knowing who it was. The trooper went to the back door and let himself in with his key. I pulled up to the back door also and went in. The trooper who made the call looked all over the station and couldn't find the dispatcher. I found him hiding in the closet where we kept the teletype machine. I told him not to tell the sergeant what happened; I knew he wouldn't. I told the other trooper we'd better take it easy on this dispatcher. We could give him a heart attack. Incidents like this happened a lot back then. Today if you did something like this, you would be brought up on charges and receive a stiff suspension or possibly be fired. The State Police has changed over the years. But I always said (back then) that if you didn't get caught, it didn't happen.

We had a bunch of recruits report to Washington Station for training. Two were assigned to our squad. Washington Station and the three Sussex Stations were GP (general police) stations and were good to break in new troopers. We got two recruits assigned to our squad, one black male and one white male. The white male looked like he was about fifteen years old and didn't shave. Both recruits had good coaches. The sergeant was a little pissed. His son had tried for the State Police but didn't make the cut. The sergeant said that the State Police was now taking minority troopers but couldn't take his son.

Both coaches came to me with their problems, if any, with their recruits. The black recruit was doing quite well with the coach program. The white recruit, not so well. His coach came to me and advised me that his recruit was terrible. I told the coach to give him some time. I was a coach many times at Somerville Station, and some recruits take more time than others. When the first 30-day period was done, the black recruit had an excellent report. The white recruit did not. The coach of the white recruit was an excellent trooper, and I told him just put down the truth on the report. He still has another thirty days to come around.

After the second thirty-day period, I was given both completed reports. The black trooper had an outstanding report. The white trooper had the worst recruit training report I had ever seen. His coach told me that he should never have graduated from the academy. I brought both reports to the sergeant for his signature. After reading the reports, he called the white recruit in his office alone. I could hear the sergeant yelling at him. Finally, the sergeant came out of his office and said the recruit was crying. The sergeant and I took the poor report to the station commander. The commander said he would notify Troop B headquarters, and the captain would probably have him fired. I chimed in and recommended that the recruit in question be transferred to a slower station, like Flemington, and be put on another 60-day Tpr-Coach program. Troop headquarters took my advice, and the white recruit passed the program finally. I said to my sergeant that the black recruit was pretty good. He admitted he was. I told him, don't judge a book by its cover. The sergeant finally agreed with me on something. Many years later, the white trooper retired as a Trooper I, and the black trooper retired as a Detective Captain. It's nice when some things work out.

One night the sergeant and I went out on patrol on the midnight shift. We usually didn't ride together, but the sergeant wanted to talk to me about the other members of the squad. We had two additional two-man patrols out. The other patrols got involved in a serious motor vehicle involving a tractor-trailer on I-78. We then received a call from the station to check on a stolen motor vehicle complaint at a residence in Franklin Township. The owner gave us the information about the vehicle, and when asked if the keys were in the car, he stated yes, over the sun visor. The vehicle information was then called into the station to be put into the NCIC (National Crime Information Center).

As we resumed patrol, I spotted the stolen vehicle parked in a tavern in Washington Borough. The sergeant wanted to tow the vehicle, but I told him, "It's 1:30 A.M. The bars close at 2. The thief is probably in the bar drinking. We should wait until he comes out and get him in the stolen car."

We hid on a side street, watching the vehicle.

At about 2 A.M., the subject came out, and when he entered the stolen vehicle, I drove up and blocked him in. I pulled him out of the car and arrested him for possessing the stolen motor vehicle.

The subject explained, "I borrowed the car from my neighbor."

The subject did live near the vehicle owner's home. We put the subject in the Warren County Jail. He did have a bad attitude and was very argumentative.

I found out about three weeks later that the subject did not make bail and pleaded guilty to the charge to be released after serving eighteen days in the Warren County Jail. I guess the county got tired of feeding him, or so I thought.

A couple of months later, the station detective gave me a warrant for this subject. He had been charged with aggravated assault in severely beating a man who was going out with his ex-girlfriend. I took the warrant and went to pick him up. It was late afternoon. The subject lived with his mother, who was divorced from her husband. I rang the doorbell, and the mother opened the door and warned, "My son has a gun and will shoot you."

She tried to stop him.

I entered the house and went to the back door, which was still ajar. He had run into the woods behind the house.

I went back to my troop car and radioed in the information. There was a State Police helicopter in the area, and the pilot heard the call and started looking for the subject along with other members of my squad.

His mother told me, "He is wanted in Belvidere for beating up someone, and he doesn't want to go to jail again. He has a small pistol, but I don't know what kind."

He was able to get away that day.

The next day the subject turned himself in to the Belvidere Police, accompanied by his father.

I then met with the Warren County Prosecutor about any additional charges. The prosecutor said, "It is your word against his mother's, and we don't have the gun."

I told the prosecutor, "That's OK, as long as he spent some time in jail for the aggravated assault complaint."

He did.

It was pleasant having State Police dispatchers at Washington Station. For some reason, the Parkway (Troop E) and the Turnpike (Troop D) still had no civilian dispatchers. The only days our dispatchers didn't work were the thirteen state holidays or if they called in sick. Our squad came to work for the midnight shift, 11 P.M. to 7 A.M., one night. The dispatcher had called in sick. Usually, when this happened, the squad sergeant stayed in for dispatch duties. Our sergeant didn't want to stay in. He was going to have a young trooper remain in.

I told him, "It's not fair for the younger troopers. I'll stay and take the dispatch duties."

He said, "OK."

It was a slow night, probably a weekday night. A local police officer arrived with a drunk driver at about 2 A.M. He wanted a breathalyzer test run. He wasn't a breathalyzer operator, and none were working in his department. I signed the police officer and his prisoner in and set up the breathalyzer machine for the test. The subject was obviously under the influence of an alcoholic beverage. As I ran the test, the subject stated he was friendly with a State Police sergeant. It happened to be my sergeant. I ignored the issue; it wasn't my arrest. I was just running the test. The patrolman then left with his prisoner.

When the sergeant came in, he read the station record and saw that his friend had been brought in for a breathalyzer test. He asked me what had happened. I told him what happened and that it was a local patrolman's arrest, not mine. Though I didn't tell him, the subject mentioned his name. The sergeant started yelling at me that I shouldn't have run the test, and now a friend of his got arrested for drunk driving. I jumped back into his face and told him that he might have talked the patrolman out of the arrest if he had taken the dispatch duties instead of going out to sleep somewhere.

While we were arguing, the janitor arrived, and he walked in the back door; seeing us arguing very loudly, he walked back out. The sergeant then said he would bring me up on charges for assisting the local police and having friends arrested. I told him when the captain gets done with an investigation, he will be the one to suffer.

The next night when we came to work, he apologized for the previous night. We got along most of the time, but it was worth the times we didn't, as long as he let me run the squad and keep everything running smoothly.

One day we were working days (7 A.M. to 3 P.M.). It was snowing while I was driving to work. During roll call, the sergeant said to be very careful and not have a troop car accident. Jokingly I said if it's going to happen, it's going to happen. He was not impressed. There's a lot of extra paperwork for a troop car accident, and I know the sergeant didn't want to do it. Troopers were not allowed to investigate troop car accidents, only sergeants. After roll call, I pulled out of the station and made a left turn heading west on NJ-57, a one-lane road.

About a half mile west of the station, I noticed a vehicle sideways, blocking the westbound lane. There was a downgrade heading west. I stopped at the vehicle. The shoulder was only about two feet wide. A young woman was standing by her vehicle, crying about her problem. It was only a spin-out, and she didn't hit anything. I asked her to get back into her vehicle and drive on, but she refused. As we spoke, another car appeared from the east and came down the grade too fast. It was apparent to me that he would hit my troop car. I told the young woman to move onto the berm, but she was almost hysterical. I picked her up by her waist and carried her to the berm as the other vehicle hit my troop car in the rear. The troop car did not hit the young lady's automobile. The young lady still would not drive her vehicle, so I had another trooper take her to a school in Washington where she was a teacher. Her vehicle was towed in.

The sergeant was pissed off when I told him about my troop car accident. He told me, "Return to the station with the other driver who hit you."

Both vehicles were drivable.

At the station, the sergeant ordered, "Get the necessary information from the other driver and write him a summons for careless driving."

I advised the sergeant, "You have to write the summons. I can't since I was involved in the accident."

He said, "I don't have a summons book."

I signed him out a summons book, wrote the summons, and he signed it.

I gave the summons to the motorist that hit me and cut him loose.

The sergeant then said, "Make out the report, and I will sign it."

It was the first troop car accident I investigated, and it was my own. In my nineteen years on the road, I only had this happen to me once, though I have seen it happen with other troopers. If a driver refuses to open or unlock his door and does not give the trooper his credentials, sometimes the trooper has no choice but to break a window to get to the driver. I have seen it done, and I think it's proper. Unfortunately, the driver usually complains about the trooper who broke his window, and you must go through an internal investigation.

The one case that I came close to breaking a window was a speeding incident on I-78. I was driving an unmarked troop car and had clocked a vehicle speeding at 80 MPH. I stopped the vehicle on the right shoulder. The driver was a white male in a business suit. He was holding onto the steering wheel and facing straight ahead. I asked him to open his window, but he kept staring straight ahead and ignoring me. I told him through the window, even though it wasn't open, that I was calling a tow truck and having him towed to the State Police Station. He did not respond.

When the tow truck arrived, the subject got out of his car and started yelling at the tow truck driver. This was my chance. I got out of my vehicle, grabbed him by the back of his jacket and shoulder, threw him over his vehicle's hood, and handcuffed him. I arrested him for interference with governmental responsibilities, a disorderly person's charge handled in municipal court. And, of course, I issued him a summons for speeding. The court clerk set bail at about $300, and the subject was lodged in the county jail. I then called his home, spoke to his wife, and advised her what had happened. She said her husband said the next time he was stopped for speeding, he would do that, and he thought the cop would go away. I told his wife I did not go away. I then advised her that she could post bail at the county jail. I was glad I didn't have to break his car window.

This incident was an excellent example of using enough physical force to make an arrest. Sometimes it's better to use extra force to let the subject know who was in charge. Today it's more challenging with all the cameras that are around. But only the trooper or police officer knows how much force was needed. If you don't use enough physical force, it could lead to more resistance and injuries. I would use more force to end the confrontation quickly so it does not escalate. If the incident was on video, I hope the officer benefits from the doubt during an internal investigation.

Most of the troopers on our squad came to me, not the sergeant because he would probably yell at them. One day a young trooper came to me and related an incident that had just happened to him. The trooper stated that he stopped a tractor-trailer for speeding. When he approached the driver for his credentials, he got out of his truck and was told he was speeding. Instead of giving the trooper his credentials, he started running around his truck. The trooper told me he chased the driver around the truck about three times until he finally stopped out of breath. The trooper said he wrote the driver a speeding summons and let him go. The trooper wanted to know if he handled this incident properly. I told him absolutely not. When he stopped running, you should have knocked him to the ground and arrested him. If he tries it again, another police officer will have to do what you didn't.

Another type of call that was difficult was domestic violence calls. They usually happened on a Friday or Saturday night and typically involved drinking. Back then, there were no specific statutes like today when the police had to arrest a suspect if there was an apparent injury to the complainant. When I went to a domestic violence call, the complainant, most likely a female, would refuse to sign a complaint against her husband or boyfriend. I would have the other trooper stay with the complainant and take her husband or boyfriend outside. I would then grab him by his shirt and throw him against the house. I would firmly tell him if we had to come back here again, I would say that he assaulted me and that I would knock the hell out of him. He would then end up in the hospital. Usually, we didn't have to go back there again. Most of these guys are cowards, and when drinking, they would assault their wives or girlfriends.

I only recall one case in which a wife assaulted her husband. Another trooper and I went to a residence on a country road in Franklin Township, Warren County. When we arrived at the house (the husband had called), the husband complained, "My wife hit me on the head with a heavy frying pan."

He refused to sign a complaint but wanted her out of the house. He had a massive bump on his head.

She agreed and left for a girlfriend's home.

Later the husband got a restraining order against his wife. It was good for six months. I happened to be on the station record and radio when a woman entered the station. She explained, "I am going home. The restraining order had expired."

I recognized her and said, "I handled the call six months ago."

I checked the file we had on restraining orders, and the one against her had expired—one day ago.

I told her, "Please wait in the vestibule. I want to contact your husband."

"OK," she said.

I called his home and told the husband, "Your wife is here and is coming home. The restraining order expired yesterday, and you never extended it."

He pleaded, "Give me a half hour to pack up and leave!"

I advised the wife of this, and she had no problem waiting a while.

When he left, she went home. I guess he didn't want to get hit again with a frying pan.

Today under the new laws, a police officer has to make an arrest for assault and take the person committing the assault to a judge or jail. This usually stops repeat assaults. Also, now, with body cameras and audio, you cannot handle a domestic complaint as we did years ago, though it usually worked.

One day I got a call from the station to check on a possible suicide in Harmony Township. A UPS (United Parcel Service) truck was in the driveway as I pulled up to the residence. The UPS truck driver was standing by the back door with tears in his eyes. The driver said he thought the resident had killed himself. An older man was lying on the kitchen floor, and there was a small revolver by his side. The UPS driver had called this in. I forced the door open and went in. I first found a small suitcase that was almost fully packed. I also found a personal phone book with names and addresses in it.

One of the addresses was in a small town outside of Allentown. I ascertained through some family pictures that this subject had a son at the Pennsylvania address. I called the local police from that town so they could make a notification of this death. I gave the information to the desk sergeant, who said he would call me back when a notification was made.

A short while later, the phone rang. When I answered it, I found that it was the son of the man who shot himself. He told me his local police told him the State Police were at his father's house and that something had happened and to call them. The local police never told him what happened. Another botched death notification, it never ends. I explained everything to the son, and he told me that he had spoken to his father earlier that day, and his father told him the doctor told him to report to Warren Hospital because he had a terrible cold. That was why he was packing a small suitcase. I still cannot understand why police departments don't want to do their jobs adequately on death notifications. These notifications should not be done on the phone.

One night on late patrol (11 P.M. to 7 A.M.), I was riding with a trooper just a couple of years junior to me. He wanted to be a detective and made criminal arrests during patrol. He was also thick-headed and made mistakes by trying to circumvent proper procedures. I didn't usually ride with him on late patrols, but this night I did. We stopped a suspected drunk driver at the beginning of I-78 Eastbound. The driver, who was alone, appeared to have been drinking. He had bloodshot eyes and an odor of an alcoholic beverage on his breath. The other trooper just wanted to search his vehicle. The other trooper popped the trunk and found about 1,500 reels of pornographic material.

There was a directive from the Warren County Prosecutor's Office going around to all police departments to look for pornographic material. The trooper thought he hit "the mother lode." I told him we had to run a breathalyzer test on him since that was the probable cause for the stop. The trooper stated he didn't care about the traffic charge, just the criminal arrest. The subject was charged with a criminal violation but did not take a breathalyzer test. I didn't pull rank on the trooper and make him run a breathalyzer test on the subject. He always cut corners, so I didn't like riding with him.

For some reason, the arrest for the pornographic material was published in the local paper, probably due to many mothers complaining about the pornographic material being sold around the county. A couple of weeks later, I got a subpoena to testify at a preliminary hearing on this case. I did not want to testify because I would not lie to make the other trooper look good. I called a friend of mine who was a detective at the Warren County Prosecutor's office. I told him the story, and he had the subpoena quashed. The other trooper testified, and the defense was able to eliminate the probable cause for the stop, and the case was dismissed. The State Police got a lot of negative press on this case. I explained the issue and my part to the station detective, who agreed with me about why I didn't testify. The trooper who lost the case continued to cut corners on his arrests. At the time, he was a heavy drinker and, while off duty, cut a corner too fast, and his vehicle turned over. Of course, being that this happened in a State Police patrolled area, he didn't get charged with anything. Finally, a while later, he was elevated to the rank of detective. God bless the unit that he was assigned to.

While on applicant investigations, I was assigned to do minority applicants who resided in New York City. As with any other time I did applicant investigations, you got some good and some poor applicants. Back then, you were allowed to give your opinion on the applicant. The last time I had this detail as a sergeant, an opinion was allowed. One applicant was a married black male living in East Chester, New York. His father was an Eastchester police officer. At the time, he lived with his in-laws, had a young child, and worked for the Con-Edison Power Company. My interview with him was pre-arranged so I could interview his wife, who was also working. I had already interviewed his immediate supervisor and previous supervisor. His new supervisor had no problem with him, but his last supervisor gave him a terrible recommendation for the State Police. The applicant confessed he had a problem with his previous supervisor, which was why he was transferred to a different supervisor. The applicant said his last supervisor was prejudiced against black people. My interview with that applicant and his family went well. I had to do another check on the applicant's previous supervisor. I interviewed six additional employees who either worked for the same supervisor or knew the applicant. None of the employees interviewed liked their supervisor. These other interviews made up my mind that the applicant should be allowed to enter the State Police, so I recommended him for entrance to the academy.

The applicant graduated from the State Police Academy. When he reported to Troop B, he was assigned to Washington Station and right to my squad. His odds of getting on my squad were about forty to one since we had ten stations back then with four squads per station. We were working a midnight shift, and he was due in by 11 P.M. At about 10:30 P.M., he called the station, and I took the call. He said he might be late because someone broke into his car and stole his issued uniform. He had it pressed yesterday and left it in his vehicle with some civilian clothes. The thief or thieves threw the uniform away in a dumpster near his home, and he found it, but it was all wrinkled. He stated he was only issued one uniform at the academy but had his class-B uniform. I advised him to come right in and that he could wear his class-B uniform. When he arrived, since I knew him, I introduced him to his coach and our sergeant. The sergeant did not say anything about why he was late, *thank God*. He was a great recruit and became an asset to the State Police, retiring twenty-five years later as a detective sergeant first class. I was glad that I continued my applicant investigation into his previous supervisor for clarification.

Another time on applicant investigations, I was assigned to New Jersey counties. While working on an applicant in Union County, I encountered unsavory characters at an employer where the applicant used to work. At his interview, the applicant told me he quit this job because of the characters that visited the shop. I started watching the shop, following some of the subjects to other locations and getting plate numbers like I used to do in Keyport Station. I followed some of these subjects for about three or four days.

I received a call from Somerville Station to go and see the Union County Prosecutor. I did not know what this was about. I got to his Westfield office, and when I entered his office, he had two county detectives standing next to him. The prosecutor asked me, "What were you doing hanging around the store in Union? My detectives got your plate number."

I told him what I was doing and showed him my notes on the subjects I followed.

He studied the notes for a while and then told his two detectives, "This trooper has gotten more information in four days than you got in a month!"

He then sent them out of his office.

The prosecutor then asked me, "Would you please make me a report on this information?"

I replied, "I have to make it out to my troop commander, but I will mail you a copy immediately. It could take two to three weeks if you wait for the report to go through channels."

I typed the special information the next day and mailed it right out. Eventually, I got a letter of appreciation from the prosecutor. I guess a "road trooper" can do an investigation as well as a detective if he has to.

As the detail on applicant investigations ended, I received a call from the lieutenant in division headquarters, who was in charge of applicant investigations statewide. He asked if I would be interested in going to the SIU (Special Investigations Unit), which did background investigations on judges, high-ranking state employees, and even political appointees. Back then, if you got assigned to a unit in division headquarters, it was marked temporary on the teletype. If you worked out, it became permanent. I knew I could always go back to the road if I didn't like it.

The teletype came out on a Friday, assigning me to the SIU on Monday at 9 A.M. I was working a day shift on Friday, and all hands, including the station commander, shook my hand and wished me well. They stated I made "the big time." I drove to division headquarters on Monday morning and entered the CIS (Criminal Investigation Section) building.

Two troopers and I, all newly assigned, were having a cup of coffee when the lieutenant in charge of the unit came in and called out, "Maggio!"

I replied, "Here, sir!"

He ordered, "I want you to return to Washington Station."

I said, surprised, "Excuse me, sir?"

He repeated, "I want you to go back to Washington Station."

So I drove back to Washington Station and saw the station commander. He said he was sorry and showed me the new teletype rescinding the one sent on Friday.

Later that day, the lieutenant who got me the job was sorry and said it should not have happened. He then offered me another assignment to the Casino Bureau to do job applicant investigations on casino employees, including dealers and supervisors. I already knew someone in that bureau who never left his office in division headquarters. That wasn't for me. I thanked the lieutenant but turned down the job. I had my assignment in division headquarters (fifteen minutes), had a cup of coffee, and returned to the road where I belonged. Of course, I found out who stole my position. He retired as a DSG (Detective Sergeant), and I retired as a Captain.

At Washington Station, the station commander would let each trooper pick which State holiday they wanted off, either Christmas or New Year's. With seniority as a guide, I put in for Christmas off and worked New Year's Eve. I found that New Year's Eve was a quiet night over the years. One New Year's Eve, I was working the midnight shift with two other troopers, one on the station record (This was a holiday, and the dispatchers were off), and one two-man patrol. The other trooper was from another squad and had three years of seniority on me. As usual, it was a quiet night. Most people are careful on New Year's Eve, have a designated driver, or watch themselves if drinking.

Around 3 A.M., the station got a call from the Mansfield Police about a slight problem at the Washington National Guard Armory next door to the Washington Station. Both the Washington Station and the Armory are in Mansfield Township. The Mansfield police also had only one patrol out and were tied up on an accident investigation. There had been a New Year's Eve party for National Guard members at the armory. The party was over at 2 A.M., and the bartender wanted to close up. He stated that the two couples just didn't want to leave. The bartender said he had not served them a drink since 2 A.M. when the party was over. My partner and I went to them and told them they had to leave. They said OK and got up and headed to the back door of the armory. I didn't expect any problem from them. Both my partner and I were in the New Jersey National Guard. I was attached to the Flemington Armory, and he was attached to the Phillipsburg Armory. The two males were too drunk to drive, and we were going to ask one of the girls to drive. They all came in one car. As we entered the parking lot, the two males started to argue.

As my partner and I got between them to break them up, one of them tried throwing a roundhouse punch at me. I blocked his punch with my left arm and struck him very hard in the face. He went down like a ton of bricks. My partner was struggling with the other male. The girlfriend of the one I struck jumped on my back and started choking me. I got her off and hit her as hard as possible with an open hand. She, too, went down like a ton of bricks. My partner had the other male by the head and was banging his head on the roof of the troop car. His girlfriend was already lying on the ground. I then ran over to stop my partner from banging the male's head on the troop car; it looked like one more bang, and his head would split open like a watermelon. I found out that the other girl had spit at my partner, and he slapped her also with an open hand.

All four subjects ended up in the Warren County Jail, where the court clerk set bail at $400 a piece. Since January one was a state holiday, I knew they wouldn't get out of jail until January 2nd. The one male that had his head smashed into the troop car did sign a complaint against the other trooper, which caused an internal investigation. The lieutenant found that we both used the proper amount of physical force to effect the arrest for drunk and disorderly and resisting arrest. They did plead not guilty, but the Mansfield Township judge found them guilty and fined them each $400 and the one day they spent in jail. I don't know what would happen with phone video cameras and such in today's environment. I still say a trooper or a police officer could and should use enough physical force to effect an arrest. The State Police and the county prosecutor's office should back any trooper or police officer where physical force was necessary and ignore social media comments. Most comments become political and should be discounted.

On a side note, I stopped at a local supermarket a few months later to pick up a few things. As I was checking out, I noticed the checker I had was the same girl who spit in my partner's face at the above-listed incident. I knew she wasn't sure if I was one of the troopers that arrested her and her friends, but she kept staring at me.

As I left, I smiled and said, "Have a nice day!"

She just stared at me as I left.

I was assigned an unmarked vehicle on patrol one day, and we were using the new K-55 radar machine. It was mounted on the dashboard. I was getting to operate this machine quite well. I would park on the shoulder, aim the cone out the back window, and clock vehicles coming towards me. Traffic was light, and I clocked a car going about 80 MPH going right by me. As I started to pull out after him, a black Mercedes coming behind me sped up and would not let me off the shoulder. I was up to over 90 MPH when I finally got in front of him to continue chasing the violator. The driver of the Mercedes started giving me the finger.

That was it. I put my hat and red light on and pulled the Mercedes over.

I told the driver, "I am issuing you a summons for careless driving," and chewed him out for what he did.

The driver said, "I didn't know you were a trooper!"

I said, "I could have been a priest or rabbi, and you gave me the finger!"

He added, "You only gave me a summons because I gave you the finger."

I just told him, "You are entitled to your opinion."

I wasn't surprised that he pleaded not guilty to the charge. In court, the subject represented himself. I gave testimony first, not mentioning that he gave me the finger.

When the subject testified, he said, "The only reason he gave me a summons was I gave him the finger."

The judge looked at him and asked, "What do you mean by the finger?"

The subject replied, "You know, the Italian salute."

The judge said, "Then I will amend the charge to a lewd act."

The subject said, "No, I'll plead guilty to careless driving."

The whole court broke out in laughter. The judge found him guilty of careless driving. It takes all kinds.

I was on patrol on a day shift on US-22 Eastbound in Phillipsburg. I spotted a Chevrolet Nova with an overdue state inspection sticker that had been expired for about six months. I pulled the car over and approached the driver, a white male about thirty years old. He gave me his credentials; the registration expired about six months ago. The vehicle was registered to a company in Montclair. As I asked him questions, he became nervous and said, "Just write me a ticket!"

A check on the plate and the vehicle was not reported stolen. I had the station call the company that owned the vehicle in Montclair. They mentioned that the driver had taken the vehicle without permission six months ago, and they hadn't seen him since. They said, "We already collected insurance on the car but never reported it stolen since we knew who had it."

I then ran the subject's name and information in the NCIC and found he was wanted for fraud in Clark County, Nevada, and they will extradite him. I found that this subject was working for a company in Clark County and stole the company check-writing machine, made himself about a dozen paychecks, and cashed them in gambling casinos on the strip.

The subject told me, "I was tired of Nevada and made the checks to have enough money to return to New Jersey."

He waived extradition and was picked up by two detectives from the Clark County Sheriff's Office the next day. It's amazing how a minor charge of an overdue inspection sticker can lead to a good arrest.

One night on a late patrol, I rode with a recruit since his coach was off. I let him drive to see how he was handling a troop car. He drove quite well.

Around 3 A.M., he asked me, "Can we stop for breakfast?"

I said, "Yes, at Louise's Diner."

He asked, "Could we stop at the big truck stop in Bloomsbury instead?"

I said, "No, gotta be Louise's."

"But I only have two dollars with me," he admitted.

I told him, "I am not happy with the truck stop in Bloomsbury because they give us free food, and we only tip the waitress."

I bought him breakfast at Louise's that morning, and I think he learned a lesson.

The same night we later received a call from the station that a white male ran into the lady's room at the Bloomsbury truck stop. The truck driver was sitting at a booth waiting for us when we arrived.

He said, "I picked up a girl outside and took her to the truck stop to have a cup of coffee. (The truck stop was where prostitutes hung out to sell their wares.) She liked a ring I was wearing. I took it off to show it to her, and she dropped it down her blouse and ran into the lady's room. Then she ran out the door, got in her car, and took off. My wife gave me the ring, and she will be furious that I lost it."

I asked him, "Will you tell your wife the truth?"

"No," he said, "I'd just tell her I lost it."

Fortunately for him, he got the Pennsylvania license plate of her vehicle.

I told the truck driver, "I will see what I can do. Stay right here."

The address was in Easton, about eight miles west of the truck stop. I radioed the station that we were still working on this case.

The recruit asked me, "Are we going into Easton after the ring?"

I believe I said, "Watch me!"

We arrived at the address in Easton. I rang the bell to this row house, and an older woman answered the door.

I told her, "Please send your daughter down with the ring she stole. If she gives it back, I won't arrest her; just give her a warning."

The young girl came down and gave me the ring. She explained, "I would have given it back the next time I saw him."

I said, "Right," and suspended her from the truck stop for one month.

We returned to New Jersey and gave the ring back to the truck driver.

I told him, "Don't take the ring off again!"

He thanked us, and we left.

The recruit asked me, "Was that legal?"

I told him, "No, but it got the job done. Don't do anything like this until you have tenure on the job in five years. If the girl complained to Internal Affairs, I could probably have gotten a summary court martial with a maximum of thirty days off without pay. Being she didn't, the incident didn't happen."

Today I don't know what would happen if a complaint was made; I would hope just a summary court martial.

I was on day patrol in an unmarked vehicle driving on a country road. I was only going about 35 MPH when a large dog started chasing my vehicle. This was not the first time this happened with this dog, a pretty gold Labrador retriever. The dog got too close this time and went under my right front wheel. I stopped, got out of my vehicle, and checked the dog. It looked like it had a broken left front leg. Other than that, it looked OK. At this time, the dog's owner came out of the house and started yelling at the dog that it was his fault for chasing cars. I convinced the dog's owner to take the dog to a veterinarian, which he did. I radioed the station and advised the sergeant of the incident. The sergeant asked was the dog on a leash, and I said no. He just said to make out an operations report.

Back at the station, I heard the sergeant answer the phone. The dog owner just got back from the veterinarian and offered he was charged $125 to fix the dog's leg and wanted the State Police to pay the bill. The sergeant asked him if the dog was on a leash; the dog's owner said no. The sergeant then told him, "The State won't pay," and hung the phone up on him. I thought the sergeant could have been a little nicer to the dog owner, but "that's the way it was back then."

I investigated my only homicide investigation at Washington Station. I received a call to check with a subject walking his dog and smelling a foul odor in a cornfield. I arrived, entered the cornfield about twenty feet off the road, and saw a very decomposed man lying face down with his hands tied behind his back. I called for a CSI on this apparent homicide and to notify the station DSG. I was told that the station DSG was tied up and to handle the scene until he arrived. I roped off the area in crime scene tape and took names and statements of everyone who came, including the man reporting the incident. Two CSI detectives arrived, and a medical examiner's office member to pronounce the body.

When DSG Jim Roseberry arrived and looked at my notes, he stated it looked like I got everything and that I should make out the initial investigation report, which I did. DSG Roseberry worked on the case and found out the victim was a missing person, and his tractor-trailer was found on the New York Thruway just north of New York City. It had a load of meat that was missing. The victim's wife gave us the names of two suspects who were her husband's friends. DSG Roseberry told me that the major Crimes Unit from division headquarters was taking over the investigation. I didn't think that it was fair that Division would take the arrests since he did most of the work. He said welcome to the real world. I found out later that the two suspects were involved with the victim stealing the load of meat. They then decided to kill him and only split the proceeds two ways instead of three. The suspects pleaded guilty to manslaughter and were sentenced to ten years in jail each. It was nice that the DSG Roseberry let me follow the case to its end.

Another homicide case I worked on was a media nightmare for the State Police and the Warren County Prosecutor's Office. In a garden apartment complex outside of Phillipsburg, an older woman woke up early and heard loud music coming from the apartment upstairs. She called the superintendent, and he called the local police. They opened the door to the apartment and found a young woman stabbed to death on the floor. The local police, a relatively new department, called the State Police for help. A couple of State Police detectives went to the scene and decided to handle the case. The victim, a white female about thirty years old, lived alone and was known to be a little promiscuous. The detectives found male underwear in her dresser with a couple of troopers' names on them. The detectives also found out from a girlfriend that the victim had a date the previous night with a male subject that lived in the same complex. He worked for a local phone company and was single. The detectives found some questionable information about the subject. They also found that he had left the area early for Carlisle, Pennsylvania, where he was originally from. They were able to get a search warrant for his car and apartment. Also, they contacted the Pennsylvania State Police, who located his vehicle.

The Pennsylvania troopers watched his vehicle for a day and advised us that he was now moving east on US-22 toward New Jersey. A New Jersey patrol picked him up as he entered the state and followed him to his apartment. We had the complex surrounded. I was located at the rear exit. The suspect pulled into his assigned parking space, and the detectives moved in as he got out of his vehicle. They confronted him and asked him to search his car, and he said, "No." The detectives showed him the search warrant. Behind the spare tire, they found a bloody knife in the vehicle, which was the murder weapon. They also found some of the victim's bloody underwear in the trunk. They found some of the victim's clean underwear in his apartment in his dresser. The Warren County Prosecutor made a big media event of this case, stating that he would seek the death penalty since, at that time, we still had the death penalty in New Jersey.

The state had to assign the case to the Public Defender's Office since the defendant could not afford an attorney. The local paper from Pennsylvania also handled Warren County, New Jersey news. The paper, known as a very liberal paper, printed articles on the case, saying the troopers themselves might be suspects. Two troopers had to testify that they had sex with the victim, and one detective testified that he yelled at her in a bar because she would not let him buy her a drink. If you read a more conservative newspaper from Morris County, you would think they were two different cases. The public defender did a good job. He put his client on the stand, and the suspect stated that he found the victim that way, already stabbed to death. He stated he cleaned up some of the mess because he was a "clean freak." He also said he took the knife and blood-soaked underwear so he wouldn't get blamed for the crime. His other comment was that he took her clean underwear because he was a "cross-dresser." Naturally, the public defender tried to blame the State Police for the crime and for covering up for one of their own.

Near the end of the trial, I was playing golf in Washington. I was paired up with three individuals who looked like local business people. When I play golf with people I don't know, and if they ask me what I do for a living, I would say that I work for an insurance company. They usually don't bother me anymore. The three started talking about this case, and all thought that the State Police did the murder and tried to pin it on the guy on trial. I knew we had a problem with the jury if they were thinking like these golfers. Sure enough, the accused was found not guilty and went free. The prosecutor took a big hit on this.

I found out later that the public defender had given a lie detector test to his client and, with the results, told the prosecutor that his client was willing to plead guilty to manslaughter. The prosecutor refused and went on with the trial and lost. The State Police superintendent was not pleased with his troopers and had some transferred, but that was all he could do. This case was the worst miscarriage of justice I saw during my carrier with the State Police. There was no such thing as a "slam dunk case." The media can sway the minds of the public and the jury.

Sometime in late 1978, I was asked by the Troop B traffic officer if I wanted to go on the Weigh Team, and I declined. I didn't mind weighing trucks at Somerville Station and Hackensack Station because they had a state scale in their area. The other reason he wanted me was that, at the time, only one marked troop car was assigned to a two-man unit, and the trooper I would be assigned with lived in the same town as me. I told the lieutenant that I didn't want to spend forty hours a week weighing trucks and having to listen to the whining of truck drivers. He mentioned I could hurt my career if I turned down his offer, and I told him I would not change my mind.

While working days, one day, I heard on the radio that there was a bank robbery at a bank in Blairstown Township, near where the Blairstown Station was. It happened at about 9 A.M. when the bank opened. There were two white males in the vehicle. The vehicle was described as a light blue Dodge Challenger with a large white racing strip down the middle of the vehicle, an easy car to spot.

There was no other activity on this vehicle until around 2:15 P.M. I headed back to Washington Station from I-78 to end my shift. At 2:15 P.M., a Blairstown Trooper stopped a suspect vehicle, a light blue Dodge Challenger with a white racing stripe, on I-80 East. The Blairstown Station DSG told the trooper to hold the vehicle so he could question the driver and passenger. At the scene of the stop, the DSG questioned the driver, who seemed to have the correct answers. The DSG didn't know that the driver was recently fired as a police officer in Woodbridge Township, New Jersey. As the vehicle was let go, the money from the robbery broke loose from under the hood in the wheel well and started flying all over the highway. As the DSG and the trooper began pursuing the vehicle, he put what was happening on the air. Apparently, the suspects hid somewhere in Blairstown and waited until they thought the coast was clear. The suspect vehicle was seen going off exit 19 to RTE 517 South. Hackettstown Police and Independence Police set up a roadblock on RTE 517 South. They never showed up.

I was near Washington Station, and I knew they might have turned down Cat Swamp Road which was a shortcut to the Mansfield Pistol Range, where we had been qualifying twice a year. I started heading up towards the range. I was in a dark blue unmarked car, driving very slowly. As I approached a slight rise, the suspect vehicle passed me, going in the opposite direction. The driver made me (the ex-cop). I made a quick u-turn, followed the vehicle, and saw that it turned into a private driveway. I radioed in my location and the suspect vehicle. The two suspects left their vehicle and ran around the house. I didn't know that my squad sergeant, who also knew the area, had left the station, and as I was entering the wooded area, he was right behind me. We chased them into the woods. They took off their clothes to blend in with the environment since the State Police helicopter was also looking for them. We caught them shortly as they tried to enter the roadway where the Mansfield police were waiting. We brought them back to Washington Station, where we met with the Blairstown DSG. He couldn't thank me enough and my squad sergeant for making the apprehension. He stated he would put us in for a commendation which he did. Unfortunately, because headquarters didn't want to promote my sergeant to SFC, we only got letters of appreciation from the troop commander. After that, I had a lot more respect for my squad sergeant, even though he was a little lazy with paperwork, and let me run the squad.

In late 1978 the State Police gave its first written examination for the rank of sergeant. Though I was eligible, I was only a Trooper II and lost points to a Trooper I. I would not be a Trooper I until July 1979. I still took the test in 1978 to get experience on the test. It took twelve years to make Trooper I, which was a time promotion. Now it's only nine years. I studied hard for the test in December 1979. We were told there would be a lot of the criminal code, 2C, on the test. I took the test and thought that I did well. There were also a lot of traffic questions on the test, which I know I maxed.

Rumors were flying on the criteria for promotion. I called Trooper I Thomas Iskrzycki, the president of the STFA. We have been good friends since our days at Howell Station in Troop C and my time as a station rep on TPU. I asked Tom about the criteria for promotion to sergeant. I told him in Troop B, we had three Trooper 1's that were acting sergeants and running squads. He asked me if I had any written reprimands, and I stated no. I told him I was just promoted to Trooper I on July 1, 1979, and on my last three or four evaluations, I was recommended for sergeant. Also, I was the senior man on my squad. He then told me that, in my case, the test was now worth 100%. Sometime in March 1980, I was doing some reports at the station, and a troop lieutenant had stopped in to see the station commander. When he saw me, he called my name, and as I looked at him, he put three fingers on his arm that simulated sergeant strips and left. I didn't know what to think. I knew I was close, but three Tpr I's were running the three squads in the troop, and they were acting sergeants.

I was flying to Florida on Friday the next day with my mom, so she could visit her brother from Canada, who had a winter home in Florida. I was off the weekend and would not return to New Jersey until Tuesday. My mom and I arrived in Florida Friday morning at about 11 A.M. We were picked up at the airport by my uncle. On all vacations, you had to leave a number about where you were staying. I left my uncle's phone number in Florida. The phone rang just as we were finishing dinner. The sergeant on the line from the station congratulated me on making sergeant. Then he gave me the bad news that I had to report to the Troop E commander, Captain Richard Kelly, on Monday at 9 A.M. and that I was transferred to Bloomfield Station. The sergeant was wrong. If he read the teletype correctly, it said that I was promoted and assigned to Troop E but not transferred yet.

I called the airline and changed our tickets to Sunday night instead of Tuesday. My mom and I left Florida at around 7 P.M. on Sunday and arrived at Newark Airport at 11 P.M. I dropped my mom off at her home, raced to Washington Station, loaded my car with all my gear, and got home at about 3 A.M. I slept a couple of hours and reported to Troop E headquarters at 9 A.M. I reported to the SFC, who advised me that he hadn't even cut the teletype yet to send me to Bloomfield Station. He went to see Captain Kelly, who wanted to see me. He welcomed me aboard and couldn't believe what had happened. He told me to see the Bloomfield Station commander, who would give me a locker for my gear. Then he told me he was giving me off until Thursday when my squad was working days. I dropped my gear off at Bloomfield Station. I found out that I and a trooper from Flemington Station got promoted to sergeant because of the test, and I was sent to Bloomfield because I was there once before, and the other trooper was sent to Newark on the Turnpike because he was there before. That was the last time a test was given for sergeant because it took too much power from the troop commanders to promote who they wanted.

Troop E Bloomfield Post, here I come again.

7

TROOP E POST: BACK TO BLOOMFIELD STATION AS A SERGEANT

I reported for my first shift, a day shift, after the troop commander gave me a few days off. I had a squad of ten, including me. My senior man, Tpr I Roy Van Tassel, was the only trooper I knew. I didn't know the other eight, although they were initially from Troop B. I sat down with my senior man, who told me about all the squad members. He told me all members were OK, but one member had a habit of not signing off at a location if he was out of the car. I didn't particularly appreciate that the Parkway and Turnpike still didn't have civilian dispatchers, which meant I would have to stay in and handle the station record and radio. A couple of times a month, you had a "power day," which meant two squads were working days. Power days were also used for training.

I introduced myself to all my squad members. I emphasized to all; please sign off to a location if you are not in the car. I wanted to ensure that the one trooper who had a problem signing off would understand. On my second day, I was on the station record. I called the same trooper who allegedly was not signing off to investigate a two-car minor accident at the Essex Toll Plaza. He did not answer. I had to assign another trooper to investigate this accident. When I finally got in touch with the first trooper, I had him stop at the station. I wrote him a performance notice for being off the air and missing a call (A performance notice was a small chit acknowledging something wrong or good. The trooper must sign it to show that he got it but may disagree. It can go on his six-month evaluation.). He tried to make some half-ass excuse as to why he was off the air, but I didn't care. I had just made him aware of this yesterday. Of course, he did it again in a couple of days. Before giving him the second performance notice, I discussed it with the station commander. He stated that maybe he's been out here too long and should go back to Troop B. When I discussed this second performance notice with him, he got angry and offered he would see the station commander. I told him to go ahead.

I noted that he had been out here almost five years and lived in Bloomfield, about five minutes from work. Maybe it's time for him to return to Troop B. Washington Station or Blairstown Station was pretty good. (Both are more than an hour from his home). He asked for another chance, and I said we would see. He became one of my better troopers, making drunken driver arrests and issuing many traffic summonses.

To myself, I thanked my previous sergeant at Washington Station for letting me run the squad and getting the experience of supervising. Supposedly I had to be here for at least one year while on probation. So I thought. After being at Bloomfield Station for about two months, I received a call from a senior sergeant I knew well. He wanted to see if I wanted to make a mutual transfer back to Troop B. He wanted my squad only because my senior man, and he lived in the same town and could ride to work together. If this worked, I would be stationed at the Netcong Station, about five miles from home. He told me to put in for a transfer back to Troop B, and he would take care of the rest.

I spoke to the station commander, who understood and said to put in for the transfer. About a week later, the transfer request was denied in that I had to put in at least one year at Bloomfield until I was off probation. I called the senior sergeant and advised him of the denial of the transfer. He was a little pissed and told me not to do anything yet.

A week later, the station commander told me that my transfer request had been changed to approved, and I was going back to Troop B and Netcong Station. I don't know how the senior sergeant did it, but it made me happy. He must have had some pull at division headquarters.

Here we go, back to Troop B Netcong Station Post.

8

TROOP B POST:
BACK TO NETCONG STATION

It was fantastic to get back to Troop B. Any station would have been great with all Troop B Stations having civilian dispatchers. Netcong Station was even better, just five miles from home. Now I could get out of the station after completing squad reports and patrol like a road sergeant. Netcong Station was responsible for I-80 from Allamuchy Township, Warren County, to Parsippany Township, Morris County, then I-287 South from I-80 to the Somerset County line. Netcong Station did the local work in Victory Gardens Borough (and still does) in that they had laid off their police department some years ago. Of course, there were a lot of accidents, especially during rush hour. I had an excellent squad but with only six members, including me. I had a great senior man who I've known for many years. My senior man had a nickname, Chief of Police of Victory Gardens. When we worked days on the weekend, he went down to Victory Gardens and enforced a town ordinance that did not allow vehicles to park on the front or rear lawns of the homes. The mayor and council wanted the ordinance enforced. So on a Saturday or Sunday morning, my senior man and usually one additional trooper would go down to the borough, write a summons on the ordinance, and tow the vehicle in. This kept the mayor and council happy. From what I remember, we were the only squad enforcing the ordinance.

I had one trooper, Tpr I David Scureman, who was pretty good at making criminal arrests. His arrests were about 75 percent white and 25 percent minority, blacks and Hispanics. This was about right on an Interstate highway and for the population of New Jersey. A younger trooper came to me and offered he wanted to make criminal arrests but wasn't sure how. I let him ride double with my key arrest man, Tpr I Scureman, and he broke him in correctly, and the younger trooper started making criminal arrests. In a couple of years, he was elevated to detective, transferred to the Narcotics Bureau, and had a fine career retiring as a lieutenant.

I had to take the station record and radio on one midnight shift because the dispatcher called in sick. I didn't mind because we had dispatchers, and I was out a lot. I received a call from one of my cars with my ace criminal man and another young trooper with him. They had stopped a car on I-287 South in Parsippany Township and had a sick motorist who was a VIP and would take him home. They were going to park his vehicle at the old Troop B headquarters in Morristown (Some units were still using this site until it was sold.). The new headquarters was now in Totowa. I figured they would tell me who this VIP was when they came in. At about 6:30 A.M., they came in, and the senior trooper explained what had happened. The trooper stated that they stopped a black sedan on I-287 Southbound. The vehicle had been weaving all over the road and driving very slowly. When stopped, they realized that it was our Troop B commander who at first resisted being stopped. He was taken out of his troop car and handcuffed. He then calmed down and offered he thought he had missed a turn. The trooper said they took his vehicle to the old Morristown headquarters and took the captain home. At first, I didn't believe them until I heard Little Falls Station direct a patrol to pick up the Troop B commander and relay him to the old Morristown headquarters to pick up his vehicle. This was why some of my hair was falling out. We kept everything quiet. The captain was an excellent commander of Troop B and had a great career retiring as a lieutenant colonel. The public might think we only let friends or other police officers go for drinking and driving. I can only speak for myself. I let at least one go for every five drunk drivers I arrested. I would give them a breathalyzer test, adjust the reading below .10 and only write them a summons for whatever I stopped them for. Today it's almost impossible to let anyone go. The new machine prints a copy of the blood alcohol reading, and a copy goes to the New Jersey DMV. So once you are brought in, "your goose was cooked." I liked the old way better; it gave discretion to the trooper.

It was a Sunday morning, and I was on the station record and radio since the dispatcher had called in sick. My ace criminal man, Tpr I David Scureman, stopped a speeding vehicle on I-80 Eastbound in Blairstown Township. He stated he was taking the violator to the Blairstown Station to have him post bail. He called me when he got there. He noted the two couples in the vehicle, which was rented, were Israeli citizens and were running late to catch a plane back to Israel from a New York airport. He added the driver called him a "Nazi" (Our winter uniform was similar to the German military uniform.). Then the driver said as the trooper gave the driver the summons for speeding, he would throw it away when he got home. So then the trooper decided to have him post bond. All four subjects stated they did not have the $50 for bail at the Blairstown Station. The trooper allowed them to make a phone call, and the driver called the Israeli Consulate in New York City. The consulate called me at Netcong Station. I advised the consulate what had happened and that her citizen threatened to throw the summons away when he got home. I informed her that if they didn't post the $50 bail, the driver would go to the Warren County Jail. The consulate called the Blairstown Station and advised her citizen to post the bail, which he did. Unfortunately for the two couples, they missed their flight back home. I think the trooper did an excellent job with this arrogant motorist, but another few hairs fell out of my head.

In another case, I was in the station, and the SFC heard one of my men calling for a wrecker to tow in a 10-speed Schwinn bicycle. The SFC told me to go out and see what's up with towing in a bike. I went onto I-80 and saw the trooper on the side of the road with the violator, who had been riding on the highway on his bicycle. The trooper had written him a summons for riding on the interstate, which was illegal. The trooper told me he gave the same subject a written warning last week, and now he's doing it again.

I asked the trooper, "Why are you attempting to tow the bike?"

The trooper said, "Because I want to."

I told him, "Not going to happen."

He got a little upset and said, "When I call for a tow truck, I should get a tow truck."

I told him, "You don't always get what you want on this job."

I spoke to the bike owner, who stated he had lost his license for drinking and driving and was going to work.

I advised him, "Use US-46 in the future, which was legal. You can pick your bike up at Netcong Station tomorrow."

I took the bike back to the station, and the trooper took the bicyclist to the next exit.

You live and learn on this job. This was the only time I saw a trooper attempt to tow a bike.

While on patrol at Netcong Station, I would write only a good summons for a serious violation. I would not set up radar. That was my men's responsibility. I would write about ten to fifteen summons a month, about 20 percent of what a trooper wrote. I was out a lot, but on midnight patrol, if I were riding double, I would let the trooper write all the summonses. There were four squads back then at all stations, and we were all on the eight-hour day since 1976. Two other sergeants were unhappy with me writing ten to fifteen summons monthly. They were talking behind my back. They just wanted to stay in the station drinking coffee. They were a little senior to me with time on the job. One day when I was stopping at the station to pick up my paycheck, I heard the two sergeants in the kitchen talking about me and saying that I was making them look bad. I stepped into the kitchen and confronted them. I told them that if they wanted to sit in the station and twiddle their thumbs, that was OK with me. But don't tell me what to do. I told them if they think I'm writing too many summonses now, wait until next month when I start writing forty to sixty a month like a regular trooper. They understood and apologized for their comments.

It was a Sunday morning, and our squad was working days. I was in the station a little longer and working on my squad's six-month evaluations. I went out on patrol at about 10 A.M. As I entered I-80 East, I heard my senior man call out a car he had clocked at over 90 MPH. He was headed west, and he had just past me. I made a quick u-turn and started following my senior man. He had just pulled the car over as I pulled up behind him. As I got out, my senior man stated there was something wrong. The driver held his hand on his right front pocket as if hiding something. I got to the car, a Cadillac two-door sedan, and ordered the driver out. As he came out, the senior man walked this white male to the rear of their car, and the driver was still holding his hand on his pocket and stating, "Don't take it; it's mine."

There were three more white males in the vehicle. I ordered them out of the car. The last one out had been sitting in the vehicle's rear left. As he got out, I saw him reach into his jacket pocket and pull out a small automatic pistol. I pulled out my service revolver and was ready to shoot. He threw his gun back into the car. I ran around their car, ensured the other two passengers were on the ground, and then I retrieved the small automatic pistol and told the subject carrying it that he was under arrest.

He yelled, "I'm not going back to jail," and ran into the woods.

I chased him for about one hundred yards until we hit the cyclone fence that kept the deer off the highway. He turned to face me. I still had my revolver out. I told him if he tried to climb the fence, I would strike him on the head with my gun and that he wouldn't wake up until tomorrow. He hesitated for a few seconds, then turned around, and I cuffed him.

Back at the car, a couple of other troopers stopped to help. My senior man and I searched the vehicle and found a kilo of cocaine, a large bag of Quaaludes, and a large bag of phony quarters that could be used in Atlantic City casinos back then.

Back at the station, my senior man mentioned, "I am taking four hours of compensatory time to go to a family christening."

I asked him, "What about this nice arrest you made?"

He didn't care; the christening was more important to him.

So, I let him go after he wrote the speeding summons. All four subjects would be charged due to the amount of drugs and the gun. I found out from the driver that he was holding his pocket because he had about $2,000 in it, and in New York City, from where they are from, the cops take their money, so they said. They all came from Queens, and after they crossed the George Washington Bridge, they must have missed the turn for the New Jersey Turnpike on their way to Atlantic City.

Along with the cocaine, I counted 1,200 Quaaludes, a couple of hundred phony quarters, which I eventually turned over to the Secret Service. Then the next shift was almost ready to take the subjects to the Morris County Jail, and the one subject with the gun wanted to see me. I walked over to where he was cuffed to the prisoner bar and asked him what he wanted. He said he wanted to thank me because the cops beat him up when he was arrested in New York City. I don't know whether he was telling the truth, but if he was, there was no reason to beat someone just because they were breaking the law. Arrests like this are why I loved the road.

Because of my activities and that my squad led the station in most activities, I was asked by the assistant tactical patrol supervisor if I wanted to take the place of the Netcong tactical patrol sergeant, who was being transferred to a road station. The SFC told me that I wasn't the first choice of the tactical patrol lieutenant, but the captain interceded. Back then, the rumor was the tactical patrol lieutenant didn't like Italians. I didn't care; I loved the two years I spent on the TPU as a trooper. I accepted the position. I had excellent troopers working for me. But as usual, there was always one that tried to test you. This individual started coming in late all the time. I advised him that I wanted all my troopers here for roll call, usually in the morning. When working days, our hours were either 8 A.M. to 4 P.M., 9 A.M. to 5 P.M., or 10 A.M. to 6 P.M. I wanted roll call to go over any new directives or wanted persons.

Conversely, if a trooper had to go someplace late in the day, I allowed them to work their way home (All tactical patrol troopers had their troop cars assigned to them.). My men wrote a lot of summonses, and we worked every other weekend at night on drinking driving patrols. My men also made their share of criminal arrests. We also handled most of the details at the troop level, especially presidential details and heads of state details with the Secret Service. The same trooper continued coming in late with an excuse or that he stopped to write a summons. Finally, I wrote him up. This was highly unusual for a tactical patrol trooper. When I wrote him up the second time, I told him I would not put these performance notices on his evaluations because he would not be here at evaluation time. Suddenly he wasn't late for work anymore. Incredible what a little threat can do (It wasn't a threat; it was true.).

I took a little heat on this arrest. My unit was working a drunk driving patrol on US-46 from Netcong Borough to Hackettstown. Around 10 P.M., I spotted a vehicle on a side road from US-46 with the trunk lid open and some people around the car. I pulled up quickly and saw a group of juveniles loading pumpkins into the trunk (It was around Halloween.). There were seven teenagers; the vehicle driver was the oldest at seventeen. The rest were between fifteen and sixteen years old. There were four boys and three girls. It was obvious that they were stealing the pumpkins from the farmer's field. They would not tell me what they were going to do with them. I suspected they would go to the local high school and throw them around, but I wasn't sure (I did it when I was a teenager.). With the help of the Mt. Olive Police, we took all seven back to the local station just down the road. I had the seventeen-year-old drive his car back to the station. The local police contacted the farmer, and he came by and picked up his pumpkins. Believe it or not, I had him sign a property report. There were about twelve pumpkins worth about $25. I told the seventeen-year-old that if he agreed to give me a statement, I would only charge him and let the other six go. The seventeen-year-old agreed, but the three girls protested. They said if I were going to arrest him, I would have to arrest all of them. I then called each of the parents of the juveniles to pick them up. I advised them of the larceny charge against their children and that it will be handled in the County Juvenile Court. Unfortunately, it involved two different counties. Four juveniles were from Morris County, and three were from Warren County. I found out months later that the Morris County Juvenile Court put the four on probation for six months and fined them $50. In Warren County Juvenile Court, the three got six months of probation and no fine. My lieutenant busted my chops about the "pumpkin arrests" and asked me if I was still trying to be a detective. He also asked me if I had ever done something like this when I was a teenager, and I told him, of course, but I didn't get caught. I even found a small pumpkin on the roof of my troop car parked behind Netcong Station, where my office was.

One of the most significant details I had on tactical patrol as a sergeant was that President Reagan would be giving a speech at the Flemington Fairgrounds. We had about thirty troopers assigned to assist the

Secret Service. The detail was on a Sunday. I met with the Secret Service, and we laid out a plan for posts of troopers. There was a good rumor that the local farmers would protest the price of grain being too low. They were going to block NJ-31 so the president could see their signs. The Secret Service had two motorcades, one for the president to go out the rear gate after his speech and a fake one to enter NJ-31.

We had a briefing at Somerville Station about three hours before the detail. I was surprised that the Superintendent, COL Clinton Pagano, was at the briefing along with the troop commander, Captain Raymond Maralla (no other Sergeants or Lieutenants, just me.). So I picked an excellent Tpr I to help me supervise. After the briefing, COL Pagano left. The troop commander approached me and offered he wanted everything to go right. He noted the operations officer was there in civilian clothes and working with the Secret Service since he was just promoted on Friday and his uniforms were not ready. The captain said he put me in charge because he knew I could do the job. Then he hesitated a minute and said, "don't screw this up; I don't forget."

Talk about being a little nervous. I was on NJ-31, where the farmers lined up their tractors just north of the main entrance. I went up to them and offered that if they kept their tractors off the road, I would let them ride up to the front gate so the president could see their signs. So they pulled their tractors on the shoulder to avoid blocking traffic and be right in front of the main entrance. As the fake motorcade came out of the main gate, the farmers raised their signs to the motorcade, but the president had already left out the back gate. I only had one problem. A weigh team trooper tried to leave early, and I chased him north on NJ-31 and stopped him. He said he thought the detail was over. I told him it was not over until I said so. It bothers me to have a specialist trooper try and leave when he doesn't even work shift work anymore; he just weighs trucks. I made him stay until I left. The detail went well without a hitch.

When there's a pending promotion to sergeant, sergeant first class, or lieutenant, division headquarters sends each eligible trooper a notice of their promotional rank to their home. In Troop B, there were close to fifty eligible sergeants and detective sergeants for promotion to SFC.

The previous notice I got was nineteen. After President Regan's detail, I noticed I was now number six. Not bad. Good thing the detail went well. Remember, the captain said, "I don't forget."

I continued to enjoy the TPU. Being out and on the road was what this job was all about. I got a call from the SFC, my immediate supervisor. He stated the lieutenant wanted me and another Unit (TPU) to work together next weekend out of the Little Falls Station and patrol NJ-3 for drunk drivers. NJ-3 runs from the Lincoln Tunnel to US-46 in Clifton. The SFC added that he wanted thirty drunk driver arrests for the two units. I told the SFC that he was nuts. You can't put a total on any drunk driver detail, only to do the best job you can. That would mean fifteen drunk driver arrests per unit. Each unit had seven men, including the sergeant. Plus, my unit was short one trooper who was on vacation. So let the fun begin. We worked as instructed out of the Little Falls Station.

At the end of the weekend, the other unit did get a total of fifteen drunk drivers. My unit got eleven, which was still not bad being one man short.

On the way home at about 5 A.M., I was driving behind the other sergeant when he stopped a vehicle. I came up behind him to back him up. He got the driver out of the car and asked if he had anything to drink. The driver had fishing equipment in the back seat. He said he had some beer the previous night but that he was going fishing. The sergeant decided to cut the driver loose. After the motorist left, I asked the sergeant if he was trying to put a nail in my coffin, but he didn't answer; he just left. He knew what I was saying. I was delighted with my unit.

My next day to work was Tuesday morning when we completed all pending reports from the previous weekend. My SFC called from Troop B headquarters, saying the lieutenant was upset about not getting the number of arrests and wanted to talk to me. He got on the phone and started yelling and ranting that I didn't do my job. Finally, I couldn't take him anymore, so I hung up the phone. The SFC called back and said the lieutenant said I hung up the phone on him. I told the SFC I didn't; we must have had a bad connection.

A little while later, the SFC called me again and added the lieutenant wanted me in his office tomorrow at 9 A.M. sharp. The SFC said,

"He's going to give you a performance notice for hanging up on him. Please don't argue with him, or he may bring you up on charges for insubordination."

I thanked the SFC and said, "I will see you tomorrow!"

Unfortunately, when tomorrow came, my troop car would not start. I finally got it started with my personal vehicle, and instead of going to my appointment with the lieutenant, I took the car to our State Police garage in Bedminster. I called the SFC and told him what had happened. He called me back and said the lieutenant was fuming. He thinks you did it on purpose. The appointment was changed to the next day.

I arrived at Troop B headquarters the next day at 9 A.M. and went to the Tactical Patrol Office. The lieutenant started to chew me out about me hanging up on him the other day.

"I didn't hang up," I said, but he still issued a performance notice stating that I hung the phone up on him. I signed the notice (Signing the notice only means that you got it, not agreeing with it.).

The lieutenant continued yelling at me, "You are the worst Tactical Patrol Sergeant who ever worked for me. What do you have to say for yourself?"

I said, "I could use a better troop car." (In 1979, the State Police ordered 1979 Ford midsize vehicles. They were the worst marked troop cars ever used for patrol. They could not get out of their own way.)

He roared, "As long as you work for me, I will not give you a better car. Now get out of my office!"

As I was leaving and passing the captain's office, the captain called me in. He must have known I was coming in to see my lieutenant because he asked, "How did you make out?"

I said, "I can handle him."

The captain just laughed as I went on my way. The captain was also Italian; I'm sure he knew the lieutenant didn't like Italians. In my mind, I don't think the lieutenant liked anyone but himself.

On another afternoon shift, my unit and I were working on a Tuesday after working the previous weekend on a drunk driving check. We were working at Washington Station. We would do our last weekend reports and then go to Louise's Diner for dinner. After dinner, it usually was about 10 P.M. I would tell my men to start working their way home. Our hours that day were 4 P.M. to midnight. I would not go home until midnight. I did not trust the lieutenant I worked for because he would love to catch me leaving early. One of my men who lived in the Phillipsburg area called in a stop and offered he was heading back to Washington Station with a possible drunk driver arrest. I advised him that I would meet him there.

When I arrived at the station, it was about 10:45 P.M. The trooper had already arrived with the suspected drunk driver. As I walked in the back door, I was surprised to see my lieutenant there in full uniform. He asked me, "What are you doing here?"

I said, "I'm working until midnight."

He looked as white as a ghost. He was obviously trying to catch me leaving early and get me transferred back to a road station. I may have my men leave a little early, but I always stayed until the shift was over. I still had about six months left on the TPU assignment. I knew when I had two years on, the lieutenant would have me transferred back to a road station. I was OK with that because I was still a road sergeant enjoying the road.

While on the TPU, I was trained as a Troop B firearms instructor. The division had decided to go to a better duty weapon after Tpr Philip Lomonaco was shot and killed in a shootout on I-80 in Warren County. The division, after extensive testing, decided on the German 9MM made by Heckler and Koch Inc. It was a great weapon holding nine rounds of 9MM bullets. Most police departments were going to a more powerful weapon since the criminals were also. All sworn members of the division had to be qualified with the new firearm. At the time, that would be about 2,500 Troopers.

The instructions would be at Fort Dix, the US Army military base. The academy instructors were in charge. I was assigned as an assistant instructor for range duty in the afternoon. Classroom instructions were given in the morning. I took the classroom instruction on my first day, a Monday. I was issued a new Heckler and Koch 9 MM with a new holster. I qualified in the afternoon. I noticed in the morning that the academy instructor giving the class was getting hoarse. I knew him because we were stationed together years ago at Somerville Station. He asked if I could give the morning class since he was so hoarse. He had been giving the course already for a couple of weeks. I gave the course for the rest of the week, and the instructor got me extended for another week. After the second week, my lieutenant got me back to Troop B so I wouldn't miss another drunk driving patrol. I enjoyed details like this. It broke up the usual routine as applicant investigations did, but you knew that you were always returning to the road.

My immediate supervisor was an SFC. He was between me and the tactical patrol supervisor, the lieutenant. The SFC called me one day and wanted to speak to me about something. We were pretty close. He always warned me when the lieutenant was gunning for me. Though he never said it, I don't think he liked our lieutenant very much. He closed the door to his office. It was a Monday morning. We were off the previous weekend. The SFC said that he had a problem this past Friday night. He said he was home sleeping with his wife, and a bunch of rowdy drunks were making a lot of noise at a bar across the street from his house. He stated he came out of his house to tell them to stop making noise. He said he didn't want to call his local police department and get these kids in trouble. They turned on him, and he took them out, all four of them.

The local police came and arrested all of them for being drunk and disorderly and took them away. The SFC wanted my opinion if he should make out a special report that he was involved in an off-duty incident. The SFC knew I was friendly with some of the local police in that town since I was still in the New Jersey National Guard with them. I called one of my friends, a detective sergeant, and he advised me the SFC's name will not appear on the arrest reports. I told the SFC not to make out any reports to the captain.

"The incident didn't happen."

I also thanked him for taking out all four drunks. We shook hands, and I told him, "Once a Trooper, Always a Trooper."

Another State Police program I liked was the warning program. When you stop someone for a minor moving or equipment violation, you get to see their credentials and look into the vehicle. On an evening on patrol working out of Washington Station, I stopped a car with a broken taillight. Another one of my men was behind me and was backing me up. The vehicle was an old Ford Mustang. The white male driver gave me his license, registration, and insurance card. The passenger, also a white male, had a female-type pocketbook on his lap and appeared to be wearing lipstick. The car registration was expired for over three months. I had the driver step out of his vehicle to inspect his broken taillight. I advised him, "I will have this car towed for an expired registration (normal procedure)."

He angrily accused me, "You are only picking on me because I am gay."

I told him, "I don't care what sexual persuasion you are. Your car is unregistered."

I had the vehicle towed in, and the other trooper and I dropped them off at the 24-hour truck stop about seven miles from where they lived in Easton.

The driver made a formal complaint against me that I threatened him because he was gay. A troop lieutenant did the internal investigation, and the complaint was unsubstantiated.

I always stop a car for a violation, not a particular person, whether the driver was white, black, brown, male, or female. Using these criteria, you cannot get in any hot water. At least when I was on the road.

Today it's different with all the cameras out there. From what I have seen, there was not only a video. It's how the footage was interpreted.

Another interesting case I had at Netcong Station was when a small bus with about fifteen students from London, England, ran onto the shoulder and stopped. The driver, a 39-year-old white male, was also the male chaperone, and there was a female chaperone. The driver had a heart attack, and the ambulance took him to Hackettstown Hospital, where he was pronounced dead on arrival. The female chaperone drove the bus with the fifteen children back to the station. They were on the way to Canada from New York City on their summer vacation. The problem was the deceased chaperone had the students' passports and travelers' checks, and the checks also needed his signature. The female chaperone didn't know what to do.

I contacted the United Kingdom Consulate in New York City and explained the problem. They gave the female chaperone the right to sign the travelers' checks, which I documented in the station record. The female chaperone said that she had no problem driving the small bus to Canada.

Now I had to take care of the deceased chaperone. Through his identification, I contacted the London Police, where he lived. They gave me the phone number of the superintendent of his apartment complex. The superintendent said the subject was single and had a brother living in Australia. He gave me the phone number of the brother. I contacted his brother, and since we were limited on time to pick the body up, I advised the brother on the phone about what had happened. This was against my better judgment to advise a person on the phone on a death notification. He hadn't seen his brother for about ten years since he moved to London. He wanted his brother cremated, and I gave him a couple of local mortuaries that did cremations.

On follow-up, I found that the body was cremated, and the ashes were shipped to his brother in Australia. Case closed. You never know what to expect on the road. This was another reason why I liked the road. Helping the fifteen children and their chaperone continue their trip to Canada made me feel good.

My time on the TPU was coming to an end in 1984. I had my two years on and was ready to return to a road station, and I also knew that the lieutenant wanted me gone. The standard policy was that when you went back to a road station, you went back to where you came from, in my case Netcong Station. The troop commander called me personally and offered he was having a problem getting me back to Netcong and asked if I would mind going to Washington Station. I said fine. Washington Station was only thirteen miles from my home.

Washington Station, here I come again, only this time as a sergeant.

2018 FTA picnic: Sal Maggio, front; Past President of FTA, Nick Soranno (left rear); Current President of FTA, George Wren (center rear); and FTA Director, Joe Craparotta (right rear).

Sal Maggio with former Col. Rick Fuentes (right) and current Col. Pat Callahan (left).

Captain Sal Maggio in his office.

Land, Sea, & Air

Captain Sal Maggio

Washington Station Annual Inspection in March of 1987 with Troop "B" Command Staff. SFC Sal Maggio is in top row on far right.

Captain Sal Maggio with the Superintendent of the State Police, COL Clinton Pagano at a retirement party in 1988

Captain Sal Maggio with COL Carl Williams, Superintendent, at a Morris County 200 Club function

Meeting with Pope John Paul II, October 5, 1995.

Captain Sal Maggio with General Norman Schwarzkoph Commander of the first Gulf war in 1991 and the father of the first NJ State Police Superintendent, COL H. Norman Schwarzkopf at the 75th State Police anniversary at the Seagirt Training Academy in 1996

Field Operations Section Supervisors with the "boss" Major Lanny Roberson front row center.

Captain Sal Maggio with former President George H. W. Bush in September 1996 at Teterboro Airport.

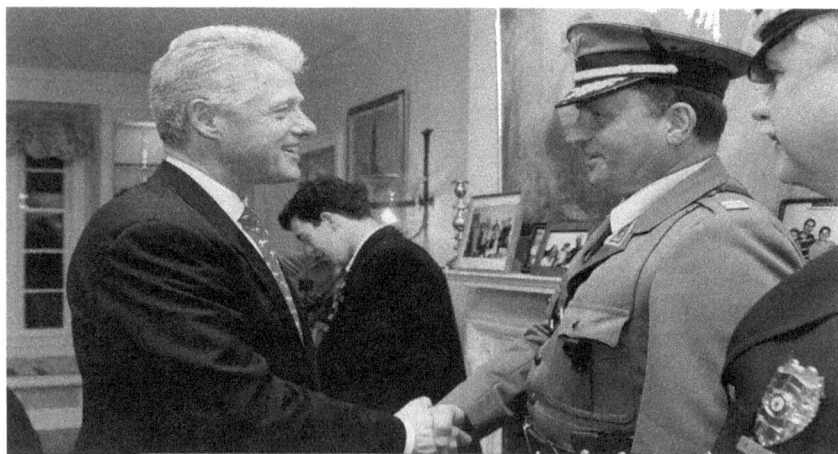

To Capt. Sal Maggio
With Appreciation,
Bill Clinton

Captain Sal Maggio with President Bill Clinton in October 1997 at a political function in West Orange, New Jersey.

9

TROOP B POST:
WASHINGTON STATION AS A SERGEANT

Well, I'm back at Washington Station, where I spent four years as a trooper from 1976 when the State Police ended the barracks life and went to the eight-hour day until I was promoted to sergeant in 1980 and was sent out to Bloomfield Station on the Garden State Parkway. Perryville Station in Hunterdon County still wasn't open yet, and we had all of their area and our own in Warren County. I like a busy road station. I had a good squad with a very able senior man who was also in the New Jersey National Guard with me. Sometime during 1984, when I arrived here, station commanders were elevated in rank to lieutenant. There was also talk of adding a sergeant first class as an assistant station commander. This was great getting more rank on the road. Our station commander, Lt. Enrico DePaolis, was great. He was my sergeant when I was a trooper on tactical patrol out of Somerville Station. I was looking forward to my time here; Washington was my favorite road station.

After a few months, there was a class transfer, and we lost an excellent new trooper. We got a replacement from Sussex Station. I called the sergeant from where my new trooper came from to see how he was. The sergeant said he was OK, pretty squared away, but he liked to take shortcuts. I said thanks for the info. I met the trooper on our following shift change. He lived in Warren County, and it was his third station, so he should be here for a while. I also made him an early man because he lived in the station area. Being he would start an hour earlier than the rest of the squad, I wouldn't see him when we started.

On the first or second day of the afternoon shift, I completed roll call with the squad and filled out the radio sheet for the civilian dispatcher. I called the new trooper and asked him for his shotgun number, which goes on the sheet. He gave me a number, but I could see that the shotgun was still in the rack at the station. I told him, "Negative; give me the correct number."

He gave me another number, but that shotgun was still in the rack, also.

I ordered him back to the station. I asked him, "Why don't you take a shotgun out on patrol?"

He stated, "I don't like shotguns and would never use one."

I told him, "I never said you had to use it. The SOP states you will take a shotgun, load it, and put it in the shotgun rack. It doesn't say you have to use it."

I wrote him up more for lying on the radio that he had a shotgun. I figured he might do it again, but I waited a couple weeks before checking him.

Finally, I saw him on I-78, clocking traffic, and parked on the grass median. I walked up to him and said I was checking all patrols. I looked into his vehicle and saw a shotgun in the rack. I asked him to take it out and hand it to me, which he did. I racked the action back, and nothing came out. The shotgun was not loaded.

I asked him, "Where are the shells?"

He showed me the shells in the glove box. He said, "I didn't load it because I will never use it."

I said, "What if you were taking fire from a perpetrator and a State Police detective came up to help, and since they don't carry a shotgun, he goes to your car and grabs your shotgun? I guess he would have been surprised when it didn't go off."

I had to write him up again and tell him, "This will go on your evaluation. You will have to go a long way to take shortcuts by me. I have been around for a long time."

We had no problem after that with shortcuts. He became a very good trooper while he worked on my squad.

We still had the nervous civilian dispatcher who, if you remember, was hiding in the closet when a trooper called and threatened he was coming to get him. My senior man and I just got back from summer camp with the National Guard, and he brought back a percussion grenade that was used for training purposes. Though harmless, they made a lot of noise and smoke. We decided on our next midnight shift to scare the same dispatcher who was always nervous. My senior man and I were the only troopers in the station. The rest were on patrol. I was sitting behind the dispatcher at a desk in the operations room, taking care of the gas slips for the day. My senior man snuck out of the station and put the percussion bomb under the window by the front porch. The window was between the dispatcher and me. When the bomb went off, the noise shattered the window, with glass raining down mostly on me. I thought the dispatcher was going to have a heart attack. He was almost crying. I ran out the front door and made believe I was after whoever placed the device there. Of course, I didn't see anyone. I calmed the dispatcher down and told him it must have been a giant firecracker. He just sat there shaking. Now I had to devise a story about how the window broke. My senior man and I decided to say he was hanging some new wanted posters up and slipped and fell into the window. The dispatcher was also advised. I stayed to see the station commander, Lt. DePaolis when he came in at about 7:30 A.M. I told the lieutenant what happened. He just stared at the broken window and finally told me to give him a special report on the window, which I did. I also decided not to tease this dispatcher anymore since he was a good dispatcher, and I didn't want him to have a heart attack while I was working. I can't say what the other squads were going to do.

We also had a new recruit on the squad. His coach had to work days for court. I decided to go on patrol with him and see how he drove. We started fine. As we were heading west on Harmony Road, a dirt bike with no plates cut right in front of us. I said OK, put the overhead lights on, and hit the siren, which he did. The subject didn't stop. As we were catching up to the cycle, he made a sharp left onto Montana Road. We followed. As we came up to a sharp curve in the road, I said to the trooper, slow down, I had to yell it again, and he slowed down. As we rounded the bend, a farmer's hay truck was turned over with hay stacks all over the road. The dirt bike had avoided all the hay and continued. We waited for the farmer to move some of the hay so we could get through. I told the trooper not to worry; we would get the bike another time. The trooper then asked me how I knew the hay truck had turned over and blocked the road.

I pointed to the three stripes on my arm and told him, "That's because I'm a sergeant and have to know."

He just said, "OK."

I was out with my senior man one night on late patrol. We received a call from the station that a young lady called and that she was breaking up with her boyfriend, and he threatened to kill himself. She said he was sitting in the living room with a rifle, and she had locked herself in the bedroom. We drove up to the house. There was snow on the ground and a full moon with about one hundred yards of open area before the house. It was very bright because of the moon and snow on the ground. I had my senior man take the shotgun and go to the left side of the house, and I took the right side. I snuck up to the side door and peeked in. The subject was sitting watching TV, and the rifle was next to him. The door lock seemed a bit flimsy, and with one kick, I knocked it open, went in quickly, and grabbed the rifle. The subject began to sob that his girlfriend was leaving him. A box of .22 caliber shells was on the table, but the rifle was not loaded. The young girl who had called then left in her car. We took the subject to the local hospital and admitted him for observation. There was no law in New Jersey for attempted suicide. It was now a medical problem. Just another day at the office.

I was alone one evening, and a call came through from the station that a female with a new baby was outside her home because a bat was flying around in her house. I happened to be near the location of the call and told the station I would handle it. I pulled into the driveway and saw the young mother with her baby sitting in her vehicle by the garage. She told me a big bat was flying around in her house, and her husband was away on business. I saw a broom on the front porch, and she said I could use it to try and chase the bat out of the house. I felt like a knight in shining armor helping a young mother in distress. As I entered the house with the broom, the lights were on, and I didn't see anything. I left the front door open, hoping I could chase the bat outside. Suddenly a bat (it looked like it had a wing span of six feet) flew right at my head. I ducked down quickly. I thought Dracula or Bella Lugosi was attacking me. The bat flew into a downstairs bedroom. I went into the bedroom and hoped I could chase the bat out into the foyer and then out of the house. I checked the room as best as possible but could not locate the bat. I put towels under the closed door so the bat couldn't escape the room. I advised the young lady that the bat was cornered in the bedroom and that she should call an exterminator in the morning. She thanked me but said she would stay at a girlfriend's house tonight but would call an exterminator in the morning. So much for being "a knight in shining armor."

I was on late patrol with a junior trooper, and it was going on 4 A.M. I was driving, and the trooper was starting to doze. When this happens, and you're not busy, I tell my men to find a place to park and not drive unless you get a call. We were making a loop of the eastern end of I-78 when I decided to take a break. I pulled into a wooded area of the median facing west and set the radar machine on 80 MPH. The device will start beeping if a car goes by over 80 MPH. I always told my men to pull over if you are too tired to drive and take a break. That includes me also.

I was sitting there resting my eyes when a car suddenly went by at 118 MPH. I pulled out, and the chase was on. I was now going over 100 MPH, and the vehicle was not in sight. We got to the Clinton exit and received a call from the station; a car was on fire under I-78 on the railroad underpass, just east of us, and the fire department had been called. When we got there, the car was fully engulfed in flame. From what I could determine, the vehicle we clocked at 118 MPH must have lost control after it passed us, hit the concrete bridge abutment, and went over and down onto the railroad tracks, about a twenty-foot drop. We investigated the accident, which had a driver and one passenger dead. The trooper asked me if he should mention that we clocked the car going 118 MPH in his report. I said no, we were not completely sure that it was the same car, and also, their relatives could say we were chasing them and "we" caused the accident. Then the state gets sued. The blood test showed that an alcoholic beverage legally influenced the driver. Case closed.

It was a Sunday morning, and I was taking a ride on I-78 toward Phillipsburg. I started clocking a speeding vehicle going a little over 80 MPH. The car had Pennsylvania plates with a male driver and a female passenger sitting right front. I approached the car and told the driver, "I stopped you for speeding and will issue you a summons."

The driver smiled and said, "Fine, you're just doing your job."

I usually would have given him a summons and let him go. But I thought something seemed strange. He seemed too eager to get a summons. I had the station run his name and license through the Pennsylvania DMV, and he had a valid driver's license. I then had the station run his name and date of birth in the New Jersey DMV database, and what do you know? His driving privilege was suspended in New Jersey for not paying three traffic summons in the last six months. I got each town's name, the charges, and the amount of money he owed. I walked back to his vehicle and got him out of the car. I placed him under arrest.

He asked, "Why are you arresting me?"

I told him, "If I issue you a summons for speeding and driving while your license is suspended, you will go home and throw it away."

He promised, "No, I won't."

But I didn't believe him. I checked his wife's license, and she was valid.

I met with the court clerk at the municipal building. Bail was set at $500 on the charges. He wanted to leave a personal check for the bail. The clerk usually didn't take checks back then for bail. I told him, If that check bounces on Monday, I will make it my life's work to have you indicted for passing a bad check (a felony)".

I gave his wife the information on the unpaid summonses that started this mess for him. I told her, "Make sure he cleans up these summonses if he wants to drive in New Jersey again."

A couple of months later, I learned from the court clerk that he had paid the fines on the two summonses I wrote him. I always wondered how long it took to follow up on the three summonses he threw away so he could get his driving privilege restored in New Jersey. I think he learned a lesson. I guess it takes all kinds to make the world go round.

I received a court notice from the Clifton Municipal Court on a contested speeding summons. The violation happened six years ago, in 1978, apparently on an overtime patrol. I could no longer prove speeding that long ago. I don't even know what car I had, but I had to appear. A note with the notice stated the subject had an attorney. The court's judge had a nickname, "Hang um Harry." He was a good judge, and the defendant was found guilty if you proved your case. While on tactical patrol, I had some drunken driving cases before him. He was fair and stern. I took the stand and testified that I could not prove speeding in this case since it happened too long ago. The judge thanked me for my honesty. The attorney for the defendant then asked for a dismissal of the charge. The judge stated that you could have pleaded guilty and paid a fine, but you decided to plead not guilty to avoid contempt of court charges. The judge told the defendant that you were OK with a California license since he had been living in California. Now you moved back to New York state and want to get your New York license back, but you must first clear up this matter. Well, the judge said he was not going to dismiss this case. See the Superior Court in Paterson and see if they will help you. I checked with the Clifton Court clerk in about two weeks and found out that the attorney appeared before the Superior Court and the Superior Court Judge ordered the Clifton judge to dismiss the case. So it cost the defendant another court appearance fee to his attorney to end the matter. "Jersey Justice at its best."

Another interesting municipal court case was a speeding case that I lost. I was familiar with the municipal boundaries of I-78 since I spent four years as a trooper patrolling this road. I stopped a car for speeding, and as he stopped going westbound, we were right near the sign that read entering "Union Township." (Hunterdon County). I wrote the summons returnable to the North Hunterdon Court, which handled Clinton Borough and Clinton Township in court matters. You can see Clinton Borough over the right guardrail when you pass the area in question. The attorney waited thirty days so that the judge couldn't amend the summons. The defense was that the highway westbound going back at least half a mile was in Union Township, not Clinton Borough. The attorney also had DOT maps stating that the route was in Union Township. After examining the maps, I had the case dismissed. Walking out of court, I thanked the defense attorney for his knowledge of the topography of the highway. I told him it would never happen again, at least not with me.

I was on the station record and radio one evening and got a call from H-1 (H-1 was the call sign for the superintendent, COL Clinton Pagano). The COL was clocking a vehicle westbound on I-78 at a very high speed. The COL wanted a trooper in a marked car to help him stop the vehicle. I gave the call to a young trooper to assist the COL with the stop. The trooper got between the violator and the COL and chased him off I-78 into his driveway. COL Pagano was right behind the trooper. The trooper introduced COL Pagano to the violator. The violator, who was Italian, looked at the name tag of the trooper, who was also Italian, and said in effect, come on guys, give me a break; we are all Italian. A summons was written, returnable to the Union Township (Hunterdon County) Court. I checked with COL Pagano's aid and found that the Col's troop car speedometer was calibrated monthly. About a month later, COL Pagano and the trooper appeared in court, and the violator was found guilty and paid a fine.

I worked the weekday afternoon shift (3 P.M. to 11 P.M.). I just finished roll call, and the troopers were going out on patrol. I will join them after I complete my paperwork. I didn't see the sergeant I was relieving yet. The dispatcher told me he had signed off at the Central Warren Court and hadn't signed on. I then got a call from the court clerk asking to send someone quickly. The sergeant there needs help. I didn't know what she meant. Then she told me he was sleeping and snoring in court. I got to the court quickly, woke up the sergeant, and took him to my troop car. He smelled of an alcoholic beverage and almost fell asleep in my car as we returned to the station. Apparently, he had stopped at a friend's house and had quite a few drinks. Back then, most judges would never turn in a trooper for something like this, and neither would I. The sergeant retired about a month later as he had his time in. Thankfully no one in the court made a complaint to Internal Affairs in division headquarters either.

We had another older sergeant at the station. His squad would always complain that when the sergeant was in the station and asked one of his troopers to pick him up something to eat, naturally they did, but it was hard getting him to pay for it. He would always say he'd pay you later and had no money. He had that reputation of being cheap. He finally retired and opened up a small diner on a busy highway.

I stopped to see him one day as I passed his cafe. I asked him, "How are you making out?"

He said, "Good, making some money. My old squad came in about a week ago, ordered a large breakfast, wished me luck, and left without paying."

I said, "Can you blame them?"

He admitted, "I know how I was; it's just my nature."

I thought that was the best payback for a cheapo. The former sergeant was OK with it. He was happy to see his old squad.

While on day patrol, I observed a late model Cadillac parked on the side of a country road with no one around and no houses. The vehicle had New York plates. It was registered to a person in Brooklyn and was not reported stolen. I got out of my troop car and heard some voices. I entered a wooded area and saw two men with something hung up on a tree limb. One of the men had a large knife in his hand. I pulled out my service weapon and snuck up on the men. I then yelled, "drop the knife," which he did. The men had a dead goat hanging from a tree limb and had cut its throat. They told me they bought the goat from a local farmer and wanted to let it bleed out. They showed me the receipt from the farmer they bought the goat from. I then asked them if they would clean up all the blood on this property, and they just looked at me dumbfounded. I told them I was kidding. All in a day's work.

We had one sergeant at the station that could be a little arrogant. He was about two years senior to me and was promoted about a year before me. We only had one unmarked car at the station, and the sergeants were allowed to take it home while working. This sergeant would always take the car home even though he lived the closest of the four sergeants stationed there. It became a joke between us that we seldom used the unmarked to go home. One night I came in the back door reporting for work on the midnight shift. The arrogant sergeant was on the station record at the time. I said hello and told him to sign me in. He didn't answer. I yelled as loud as I could, "hello," and he finally answered, "OK." The dispatcher wasn't due until midnight, and I would have to take the record for one hour. I dressed quickly, found the sergeant signed off of the station and went home with the unmarked car. As I was ready to sign on the station record, I got a call from the sergeant that he had struck a deer on NJ-57 just west of the station. Boy, I said to myself, "payback was a bitch." I drove to the accident scene, and the sergeant was standing in front of his vehicle. I asked him, "Where's the deer?"

He said, "It ran away," and tried to show me deer hairs in the smashed grille.

Of course, I first said, "I can't see any deer hairs."

And, of course, he continued to show me the hair.

Then since the vehicle was drivable, I had him follow me back to the station, where I started to do the paperwork for a troop car accident. I took my time doing the report, and then the sergeant left for home in his personal vehicle. I am glad this sergeant didn't take the unmarked car home for at least six months.

Unfortunately, the worst job any sergeant could have at a road station was to be in charge of transportation. When the station commander found out that I was in charge of transportation at Netcong Station, he put me in charge at Washington Station. The state was changing over to all-white vehicles from the traditional black-and-white. The state saved $50 per car by having a solid color. The local police using the state contract could have any color as long as it was one color. The State Police chose white. The State Police also added the blue and gold stripe on the front doors originally designated for the TPU. We still had a few midsize Ford Taurus cars at the station. The new ones were Ford Crown Victorias (Crown Vics), which had a more powerful engine and more fun to drive. When I was on TPU, the lieutenant assigned me a 1979 Taurus, which was terrible, so I knew the vehicle.

Unfortunately, being in charge of transportation, I had to ensure the 1979 vehicles were being used. One evening a young trooper on another squad, while driving a Crown Vic, scraped the right side on a telephone pole while exiting a parking lot. The sergeant called me and offered he thought one of our tow company body shops could fix the vehicle to avoid a troop car accident. I told the sergeant OK and that I would check the car tomorrow when I came in. I took the vehicle to a body shop that towed for us the next day. They said they could fix the scrapes quickly, but they couldn't fix the chrome strip that ran the length of the vehicle. The chrome strip cost $18. I advised the other sergeant, and he agreed that the trooper would pay the $18 to the body shop. He also decided that the trooper in question would not drive a new Crown Vic patrol car, only a 1979 Taurus, until further notice that he couldn't handle the bigger vehicle (That's how you get more mileage on older patrol cars).

Back then, the local body shops that towed for us used to fix minor damage on a patrol car, and we would throw them some extra tow jobs. That does not happen now. Everything is by the book, with estimates and state contracts to fix a vehicle. I even took advantage of this process myself. One night while working midnights, I was using the station commander's brand-new Crown Vic while he was on vacation. He let me use the car mainly because I was in charge of transportation and knew what a pain in the neck that job was. I was traveling west on US-46 when a large herd of deer ran in front of my car. I missed the first six but struck the last one in her rear. Of course, the deer got up and ran away. I checked for damage and found a large hole in the grille, which was made of plastic. I got to the station at about 10 P.M. I called one of our State Police mechanics at his home, and he advised me to have the vehicle at the Bedminster Garage tomorrow, and he will take care of it. It's much better than making a sergeant come out and make a troop car accident for such minor damage. It was like it didn't happen.

We used to have annual inspections at the stations once a year. The troopers were responsible for their gear, the station commander for administrative reports, the detectives for criminal reports, and the evidence locker. Unfortunately, I was in charge of transportation. I had the cars brought to the local body shops that tow for us, and they steam-cleaned the engine and buffed up the outside. I, along with troopers, cleaned the inside as best we could. The cars were lined up, and the troopers that were working stood the inspection. My old TPU also stood the inspection.

The troop commander and his staff did the review. You can only have three grades, exceptional, satisfactory, or unsatisfactory. An unsatisfactory meant you had to stand inspection again. As the captain checked all the cars, he noticed the TPU cars had freshly painted engine blocks and air cleaners. The captain told me he's giving the TPU an exceptional for their vehicles. He only gave our station a satisfactory for the station cars. I was OK with that. He didn't know that if you don't use the right paint, you could cause an engine fire. I didn't have the time to paint engines for fifteen marked vehicles. The TPU troopers took their cars home with them.

Another item we had was the "three o'clock call." The deputy troop commander was a lieutenant. Every shift had a duty sergeant except the day shift during the weekdays. The duty sergeant would be called by any station in the troop that had a problem or serious incident. The duty sergeant would contact the duty officer if warranted. This was fine, but the deputy troop commander wanted a call from the duty sergeant before 3:30 P.M. to see if anything was happening. Of course, it was only on the afternoon shift during weekdays. All sergeants thought this was stupid. The first half hour of the afternoon shift was very busy with roll calls and sometimes meeting with the station commander. The deputy should call if something were going on. If you forgot and didn't call the deputy troop commander, he wrote you a performance notice which, if you got two, he would have it put on your evaluation report. I found out from headquarters that he headed home to beat the commuter traffic after he was called. So he would like to leave at 3 P.M. if the call was made to him early. If you remember, in chapter one, an instructor used me to demonstrate how to get someone out of a vehicle. I didn't forget how he threw me to the ground about four times. This instructor back then was now the deputy troop commander. So I figured I'd give him some of his own medicine, not that I minded him as an instructor. He was a good instructor who taught us well. When I was the duty sergeant, I would call him from around 3:25 P.M. to 3:28 P.M. I knew this would cost him some time on his commute home. About the fourth or fifth time I had the duty, he told me very harshly, "3:28 P.M." I knew he was getting on to me, so I started calling at 3 P.M. when I got in. The lieutenant retired in a while, and the 3 P.M. call went with him.

We got a call one night about a fight at a restaurant in our area of responsibility in Harmony Township. The fight involved two high-ranking State Police officers from division headquarters, one major and one captain. Apparently, they were good friends, but something happened, and they ended up in a fistfight. I was on the station record and could not respond. I had two troopers respond. The captain had fallen and apparently broken his arm. He was taken to the local hospital by the First Aid Squad. Naturally, neither officer wanted to sign a complaint. I told the trooper to make an operations report with all the information he would make on a typical fighting complaint.

The next day the trooper submitted the completed report to me, and after checking it, I gave it to the station commander, who wanted to see it. He called me into his office and said, "Troop B headquarters wants the report typed."

I told him, "It should not be typed, it's an operations report, and CJRB (Criminal Justice Records Bureau) states it should only be handwritten."

I had the trooper type the report, and I submitted it to Troop B headquarters as instructed. Of course, the report came back from CJRB, and we were told it had to be handwritten only, as I suspected it would.

Of course, there wasn't an internal investigation into this fight between two high-ranking officers. I didn't think there would be. Rank has its privileges, sometimes.

I stopped a State Police Academy recruit on US-22 once. He was with another person. I asked him, "License and registration, please."

He gave them to me and mentioned, "I'm in the academy. My uncle is a State Police lieutenant." (whom I knew.)

I asked him, "Should I notify the academy on Monday that you were speeding?"

He didn't know what to say, but he looked like he was getting nervous.

Of course, I wouldn't notify anyone, including his uncle, that he was stopped. He did graduate, became a detective, and retired as a major.

On another night, I was on I-78 eastbound and saw a vehicle in front of me going at a high rate of speed. I started to clock the car, and it kept losing me, though I didn't think the driver realized I was a trooper. I had to go over 100 MPH to catch up to him. Finally, the car pulled over onto the shoulder when I put on my overhead lights. As I walked up to the vehicle, I quickly noticed the white male driver was in full State Police uniform. I recognized him as a detective. I asked him, "Where were you going?"

He stated, "I have a supplemental patrol out of Somerville Station and was late."

He was driving an unmarked State Police vehicle.

I asked him, "Do you have a radio in the car?"

He said, "Yes, but it is in the glove box, and I couldn't get to it when I put my overhead lights on."

Just because I was a sergeant and outranked him, I wasn't going to chew him out for driving at an excessive speed.

I told him, "Put your radio on in the future to avoid a chase."

While on the road, troopers didn't turn in troopers or local police officers for traffic violations, even drunk driving.

Today it's different. I understand they even teach recruits how to make out a complaint form against another trooper. Unless it's a criminal offense, I left it to Internal Affairs to do their job. That's what they get paid for.

The bargaining agent for the rank of sergeant and sergeant first class was the STNCO (State Troopers Non-Commissioned Officers Association). The president asked if I wanted to be the association's Troop B representative. I accepted the position. The meetings were held about once a month at the Robbinsville Airport outside of Trenton, about one and a half hours from my home. This meant that I would attend the meetings and give the necessary information to the entire troop's sergeants and sergeant first-class personnel. Division headquarters was having a problem with the ranking officers because they didn't want to retire at the mandatory age of 55. The ranking officers called themselves SPAAD (State Police Against Age Discrimination). SPAAD was taking the State Police to Federal Court. COL Clinton Pagano, the superintendent, put a temporary hold on retirements while this case went through the courts. The state had to establish a BFOQ (Bona Fide Occupational Qualification) to show that age was a factor in the employment of troopers.

One way was to have an SOP indicating a physical fitness test you would have to pass. The first SOP stated that you had to work out at home. At an STNCO meeting, I was told by the president to notify all my sergeants in Troop B to put in a grievance in that we wanted to either get paid or compensatory time for working out at home. I called all stations and advised all sergeants of the grievance, and of course, I put in one. With about 350 to 400 sergeants in the division, I expected at least 100 to 150 grievances, even though division sergeants probably wouldn't. Division headquarters then changed the SOP and eliminated working out at home. There were only twelve grievances put in. I couldn't believe the president of the STNCO didn't even put in a grievance himself. In all his wisdom, COL Pagano found in favor of the twelve grievances and awarded all twelve of us thirty-two hours of compensatory time or an additional four days off. I let my Troop B sergeants know how stupid they were in being afraid of filing a grievance on this matter. So far, I have put in two grievances against the State Police and won them both.

Now comes the fight with SPAAD. In 1984 COL Clinton Pagano tried to get his staff exempt from the age 55 retirement age, which included himself, eight majors, and two lieutenant colonels. This was fought with vigor by the STFA and its president, Trooper 1 Thomas Iskrzycki, who opposed the State Police on this. In the end, only COL Pagano was exempt since the governor appointed him. The rest had to go at age 55. So the State Police goes to court against SPAAD. As the case dragged on, there was a rift between the members of SPAAD and the younger troopers.

For example, while I was in the Washington Station, a Troop B lieutenant stopped in on inspection in full uniform. As a firearms instructor, I knew that if you looked closely at the 9MM automatic we were carrying, you could see if a round was in the chamber. You could see the brass at the end of the slide. A young trooper questioned the lieutenant as to why his gun was not loaded correctly. The lieutenant mentioned that it was. The trooper challenged him, and the lieutenant went to the dispatcher and had him sign him out. He never started the inspection. The 55 case was heard in Trenton Federal Court by Judge Maryanne Trump-Barry (the sister of former President Donald Trump). She ruled on the case in late August 1985 in favor of the state in that they proved they had a BFOQ. The SPAAD members were told they would be arrested for trespassing if they showed up for work on September 1, 1985. They all left. It's a shame how they went, there were no retirement parties for them, and they left bitter after their excellent careers. They all signed up knowing that the mandatory retirement was 55. I left in the year 2000. I thought by now, the age might have been administratively changed to 60 or 65, as the local police retirement age is. Years ago, federal agents, including the FBI, changed their retirement age administratively from 55 to 57. As far as I know, the New Jersey State Police is the only police agency in the country with a 55 mandatory retirement age. I guess one of the reasons it hasn't been changed or challenged was that most troopers today leave after twenty-five years which was the most lucrative retirement package.

Things opened up after they left. Along with SPAAD members being forced to retire, COL Pagano, the superintendent, initiated a new rank on the road. The position of assistant station commander was born. It carried the rank of SFC, who would be right under the station commander, who was already a lieutenant. This just about guaranteed my promotion to SFC. The bad thing about being promoted to this rank was that I would not be on the road dealing with the public. After nineteen years on the road as a trooper and road sergeant, I still wasn't burnt out, but life goes on, and you take what you can get. The benefit of the promotion was a significant raise in pay. Back then, this was the most significant pay raise for any rank. For a road sergeant, it also meant being assigned an unmarked patrol car to take home. Naturally, it also meant the end of shift work with weekends and holidays off. The hours for the new job were 3 P.M. to 11 P.M., which changed when the station commander wanted you in. I guess it was time for a change after nineteen years on the road as a trooper and road sergeant. I stayed right at Washington Station as the assistant commander. I took on a lot of paperwork that the squad sergeants were doing. I took on updates on fatal accidents, closing out or updating domestic violence files, junk title applications, and station transportation.

I also took over the station fund. The fund was used to buy coffee, milk, crackers, peanut butter, and flowers for a trooper if he had a death in their family. All troopers and sergeants contributed $2 a pay or $4 a month to the fund. I had one trooper who would not join the fund. He was also single. He said, "I don't drink coffee or eat at work but I will donate $2 for flowers if a troopers family member passes."

I was suspicious of this. Once on a Saturday morning, I had to stop at the station to pick up something. I walked in the back door, and when I looked to my left into the kitchen, I saw that same trooper ready to put a cracker into his mouth.

"Put that down!" I yelled.

He did. He was also drinking a cup of coffee. I couldn't believe it.

"You join the station fund now!" I said angrily.

He stammered, "But I am on the station record and didn't have anything to eat."

I told him, "It doesn't matter if you join the fund because I will do my best to transfer you to Totowa Sub Station, the farthest station from where you live."

He joined the fund. Talk about being cheap.

During my assignment and promotion, I wanted to relate my job to the road troopers and how I helped them deal with the job using my experience as a road trooper and road sergeant. It even helped that I went through a divorce in 1976 and could relate that to a trooper having marital problems. I finally got to do my first internal investigation on a trooper. Usually, in Troop B, only an SFC or Lt. did internal investigations. My first one was charging a trooper for not going to court on a traffic summons even though he received written notice on the case. If found guilty, the trooper would get a written reprimand if this was his first offense. I first interviewed the court clerk. She showed me the notice she sent to the defendant and the trooper. She also told me that the trooper stopped the other day, knew about the internal investigation, and tried to ask her to cover for him, but she could do nothing. The judge dismissed the case for lack of prosecution. I then interviewed the trooper.

Before the start of the interview, he had to sign a form stating that he was aware of the investigation and that he was entitled to a union representative if he wanted one. Before he signed the form, I told him, "I want to speak to you off the record."

He agreed and told me, "My young child was sick, and my wife was at work, and I couldn't leave the house to go to court."

I told him, "I already spoke to the court clerk and know you were down there the other day."

He then asked me, "What should I do?"

I said, "If I were you, I would admit that I missed court and there was no excuse and accept the consequences."

He signed the rights report and made no excuse for missing court. He did receive a written reprimand. More importantly, I think he learned an important lesson: accept your mistakes as well as your accolades. He retired years later as a lieutenant.

For all you road troopers and road sergeants, it's a significant change going from the road to the "office" as a manager and supervisor. That's why I took on a lot of extra work for the day to go by as fast as it did on the road. Of course, taking care of transportation kept me quite busy. Speaking of transportation, I came to work one day and saw the rear seat of a newer Ford troop car lying up against the garage. It was stained with a lot of blood. I found out the late patrol was taking a pregnant woman to the hospital, and she delivered the baby in the back seat of the troop car. The baby was OK, but the car seat was not. I got a rear seat the same color from a local junkyard, so the car was back on the road lickity split. If I had to order a seat, it would have taken at least a month to get it. As time passed, I started getting used to working regular hours and being off on weekends and holidays. It was also nice to have an unmarked troop car to use.

The new station commander was also a newly promoted lieutenant. We got along fine, and the station ran like a well-oiled clock. The station was still very busy, but the plans were set to build a new station on I-78 called Perryville Station. This would reduce the workload at Washington Station to a more manageable level. The Perryville Station would replace the old Clinton Station, which closed in the mid-1970s. New stations were now leased from a builder who would build the building in less than a year at our specifications, and the state would sign a ten-year lease with the option to buy. To have the state build a new state building could take as long as eight years.

My goal was to become a lieutenant station commander and retire at that rank. I didn't see how I could miss it. I was only forty-one years old and had plenty of time left. I will always be thankful to COL Clinton Pagano for the increase in rank on the road. When I graduated from the academy in 1967, the division only had about 1100 troopers, with most on the road. A station had a station commander with the rank of SFC, one sergeant, and the senior man who was God. Most stations also had a detective or detective sergeant or both depending on how busy the station was with criminal activity. Now in 1986, station commanders were lieutenants. There was an assistant station commander (SFC) and now five squad sergeants. There are also six lieutenants at troop head-quarters, including the deputy troop commander. So now, most road troopers have an excellent chance to become lieutenants before retiring. Of course, at the time, there was only one captain, the troop commander, and that position was much harder. You must be in the right place and time to make captain. Now the troop commander is a major, the deputy troop commander is a captain, and there are two regional captains in each troop.

Another job I liked as an assistant station commander was attending council meetings with the mayor and council in the towns we patrolled that didn't have a police department. At the time, we had seven munici-palities that we patrolled. If they had a police matter, I would usually at-tend the meeting. This proved to be good public relations in these towns.

I was still in the New Jersey Army National Guard, and now, being off on weekends, I could do my military drills on weekends with my unit. Until now, I did my drills during the week when I was off. I had already reached the rank of staff sergeant but could go no farther unless I did my drills with my unit. When the full-time major at battalion headquarters in Phillipsburg found out that I could make regular weekend drills, he transferred me from the Flemington Armory to brigade headquarters in Woodbridge. The major was also going to brigade headquarters. He immediately put me into an SFC slot in a new position, brigade legal NCO. I had to go to Legal NCO school in Fort Meade, Maryland. What was good about the Jersey Guard back then was if you had to go to a school, you did it instead of summer camp, so my active military duty was still only two weeks a year. I have attended other military and State Police schools, but this Legal NCO School was the most challenging ever. They squeezed a six-week course into two weeks. After graduating, I was promoted to SFC (E-7) in the National Guard. In future summer camps, I was a liaison for our unit and the post-military police. This liaison worked well when the military police discovered that I was a Jersey trooper, whether at Fort Drum, New York, or Fort Pickett, Virginia. The New Jersey State Police was a highly respected law enforcement agency at all military schools or bases where I trained.

After six months as the assistant station commander at Washington Station, I was transferred to Totowa Sub Station in the same position. The Sub Station was downstairs from Troop B headquarters. I never found out why I was transferred, and I didn't ask. I knew I didn't do anything wrong. I was still the Troop B representative for the NCO Association. Maybe the troop commander, Captain Peter Hausch, wanted me close for meetings or questions on our rules and regulations that would affect possible grievances since I was still the representative for the STNCO Association. I still wasn't sure why I was being transferred.

Totowa Sub Station and Troop B headquarters, here I come.

10

TROOP B POSTS:
TOTOWA SUB-STATION & HQ

I arrived at the Totowa Sub Station in the fall of 1986. It was very different than Washington Station. Totowa Station had no local area to patrol. It was a highway patrol station. They patrol I-80 from Parsippany to its end east in Teaneck; I-95 from Teaneck to the George Washington Bridge; I-280 complete; and I-287 from the New York state line in Mahwah to I-80 in Parsippany. A new station was looked at for I-287 in Riverdale, near New Jersey National Guard Armory, but it never happened. There would be no meetings with local mayors and councils here at Totowa Sub Station. My new station commander, Lieutenant Dennis Niegele, was about three years senior to me. We both came from lower Passaic County, he from Clifton and me from Passaic. We both knew a lot of the same people in the area. He was an excellent station commander. He knew what was going on and did his share of the paperwork. This made my job a lot easier. One of the unique directives we had was a contract the lieutenant had made up by a lawyer friend. The agreement was with local tow truck companies. It stipulated their equipment, yard space, a bathroom for customers, and insurance. The lieutenant also limited the number of tow companies he needed so all companies on the list would make some money when they were called in rotation. Of course, this was against the SOPs of the State Police. The Traffic Bureau in division wrote the SOP on towing. It was about two pages long and didn't say anything. The lieutenant would not allow new companies on the list, and

some would call division and make a complaint against us for not allowing them on our list. An officer from the Traffic Bureau would call and
tell the lieutenant that he could not keep other companies off the list.
He would tell them to go to hell. I run my station, not you. Then they
would call the troop commander upstairs, and the captain would come
down and talk to my lieutenant in private. I don't know what was said at
the meeting, but we continued to use our contract and keep a workable
list. The only problem I found at this station was junk titles. A junk
title was obtained from the DMV for vehicles left at tow companies and
never picked up. The junk title let the tow companies legally have the car
crushed. At Washington Station, I did all the junk titles. We had about
twenty to twenty-five a year. I could not do all the junk titles at Totowa
Station. Totowa Station had over two hundred junk title investigations
per year. When I got there, we had around one hundred pending junk
titles. So I pulled a trooper off one of the squads who used to be a DMV
officer and knew how to do junk titles. I put him on steady days, and
he cleaned up the junk titles in about two months. When the junk titles
started to back up, I would put the trooper on days again, and he would
clean up the pending junk titles.

Of course, I did some internal investigations on some of my troopers. But the one I remember as if it happened yesterday was one internal
that was a least twenty to thirty pages long. The subject was involved
in a minor accident on a ramp from I-80 into Teaneck. The local police arrived first and advised the motorists that the State Police would
handle the accident. One motorist wasn't happy and started giving the
police a hard time. The troopers pulled up, and the local police left. Now
the one motorist started giving the two troopers a hard time, and they
started giving some of his guff back. The motorist recorded their names
as he did the two Teaneck police officers that had already left. Now, this
disgruntled motorist drives from there to the Totowa Station. He speaks
to the sergeant and lodges his complaint against the two troopers at the
scene of his minor accident. The sergeant takes his complaint and he
starts giving the sergeant a hard time. Finally, the sergeant and a couple
of troopers escorted him out of the station to his vehicle and told him to
leave or be arrested. He leaves but has taken the names of all the troopers

that were there in the parking lot. The complaint went to Troop B head-quarters, division headquarters, and back and was finally assigned to me to investigate. It was a straightforward attitude and demeanor complaint, but I had seven troopers to list as principals. The two Teaneck officers he complained about would be done by the chief of police of that town. I spoke briefly to the sergeant to get an idea of who I was dealing with. Before interviewing the complainant, I found that the complainant was a New York City school teacher assigned to the "rubber room." The rubber room was a slang term where a teacher was assigned if he was pending charges. He was paid but reported to this "room" to wait on the charges made against them.

I also stopped at the local police station where the subject lived in lower Bergen County. When I mentioned the subject's name to the desk sergeant, he laughed and said wait here to find out what he does. The sergeant introduced me to a captain, and we went into his office. The captain told me this individual had been nothing but trouble to this police department. He complains about everything in Town. He drives around looking for a car parked in a handicapped space without a sticker or handicap license plate. He then calls for a patrol car to write a sum-mons. He complains to the Mayor if the patrol car doesn't come in time. The captain added that he's a New York City teacher but thinks he was suspended.

I then went to the complainant's residence to interview him on his complaint against my troopers. When I first entered his apartment, he showed me a large file cabinet with numerous civil suits he had on many different government agencies. I started to understand now where he was coming from. He complained about how the troopers spoke to him but said nothing serious. It was a typical attitude and demeanor com-plaint. I took his statement and left. I then completed my interviews with the seven troopers who thought the complainant had a screw loose. I tended to agree with them, especially after interviewing the captain of the local police department where he lived. Now I had to type up the report. Back then, in Troop B, we didn't have secretaries at stations, and we used a regular typewriter with an eraser to correct mistakes. I had a month to complete the report. It's time-consuming to type on a typewriter correcting your errors as you go along. It's much better today with a computer. I got down to the day before the report was due at headquarters, and I didn't want to ask for an extension, which I'm sure they would give me due to the report's length. My hours the day before the report was due were 11 A.M. to 7 P.M. Well, when 7 P.M. came, I still wasn't done. Fortunately, it was quiet that evening, and I continued on and finally finished at 3 A.M.

I put the report in the deputy troop commander's box and went home. The next day I came in at 11 A.M. Around 3 P.M., a staff officer came downstairs and told me he had checked my report. He said he was very pleased with such a long report and didn't find any mistakes. He then said he would give the completed report to the troop commander for his approval. The report went right through to Internal Affairs Bureau. I was satisfied that it went through, and I did not recommend any discipline for any of the seven Troopers. At the time, I forgot about the individual who made the complaint. About five years later, when I was a staff officer in Troop D headquarters in New Brunswick, on the Turnpike, I received a phone call. The phone call was from the same individual who had made the complaint against the seven troopers from the Totowa Station. At first, I didn't remember who he was, and then I recognized his voice. He thanked me for my investigation five years ago even though the seven troopers were exonerated. He then told me he was going to run for governor of New Jersey, and when he won the election, he wanted me to be his superintendent of the State Police. I thanked him for his faith in me. I wished him luck in the upcoming election (It's nice to have "friends" in high places). Fortunately, I never heard from him again.

Another incident that got me out of the station was a complaint made by a female motorist against a tow truck driver. This particular tow truck driver was not on our towing list. He would sneak onto I-80 and I-95 in Bergen County looking for work. One day he stops by a woman who was broken down. He told her it would cost her $40 to tow her to a gas station that does mechanical work. The incident took place in Teaneck on I-80 Eastbound. He hooked her car up to his wrecker, and with her in her vehicle, he started to drive. As he pulled out, the front bumper came off, and the car fell off the wrecker. The driver got out of his truck, looked at the bumper, returned to his vehicle, and took off. He didn't hook the car up properly.

Fortunately, the woman obtained his license plate number. When a patrol got to her, he called one of our listed wreckers. The trooper stopped at the station and advised me of what had happened. We got a lookup on his license plate, and it came back registered to a house in Leonia. I checked with the prosecutor's office, and they gave me a disorderly conduct statute covering the event though it was primarily civil. I then sent the trooper and the station detective to pick him up. They went to his house and saw the wrecker in the driveway. No one would answer the doorbell. They felt that someone was home since another vehicle was in the driveway.

The detective and the trooper then pulled away and parked in a nearby side street where they could see the house. They only had to wait about twenty minutes, and a female left the house; as she was getting into her car, they pulled up behind her. They asked her if the owner of the tow truck was home. She explained her husband wasn't home, and she didn't know where he was. The detective gave her his business card and told her to give it to him and have him call us. They then left and came back to the station. When they told me what happened, I said, OK, we will wait a couple of days, and then we'll get him. A couple of days later, the same trooper and I left the station a little after 5 P.M., went to the suspect's home, and hid on a side street. The tow truck wasn't there. We only had to wait about a half hour when the tow truck pulled into the driveway. I pulled right behind him as he got out of his vehicle; he was arrested by my trooper and handcuffed. I advised him of the charge (We used a new statute, "Interference with governmental responsibility"). It was a stretch, but I just wanted him to pay for the car he damaged. His wife came out and started to yell at us. I advised her that I would call her when bail was set, and she could bail him out at the Bergen County Jail.

Back at the station, after I advised him of his rights, I suggested he get an attorney to represent him in court. I also told the suspect I would have him incarcerated again if I saw him on I-80 or I-95. I then advised the victim of the arrest, and she was delighted. The trooper took the arrest, and later in court, the judge told the suspect's attorney that after he paid the $700 to fix the victim's car, the charge would be dismissed by the State Police. Case closed. I was happy to get out of the station, and it reminded me of my days as a road trooper and road sergeant.

One day I was working days, the superintendent, COL Clinton Pagano, was upstairs speaking with the troop commander. I knew he would come downstairs to the Sub Station and say hello to the men if he had time. Sure enough, he came down and talked to a young trooper while I talked to another trooper about his application to be transferred to the Aviation Unit since he flew US Army helicopters while in the service. The first name of the trooper I spoke with was Clinton, the same as COL Clinton Pagano. The COL was standing with his back to me when I yelled "Clint" to the trooper I was speaking with, and COL Pagano turned to me, and if looks could kill, I was dead. I told COL Pagano that I was talking to this trooper with the same first name as his. I told the COL that this trooper wanted to be a State Police helicopter pilot, and we were working on his application. The COL spoke to the trooper briefly and said that he thought they were the only "Clints" in the State Police (A couple of months later, Trooper "Clint" was assigned to the Aviation Unit).

One night while I was working the afternoon shift, I believe it was a Friday night, a State Police Detective assigned to the ABC Unit (Alcoholic Beverage Control) came in to see me. I knew him well when he was a road trooper with me at Washington Station. He told me, "Me and another detective are going to a bar in Paterson to check on a complaint that the go-go girls are letting customers put dollar bills in their g-strings. It's against ABC law. We will only arrest the girls, not the customers."

When he called, he asked, "Can you send a couple of troop cars over to bring them to Totowa Sub Station for processing?"

"Of course," I said.

We had a cell in the station that was big enough for up to ten people, but there wasn't a bathroom in the cell (I couldn't believe that when this building was built from 1980 to 1981, they never thought to put a bathroom in the cell). If a prisoner had to go to the toilet, you had to take them out to the public restroom in the foyer, which was near the front door. This was very unsafe.

We ended up having five girls in the cell. They were all scantily dressed. At first, they were upset about being arrested, but they started singing when they found out there would be no bail to post. Of course, they all had to go to the bathroom while they were there.

I helped escort them one at a time to the public restroom. They were all between the age of eighteen and twenty-two. They were all pretty and smelled great.

One asked me, "How old are you?"

I said, "Too old for you."

It was a great way to end my shift. These events don't happen in division headquarters, only on the road.

When I got home, my wife asked me, "How was your day?"

I said, "Just another day at the office!"

Another detail I liked was being an assistant range instructor at the pistol shoot. I started doing it as a tactical patrol sergeant and have continued till now. We were using an excellent range in Mansfield Township, Warren County. I will be talking more about the pistol shoot in a coming chapter, but this incident happened when I was assigned to Totowa Sub Station as an SFC. At the range, we had about eight to ten troopers on the line. We usually put through approximately 600 troopers twice a year, including all Troop B stations and troopers assigned to division headquarters who live in north Jersey.

I was standing at the end of the line of shooters when I noticed a young trooper firing his gun with a haphazard motion. When I checked his target, I saw he only hit it twice and failed the course. I asked him, "What's wrong?"

He said, "I have trouble shooting when other troopers are shooting next to me."

I told him, "I want you to shoot again during lunch."

I called his station commander and advised him that I was holding the trooper over to shoot again.

At the lunch break, he shot again and did qualify this time, but he just made it, and there was no one shooting next to him.

I advised him, "Practice when you're off because if you fail the next shoot, I will contact the academy and request that you have remedial training."

On another note, division headquarters wanted us to continually shoot rounds out of the weapon to see how many rounds we could fire before the gun started jamming. We used the Hechler & Koch 9 MM model P7M8 made in Germany. As the pistol shoot continued, all the instructors took turns firing the weapon. After about 900 rounds, the gun started to jam a little. It was and still is a great weapon. I know now the troopers use the Glock, which I believe holds 15 or 16 rounds. The Hechler & Hoch held only nine rounds, but it was much better than the revolver we used to carry. It was also a very accurate weapon.

An incident I had with one of my sergeants involved a troop car accident with a detective from division headquarters. It was snowing, and the roads were getting slippery.

When the detective called in the accident, I sent the station sergeant out to investigate it.

When I told the sergeant the detective's name, he said he knew him well.

When the sergeant returned with the accident information, I asked the sergeant, "What happened?"

He stated, "The detective was turning into a driveway for a shopping center, and the car slipped on some ice and struck the left side of a vehicle that was leaving the parking lot."

I just knew my sergeant would try and cover for the detective. Now to have some fun with the sergeant. First, I asked him, "Why did the detective turn into a shopping center and not go straight home?"

He said, "The detective said he would pick up some pencils for the office."

I saw the sergeant was getting a little defensive, so I continued and asked him, "Who caused the accident, the detective or the other motorist?"

The sergeant said, "The environment—the road was icy."

I said, "No, charge the detective with being wrong on the accident, and issue him a summons for careless driving (The State Police does not issue a traffic summons to troopers involved in an accident even if they are wrong)."

The trooper was charged on the accident report, and the accident was listed as "preventable" in his personnel file. If you had more than two preventable accidents in a calendar year, you were sent back to the academy for a driver's training course.

The sergeant looked perplexed and offered, "I never wrote a summons to a trooper involved in an accident with a troop car."

I said, "There's always a first time."

The sergeant said, "I don't mind charging the detective on the accident report if he was at fault, but I don't think he deserved a summons."

I said, "OK, charge him with being wrong in the report but don't issue him a summons (Now I had him)."

The sergeant continued, "What about him stopping to buy pencils for his office?"

I just said, "everyone needs pencils," and left it at that.

I investigated my share of troop car accidents when I was a sergeant. One like the one listed above was when a detective from division headquarters who lived in north Jersey had an accident on a Sunday morning. Division detectives don't work weekends unless they are on a critical case. The detective was not wrong in the accident. He was turning left into a shopping center and was struck in the rear (The other driver got a summons for careless driving).

Regarding using the car on a Sunday morning, the detective said, "The troop car was blocking my personal vehicle at home, and my wife needed some medication because she was ill. I was on my way to the drugstore to fill a prescription."

I said, "Do you really want me to put that down in my report?"

He said, "Yes."

Of course, when some officer from his command saw my recommendation on this internal investigation, he got a written reprimand for misusing a troop car. Most everyone who was assigned a troop car (unmarked, of course) uses it while off duty, including me. It took me nineteen years to have an unmarked car assigned to me when I was promoted to SFC, and I started to take advantage of it.

Once I even took my wife to a Broadway show in New York. City. I only did that once and was worried about it during the show, even though it was parked in a parking garage. The jest was don't get caught, or you will pay the price of a written reprimand. I even remember, while down at the Sea Girt Beach by the academy, a troop car parked by the beach with a towing hitch. I couldn't believe a trooper would put a hitch on his troop car to tow his boat. I found out later that this detective from the Major Crimes Unit had to take the hitch off. Could you imagine if he had an accident towing his boat? What would have happened? I think it would have been a lot worse than a written reprimand.

One of the worst troop car accidents I assisted in was on NJ-22 West in Greenwich Township, Warren County. I was picking up a new marked troop car from the Bedminster garage to return to our Totowa headquarters garage. While leaving the garage, I heard a chase going on I-78 west. About eight to ten miles from the pursuit, I decided to assist the trooper anyway (Once a trooper, always a trooper). I was traveling about 90 to 100 MPH and catching up to the trooper giving chase. The trooper was chasing the violator in the left lane, only going about 80 to 85 MPH.

Then somewhere around Bloomsbury, the right rear tire blew on the violator's car. The tire came off, and he rode on the rim and went slower. I told the trooper on the radio, "Keep following him—the rim will finally break, and the car will stop."

The trooper said, "OK."

The violator got off the US-22 exit for Phillipsburg, and as they got near the intersection of US-22 and CR-519, a traffic circle back then. The trooper decided to stop the vehicle and drove in front of the violator. The violator crashed into the troop car, going through the traffic circle and into a gas station located on the northwest corner of the circle. He pushed the troop car into a gas pump and knocked the gas pump over before all vehicles stopped. Fortunately, the gas pump didn't explode. The trooper and the violator were lucky that there wasn't an explosion. The violator was a mentally challenged Army veteran who had left Lyons Veterans Hospital and made the wrong turn on I-78 west instead of I-287 south toward home.

I told the sergeant going to investigate the accident, "The trooper was incorrect to get in front of the violator to stop him. It caused the accident and also put his life in danger. I would never pull in front of a violator to try and stop him. Just follow him the best you can until you have help."

I have been involved in many high-speed chases and never had a troop car accident on a chase. (The young trooper was eventually charged with a preventable accident on his record).

While working a scheduled noon to 8 P.M. shift, it started to snow around 1 P.M. It was snowing hard. We started getting hit with accidents around 2 P.M. I was advised by headquarters upstairs that they were assigning two tactical patrol troopers and two TEAMS (Technical Emergency And Mission Specialist) troopers to assist the station with calls. The TEAMS Unit handles all troop training and emergencies like hostage situations, barricading armed subjects, etc. So now I had two TEAMS and two TPU troopers to help with calls. I was handling the radio, and troopers coming in for the afternoon shift had trouble getting in. Some even parked their vehicles at a parking lot on US 46 and walked the rest of the way. It was after 4 P.M., and I tried to reach one of the TEAMS troopers assigned to me. He didn't answer the radio after I called numerous times. I called his home, and he answered the phone. I asked him who permitted him to go home, and he stated his hours that day were 8 A.M. to 4 P.M. I ordered him back on I-280. Then I checked the two TPU troopers. One was there, and one was not. I called his home and ordered him back on I-80, where he was assigned. I don't understand these two troopers leaving their post to go home. I guess I never will. I-280 going west closed itself because of icing on the highway in West Orange. The troopers had to back vehicles down the highway to the next available exit so the Highway Department could put salt on the roadway. After 6 P.M., the phone was ringing off the hook by mostly females wanting to know where their husbands were. They were all told about the problem on I-280 and to be patient. The highway wasn't cleared and opened until around 11 P.M. I didn't leave until after midnight. I made sure all my sergeants knew the great job their men did. I didn't turn in the TEAMS and TPU troopers who went home. I hope they learned a lesson that night. Just another day at the office.

On another day, I was scheduled to work a noon to 8 P.M. shift. I walked into Lieutenant Niegele's office, and he had a tow truck driver there who wanted to get on our list. At first, the lieutenant was polite and told him he wasn't needed. The tow truck owner started complaining to the lieutenant (Boy, I knew what was coming), and the lieutenant threw him out of the station. Boy, I loved working for this Lieutenant. He knew how to run his station. The lieutenant advised me that the troop commander wanted to see me and I went upstairs. The troop commander was Captain Peter Hausch, a real gentleman. I went upstairs to the Troop B headquarters and into Captain Hausch's office. We had some small talk. He then told me he was making some transfers and promotions and wanted to know if I would like to come upstairs and be the assistant operations officer. He stated my background as a firearms instructor, and still, the troop representative of the NCO Association made him pick me for the position. I had my run as assistant station commander, six months at Washington Station and six months at Totowa Sub Station. Now it's upstairs as assistant operations officer.

One thing I knew of all the positions in headquarters, this was the best for me. It meant I would get out of the office for many different assignments. The pistol shoot runs for about three weeks in the spring and then three weeks in the fall. Then there are the details of the Secret Service with the president and heads of state. The Operations Office was made up of the lieutenant, me, one Tpr 1, the TEAMS Unit, and the Educational Services Unit that gives classes at local schools. There was also essential responsibility with paperwork. Operations schedules all the schools for all troopers in Troop B.

The tactical patrol assistant supervisor was handling the federally funded overtime patrols. He was a good friend when we worked for years in Washington Station. He asked me if I could help him with the scheduling of overtime patrols. Of course, I said yes.

When I started looking over the overtime patrols, I noticed certain troopers were getting three to four patrols a month and other troopers only one or two. I asked the TPU SFC, "Why is this happening?"

He said, "If a trooper can't work a patrol, he gives it to someone else who is free."

I told him, "If a trooper cannot work an overtime patrol, he should call us, and we will reschedule the trooper next in line."

The way it was now, it was ripe for abuse. Boy, did I find abuse? Some troopers would put in for two patrols a month and never work one. They would give them to someone at their station. I even found a senior sergeant averaging five to six patrols a month, and three or four were assignments from other troopers who only put in for patrols but never worked one.

Here we go. I am only in headquarters for one week and have to see the captain. In troop headquarters, any sergeant or SFC can see the captain without using the standard chain of command. When I saw Captain Hausch, I explained what was happening with the overtime patrols.

He was surprised. He asked me, "What do you think we should do?"

I said, "When a trooper puts in for a patrol, he cannot give it to whom he wants. He gives us a call, and we schedule the next available trooper. Also, if he puts in for patrols and cancels over two in a row, he will be suspended from overtime patrols for three months."

The captain agreed and put out an IOC (Interoffice Correspondence) with the new directive.

During that week, a senior sergeant from one of our road stations stopped to see me. He said, "I am upset with the new rules on the IOC. You are taking food out of my kids' mouths."

I told him, "What about the food you're taking out of the mouths of troopers' kids who are getting short-changed because of you and others like you?"

I was shocked he had the nerve to even complain to me. That Sergeant went from five or six patrols per month to two or three. His seniority gave him a little more over the younger troopers. Like anything else in this world we live in, money talks. Even troopers will screw their fellow troopers over the almighty buck!

When the next pistol shoot came around, I was settled in my new position. I was looking forward to getting out of the office and going to the range in Mansfield Township, Warren County. The range was excellent, and Troop B had been using this range for quite a while. There was also a building for classroom instruction. One morning, I was doing classroom instruction on the attorney general's directive on deadly force. The SOP was very explicit. You wouldn't use deadly force (pistol, shotgun) unless deadly force was being used against you. I noticed a young trooper dozing a little, and I made an example of him by waking him up.

I asked him if he wanted to stay with the afternoon class all day. Now the class took note. Lately, troopers have been shooting at cars during high-speed chases. Most, if not all, internal investigations were in favor of the trooper. The trooper would say he was protecting the lives of the public down the road. I didn't buy it. I never shot at a car during a high-speed chase, and I don't think it's right. All the driver was guilty of was eluding, which was only a disorderly person's offense. First, you don't know who was in the vehicle, which could be a child. This all came to a head in 1998 with a horrific shooting on the New Jersey. Turnpike, which will be discussed in a future chapter.

Sometimes deadly force can be used if a motor vehicle was used as a deadly weapon. A young trooper attached to the Troop B Educational Services Unit was driving northbound on the Garden State Parkway. A car passed him at a very high rate of speed even though he was driving a marked unit. Then just as fast, two marked Hillside patrol cars also passed him, apparently chasing the speeding vehicle. The trooper, who was black, also gave chase. They all exited the Parkway just north of the Essex Toll Plaza. The speeding vehicle was then chased down a street in Belleville that was a dead end. The two Hillside police cars blocked the road, got out of their vehicles, and started approaching the driver, a young black male. The young trooper was right behind their vehicles. The driver of the suspect vehicle then started driving at the two patrolmen.

The patrolman started running back towards their vehicles, but the trooper didn't think they would make it and fired one shot at the vehicle hitting and killing the suspect. This was ruled a good shooting because the suspect's vehicle was being used as a weapon. But the next day, the black mayor of Newark commented to the media that here we go, the police again killing young black males. I found out later when the mayor found out that the trooper who shot the suspect was black, he didn't make any other comments about the incident, nor did any black associations like the NAACP. It's a shame. The mayor should have waited until the attorney general's investigation was complete before commenting to the media. The trooper was cleared, but if he was white, I am sure the black associations would have made a stink even though the trooper was cleared. It's a shame that politicians seem to bring race into everything, even though race mostly plays little in the incident. But this was the world we live in today. The black trooper had a fine State Police career retiring as a major. Today's troopers and police officers must be very careful using deadly force. Especially if firing a weapon, they should know where the bullet may go if they miss.

When I made SFC, I didn't carry a summons book. I wrote my share of summonses when I was a road trooper and road sergeant, especially on the TPU. If I saw a serious violation, I would stop the vehicle and call a road trooper to handle writing the summons. Sure enough, driving home one day, I saw a motorist driving in front of me with his left leg out the window. I have never seen this before in my years on the road. I pulled the vehicle over on I-80 Westbound. I was curious walking up to the car, and when I looked in, I noticed that the vehicle was a standard shift vehicle with a clutch. I asked the driver, a white male with one passenger, why his leg and foot were out the window. He mentioned it relaxed him. I told him to stand by while I called a uniformed trooper. The trooper arrived, and I gave him the driver's credentials and advised him to write the driver a summons for careless driving. I didn't know the trooper who was stationed at Netcong Station. The trooper didn't know me either. I told the trooper to wait as I gave the summons to the driver.

After the driver pulled away, I asked the trooper, Do you know my name?"

He said, "No, I don't."

I said, "If the driver goes to court and pleads not guilty, how will you proceed on the summons if you don't know how to reach me to testify?"

He just looked dumbfounded. I had him write my name and phone number on the back of the officer's copy of the summons.

Fortunately, the driver pleaded guilty since I never got a notice to appear in court.

A few months later, I was in my office and got a call on the interoffice phone from Captain Hausch, the troop commander, to come to his office. Captain Hausch advised me that he had a trooper coming in to see him as he was AWOL. The deputy troop commander was also there.

The captain wanted me there since I was the troop representative for the NCO Association, and he wanted me there as a witness to what was happening. The trooper came in and was in civilian clothes. Surprisingly, the same trooper wrote the summons for me with the motorist who had his leg out of the window. The captain asked the trooper, "Where have you been for the last two days?"

The trooper said, "I befriended a homeless young lady, took her to a motel, and lost track of time."

The captain asked him, "Did you have sex with this woman?"

The trooper said, "No, I was just helping her."

The captain asked the trooper, "Did you have anything to drink while you were with her?"

The trooper said, "No, but I might have had a beer."

The captain continued, "Just one beer?"

The trooper admitted, "Well, it might have been about a six-pack."

The captain said, "You will give us a urine sample to make sure you can return to work."

Of course, the trooper said, "OK."

The urine sample was then taken to the Little Falls State Police lab and returned positive for cocaine.

Of course, the captain called the superintendent, COL Clinton Pagano, who had a zero-tolerance for drugs, and the trooper was suspended immediately without pay.

He was not the first, nor would he be the last trooper who lost his job over drugs. This trooper, though, apparently needed money to live and buy drugs. He started holding up drug dealers that he knew in Hackensack. At first, they were afraid of him since he was a trooper. Then when they found out he had lost his job, they turned him in to the police, and he went to jail for a long time, only in America.

I was in my office one morning reflecting on my job. I had been an SFC for about twenty-two months, an assistant station commander at two different stations, and for almost a year now, I was the assistant operations officer in Troop B. Down the road, I felt I couldn't miss becoming a station commander, my original goal when I joined the State Police, especially now that station commanders are lieutenants. Life was good.

It was about 9 A.M. when the phone rang. It was Captain Hausch, the troop commander, and he asked me to come to his office. There was someone there who wanted to see me. As I entered the captain's office, I saw in civilian clothes the Field Operations Supervisor, Major Gary Buriello, who was responsible for over 1800 troopers in the Field Operations section. I never met him, but I did know what he looked like. The major and captain had been trying to pick a new commander for Newark Station in Troop D on the New Jersey. Turnpike.

The major asked, "Are you ready to go to Newark Station?"

I was a little stunned. I said, "You mean as an assistant station commander?" (The assistant now was an SFC who was senior to me, and I first thought that I would end up being his assistant.)

The major continued, "No jerky, as the station commander."

I said, "Yes, I am ready." (Never turn down a promotion in the State Police; another one may never come.)

The major further noted, "I want to try a trooper who has never worked the Turnpike. You were on the Parkway as a young trooper and a sergeant for a short time. The troopers ran the station, not the supervisors, and I want it stopped. I am sick of the traffic activities out there. They stink."

It was a Thursday, and I waived the ten-day minimum for a transfer and was to start on Monday.

The major added, "I will push to have you promoted as soon as possible because I don't want an SFC running a station of that size."

The major left, and I thanked Captain Hausch for considering me for the promotion.

Captain Hausch said, "You earned it. I hate losing you, but time goes on, and so does the New Jersey State Police."

Troop D, Newark Post, here I come.

11

TROOP D POST: NEWARK STATION

Troop D Newark Station at the time was the largest State Police station. There were seventy troopers, including the sergeants, three detectives, and two secretaries. Of course, I was now the station commander and had an SFC as my assistant. Within the first ten days, I was promoted to lieutenant. (I guess the major had some pull). The major wanted me to increase the traffic activities on such a major highway. The criminal activities were good. When I arrived, the station issued about 950 a month, which worked out to 14.6 summons per trooper per month. As far as I was concerned, this was almost criminal on such a superhighway.

The major added that they would be transferred off the Turnpike if I found out who the "culprits" were. He gave me two weeks to get my first list for transfers, one off each squad for a total of five troopers. He told me not to deal with the Troop D commander (my captain). I will be dealing directly with him (Though I didn't feel comfortable with this, I didn't have to call him directly; he would call me). I first sat down with my assistant, SFC Edward Pahler. My assistant had been in Newark Station for the last twenty years. He was promoted to sergeant and SFC in Newark Station. I told him what the major wanted, and he first stated it couldn't be done. I told him that if you don't want to help me, he would be the first to be transferred back to Troop B. Of course, he didn't want to go, and he expressed a good attitude to help me bring the traffic activities up. I told him we might not do it, but we would give it the good old college try. At the station, we had about fourteen black troopers, four Hispanic troopers, and four female troopers. The rest were all white males. I had never supervised female troopers before and was about to learn. During my tour at Newark Station, the females were the easiest troopers to supervise. They were much more mature than the male troopers and never gave me a problem.

Of all the white troopers and the fourteen black troopers, about 10 to 15 percent were making most of the criminal arrests. The other white, black, Hispanic, and female troopers were afraid to write more summons because they were intimidated by a group of troopers who wanted to keep the summons output down. This apparently has been going on for the last twenty years or more. My SFC and I would attend roll call at 7 A.M. and 3 P.M. to advise the men and women what was going on and that I wanted an increase in summons output from the so-called "traffic troopers." The troopers making a lot of criminal arrests were basically OK in that their hours were covered by the activities generated by the arrests. By attending roll calls, I was able to see the looks on the faces of the troopers that didn't like what I was saying (As I was making my first transfer list for the major). Sure enough, on the second Thursday that I was there, the major called and wanted five names, one from each squad to be transferred back to Troop B, and of course, we would receive five new troopers. The transfer teletype came out on Friday. There was a little grumbling but not a lot. When the new troopers reported to me, I told them upfront about the summons problem here and not to be intimidated by some senior men because they would not be here very long. After the third wave of transfers (a total of fifteen), the troopers wanted a station meeting with me and the SFC. I obliged, but I told them they could come to the meeting if they were not working, but I would not pay them. In the past, if a station meeting were called, the troopers who came would get three hours' pay according to their union contract. The troopers thought, who cares if the Turnpike pays? I care, I told them (The Turnpike Authority rents the troopers from the state and pays the troopers' salaries and benefits).

I will get into this further when I become the troop administrative officer. Well, we had our meeting. There had to be about fifty troopers there, even though none that were off were paid. Of course, they had a spokesman. He was complaining about the transfers and what was going on. I told him he didn't have to worry since he was going to be on the next "bus" back to Troop B. He couldn't believe it, so I told him to see me and the SFC in my office after the meeting. He was transferred back to Troop B, but I found out years later that he became a very productive trooper both in Troop B and Troop E (Garden State Parkway), where he worked. Sometimes a transfer was good for a trooper (Personally, I was transferred nineteen times in four different troops but never for any disciplinary reasons. All transfers were for need somewhere else or promotion).

With all this going on with transfers and productivity, I didn't need a problem trooper coming on board. This trooper transferred from Troop B seemed OK initially. Nothing special about him. I checked his personnel file. He lived in Elizabeth, so I thought, and he had a college degree from some small college down south. A couple of days later, I got a call from his old squad sergeant from his last Troop B station. The sergeant stated that the trooper investigated an accident right before he left and didn't turn in the summonses he wrote to the driver. So I went into his locker and briefcase and not only found the blue copies, which should have been turned in with the accident report, but I found all four copies of the three summonses, the court copy, the officer's copy, the defendant's copy, and the division's copy. I advised the sergeant that I would mail the summonses to him, and he could put them in the system. I will deal with the trooper later. I admit I was a little harsh with the trooper when I saw him, but I was doing two internal investigations, and I had another one in my inbox that I didn't even start. I asked the trooper why he didn't complete the summonses he wrote, and he could only tell me he ran out of time before the transfer took place. I didn't have time to argue with him; I was too busy. I just told him that's one strike against him. You hit three, and you're going back to Troop B. He said he was sorry and it would not happen again.

For a couple of weeks, everything seemed OK with him when I checked with his sergeant. Then I got a call from a finance company stating that this trooper was behind in his car payments. The finance person said the trooper's first name was William, but I said we didn't have a trooper named William with that last name. The trooper's first name was Jerome. I again checked the trooper's personnel file, and sure enough, his first name was listed as Jerome. The trooper came in that day to work an afternoon shift, and I brought him into my office. I first asked him, "what was your first name?" At first, he said Jerome, then he corrected himself and said his given name was William. His name tag had a "J" in front of his last name. I don't know how it happened, but the trooper who did his background investigation should have caught the mistake. I just didn't have time to correct this at this time. I told him to contact the finance company, or they will repossess his car. I also made the sign of the cross and anointed him "Jerome." We would deal with his name at a later date. I also advised the trooper that this was strike number two and to watch out, or it was Troop B; here you come.

About a week later, the major called me and said I had a "dirty Trooper" at my station (surprisingly, it was the same trooper who had just come to me and had a problem with his first name and car payment). He advised me that the IAB would contact me and the trooper would be taken down in two days. An undercover detective had been working with the trooper, and the trooper thought the detective was just a drug dealer. The detective rented a car that resembled an unmarked patrol car. The trooper had taken his uniform home. He was off duty that day. He was told to stop a specific vehicle near downtown Newark take the kilo of cocaine under the driver's seat, and then let the driver go. (This driver was also an undercover detective). He was told to take the cocaine back to his girlfriend's house and call the undercover detective. The IAB captain, a federal agent from the DEA (Drug Enforcement Administration), and I were parked in my unmarked car by the trooper's girlfriend's home. I was the only one in uniform, and the trooper naturally knew me. When he arrived at that location, he got out of the rental vehicle, locked it, and started walking towards the door. We rushed him, and I turned him around, cuffed him, then took away his weapon. I will never forget when he said, "You set me up."

I said, "That's right; we set you up."

We took him upstairs and also arrested his girlfriend. We had him change out of his uniform and put on a sweat suit. We took him with his girlfriend to DEA headquarters in Newark for processing. While be-ing processed, a urine sample was taken, and it came back positive for cocaine.

I went back to Newark Station. I had to notify someone in his fam-ily about this arrest. He had told me he was living with his mom in her home in Elizabeth, but he was staying with his girlfriend in Newark.

By now, it was going on 4:30 P.M., so I took one of my detectives and went to the address in Elizabeth. A neighbor said his mom worked at a hospital and should be home by 5:30 P.M.

When his Mom arrived home, she saw me in uniform and thought something had happened to her son. I quickly told her, "He is alright. Can we talk?"

She said, "OK," and called her daughter, who came in about ten minutes.

I told them, "He was arrested for drugs and would be held until bail was posted. Bail had not been set yet."

His mom told me, "I knew something was wrong when he started living with that girlfriend. He was a good boy, graduated college, and never got in trouble with the law."

Apparently, the trooper came from a very good family but got in-volved with the wrong person.

I told his mom, "I will keep you advised of what was happening with him."

I stayed with the detective until bail was set and the division had decided to put him in the Hunterdon County Jail in Flemington for his safety. I left for home that day at about 8 P.M. (Just another day at the office).

I was advised later that bail took a while to be posted because the trooper's mother and father were separated, and the father lived in Texas.

Finally, after about two months, bail was posted, and he was released. Both the trooper and his girlfriend applied for and got a public defender.

On the first hearing at Essex County Superior Court, the public de-fender asked to dismiss the charges because his clients were entrapped into committing a crime. The judge agreed and dismissed the criminal charges.

The state appealed to the State Supreme Court, overturning the judge, saying the state was entitled to a trial.

At the next hearing, the trooper went before a Superior Court Judge and was told that he could get ten years in jail if he went to trial and was found guilty. The trooper would not take a plea deal offered by the prosecutor's office.

Months later, we went to trial in Essex County Superior Court, and the jury found the trooper and his girlfriend not guilty since he had already lost his job and were both entrapped.

As a side note, two years later, when I was a staff officer in Troop D headquarters, I received a phone call from a drug rehab center in Morris County. I was told that the ex-trooper had used my name as a "voucher" for a job at the center. I told them I could not tell them why he was not with the State Police anymore and gave them the phone number for human resources in division headquarters. Boy, you live and learn on this job.

New Year's Eve 1988. I had the duty for the whole Turnpike. I always thought that being the duty officer on weekends and holidays should be handled by staff officers, not station commanders. But now I had the duty. I was having dinner with my wife and friends at a nice restaurant in Warren County. As the prime ribs came down the aisle, my beeper went off. That's why I took my troop car; if called, my friends could take my wife home. Sure enough, when I called in, I was advised by the division duty officer, a captain, that one of my troopers was in jail for domestic violence in Newark and that the deputy superintendent (lieutenant colonel) did not want a trooper spending New Year's Eve in jail. I'm on my way again.

At the station, I learned from the sergeant that the trooper was arrested for domestic violence where he lived with his wife. The Newark police arrested him. There was no bail set yet. The judge on duty, whom I knew by her name, had been married to a state police detective and recently divorced. The sergeant briefly talked to the trooper on the phone when he was arrested. The trooper told the sergeant that he had never touched his wife. They just argued. He added that the patrolmen were black, and one of them was making eyes at his wife. Well, a black trooper, two black arresting officers, and a black judge married to a black state police detective. I called the judge and told her that the trooper was under house arrest and would not leave the station until his arraignment in the morning, as ordered by the Deputy Superintendent of State Police. I also suggested that there should be no bail because if he screws up, he could get fired. She followed my suggestions, and the trooper was picked up and taken to our station on the Turnpike (His wife dropped the charges the next day). After all, was said and done, I asked the sergeant if he had any "booze" hidden since it was 11:50 P.M. He said he didn't, so we had a cup of coffee, and I drove home. Happy New Year!

Now things were getting a little dicey. I had talked some troopers into writing more summonses, both white, black, and Hispanic. As they wrote summonses, some of their gear became missing. I got stuck doing the internal investigations, and IAB said I had to find them guilty of losing their gear. I said no, the gear was stolen. I proved that a white trooper and a black trooper had their hats taken from their locked locker by squeezing a hand through the air hole and pulling out the hat, and one trooper lost his shoes from down below. I then had the Turnpike Authority put metal strips along the top and bottom of the lockers so a person could not fit his hand into the locker (The major got IAB off my back). This was not a racial or gender issue. It was troopers just wanting to do their jobs. I had some very good black and white troopers who were not afraid of the older senior troopers who tried telling them what to do.

Things started settling after I transferred about twenty-five troopers back to Troop B. The traffic summonses kept going up, but the criminal arrests did not go down but stayed about the same. By the end of 1989, the station was running like a well-oiled Swiss clock. The major called me and advised me that he was retiring and thanked me (and my SFC) for doing such a great job in changing the attitude at Newark Station. He informed me that Newark Station wrote over 2,300 summonses the previous month, which worked out to an average of thirty-five per trooper. He said he didn't know how I did it. I told him I couldn't have done it without his help transferring troopers who were troublemakers, but he said that was only part of it. He said you and the SFC convinced the new troopers to write more summonses if that was what they wanted to do on such a heavily traveled highway. He added he couldn't do it when he was station commander years ago. Also, my SFC could not believe that we increased the summons output by so much. Well, I said you had been here for over twenty years, which was better, the old or new way. He liked the new way better and how it made the troopers mesh together whether they liked traffic or criminal arrests.

The only time I almost got killed on the Turnpike was one morning I came in early looking at a troop car that was involved in an accident the night before. As I examined the vehicle, I heard a thunderous noise above me.

I stood under the ramp from Interchange 14 to the Turnpike-North roadway. I looked up and saw a tractor-trailer laying and teetering on the guide rail above me. I then saw the driver trying to exit his vehicle through the driver's door. I immediately called it in to the station, and I got a reply, "yea, we got it, lieutenant." If the truck had fallen over the guide rail, it would have landed right on top of me, and I would have been toast. All's well that ends well.

The Turnpike and Parkway still did not have civilian dispatchers. The squad sergeant would assign one of his troopers to the station record and radio daily. During the day shift, the phones were always ringing off the hook, and the radio never stopped. Basically, the station operations room was a madhouse. I always got in early, around 6:30 A.M., so I could talk to the midnight sergeant who got off at 7 A.M. One morning the captain from IAB came in to catch a plane. While waiting for his ride to the terminal, he asked me, "How can you work here?"

I replied, "Excuse me?"

He said, "It's so noisy in here I can't even think."

"Well," I responded, "this was where I work, and I found it invigorating."

He just left, shaking his head.

One of my sergeants had two tickets to a retirement party for the Troop C commander, Captain Russell Mac Arthur. The party was in a country club in Monmouth County. At first, I didn't want to go, but the sergeant talked me into it. I have been to numerous retirement parties during my career, but other than the one I attended for COL Clinton Pagano, which had about six hundred attendees, the one for Captain

Mac Arthur had over four hundred, which was the most people attending a retirement party except COL Pagano's.

At the party, the sergeant and I saw that COL Pagano was there. The sergeant said to me let's say hello to the colonel. I said no, I didn't want to bother him, but the sergeant demanded, so I agreed to speak to him. As we walked up to Colonel Pagano, he looked at the sergeant and, calling him by his first name, asked him how he was doing.

The sergeant said, "fine," and then pointed to me, "Do you know who this is, Colonel?"

I had never met the Colonel formerly, so he apparently didn't know who I was. Everyone knew the sergeant; he was one of those characters that everybody knew. The sergeant kept questioning the colonel that he should know the station commander of the biggest station in the Division of State Police.

I saw the colonel getting perturbed a little, so I identified myself. I knew the colonel, for some reason, had a knack for never forgetting the name of someone he met. I could see by his look that he would never forget that he had met me or forgotten my name. And he never did. When Colonel Pagano flew out of Newark Airport, he usually left his troop car at Newark Station, and I would find out when his return flight was and have his car washed and delivered to him at the terminal when he arrived. He once asked me how I did that; all I said was that it was a Newark Station secret.

Another problem at Newark Station was the constant media attention on the theory of racial profiling. Colonel Pagano held a news conference and said that the New Jersey Turnpike was a conduit for drugs, guns, and money between New York, Philadelphia, Baltimore, and Washington, DC, where many minorities live. The troopers are the same whether working I-80, I-287, I-280, I-295, I-195, and the Parkway. Yet most drug arrests are on the Turnpike, at all three Turnpike Stations. Though I believe most of this was true, I still feel that some troopers used race to stop vehicles. My SFC assistant and I read all criminal arrest reports before they went to the detective for further checking. I would read the report, and no mention of race was given on the stop. You can't look into the trooper's head and see why he stopped the vehicle other than a routine traffic violation. Also, on consent to search forms, about eight out of ten motorists consented in writing to have their vehicle searched. I could never understand why a motorist would consent to have his vehicle searched if he knew he had contraband in his vehicle. All he had to say was no, and the trooper would not search his vehicle.

The NAACP, the Reverend Jackson, and the Reverend Sharpton continued to say that the troopers on the New Jersey Turnpike were profiling blacks and Hispanics to make drug and gun arrests. There was never any solid proof of profiling on the New Jersey Turnpike though I am sure it went on sometimes. The New Jersey Turnpike was where the drugs and guns were, and the troopers were doing their best to stop it.

Now I understand to present a consent to search form to a motorist; you have to have a supervisor approve the signing of the form. As you might expect, the number of signed consent forms has been drastically reduced. Now the drugs and guns run almost free now on the New Jersey Turnpike. I hope the Reverend Jackson, the Reverend Sharpton, and the NAACP are happy.

Most people don't remember. The first State Police agency that the Federal Government stopped for alleged profiling was the Texas State Police. Then came the Maryland State Police on I-95. Soon to follow was the Florida Highway Patrol on I-95, making numerous cocaine arrests of Hispanics. Last but not least was the New Jersey State Police on the New Jersey Turnpike, which was I-95. So by putting handcuffs on the police, I guess the Federal Government was happy with the uptick in drug overdoses in this country. I could argue about the subject of racial profiling forever. Racial profiling was wrong, but profiling was good police work. The two should not be mixed up. If a trooper on a motor vehicle stop has probable cause to search a vehicle, he should do so regardless of the driver's race.

Another area that I was almost shocked to see was a plain clothes detail at the Vince Lombardi Service Area on the Turnpike in Richfield Park. I even went there myself one evening to see what was going on. Apparently, it was advertised in gay magazines that this Turnpike rest area was a good place to meet people. And so they did. The Turnpike Authority had been getting complaints from the public that sexual acts were happening in the bathrooms. So before I got to Newark Station, the detail was formed.

Troopers would dress in civilian clothes, enter the bathroom, and make believe they were urinating. A subject standing in front of a urinal would turn and show his penis to the trooper, and then he was arrested for lewdness. The trooper would get a minimum of three hours of pay for the detail. The cases were heard in the Richfield Park Municipal Court. The judge would fine the suspect $750 for the first offense and advise the subject that if he was arrested again, he would face a $1,000 fine and thirty days in the County Jail. I don't recall anyone being arrested twice.

I found that our detective sergeant would try and find out who the individual was. He would notify the diocese where the priest came from if it was a priest. We had some high-ranking state officials, medical doctors, and even one police officer. I was working late on an internal investigation when the police officer was arrested. I advised the arresting trooper to bring him to the station. He was a police officer in a town just north of New York City. I called the town and advised the lieutenant on the station record of the problem. The lieutenant said he was sending two detectives down to our station. They arrived in about an hour. They advised the patrol officer that he was suspended without pay and took his badge, police identification, and weapon. They didn't even take him. We transported him to the Port Authority Bus Station in Manhattan.

Another incident related to the above incident was when I got a call from a staff officer about a demonstration of gays at the Vince Lombardi Service Area. I told the lieutenant that I would take care of it. I think he thought I was going to become physical with them. I sent about ten troopers up there, including tactical patrol troopers. I also went. To demonstrate on the Turnpike property, you need a permit. The Turnpike is a "private roadway."

When I arrived, the ten troopers were already there, and I could see the demonstrators were intimidated. The demonstrators had signs that stated, "Let me pee in peace." I was in civilian clothes, but I asked for their spokesman, who came right out of the crowd.

I told him who I was and advised, "You can demonstrate, but you need to get a permit from the New Jersey Turnpike Authority office in New Brunswick."

There was also a radio station there from New York City, and I gave them a statement on the rights of the protesters, but they needed a permit. I remember I told them it was their right under the 1st Amendment of the US Constitution. Apparently, they wanted to protest the arrests we were making for lewdness in the rest area bathrooms. I would like to have told them to stay out of the bathrooms unless they had to pee, but I didn't.

They then put their signs in their vehicles and left. I don't think that they ever got a permit. Detail complete. I then returned to the station and called the lieutenant. I advised him what had happened, and he said he thought I would assault the demonstrators. I don't know where he got that idea. It was the farthest thing from my mind unless the demonstrators did something stupid, which they didn't.

During my career, I did fifty internal investigations myself. I kept a copy of each one for a while when I retired. After a couple of years, I shredded them all. Old history. Most were done while I was Newark Station commander, and some while I was a staff officer in Troop D headquarters in New Brunswick. One of the ones I remember was a complaint against one of my troopers for a poor attitude and demeanor. The complainant was a deputy attorney general from Connecticut. The IAB told me that the subject's interview would be in person in the Connecticut capital of Hartford, where he worked. I felt like saying to IAB what about me, but of course, I didn't. The ride to Hartford was two and a half hours each way.

I decided to interview the trooper first. The trooper said that the complainant was driving too fast for the conditions in the parking lot of the Vince Lombardi Service Area. He said the subject became arrogant and questioned why he was stopped, and the trooper said he told him twice. The subject told the trooper that he would report him to Governor Cuomo on his attitude (Mario Cuomo was the Governor of New York). The trooper told the motorist that he didn't work for Governor Cuomo; he worked for Governor Kean since we were in New Jersey. The trooper also said after their short conversation, he let him go without issuing a summons. Apparently, the complainant was upset that he didn't know which state he was in, New York or New Jersey.

I then made an appointment to see the Connecticut Deputy Attorney General at his office in Hartford. With traffic, it took me three hours to get there. As we entered a conference room, another deputy attorney general was there to record the interview. I did not record my interview with him. I had a yellow legal pad and advised them that I would write every word that was said no matter how long it took. They asked me if I was upset that they were recording the interview, and I said no, it was their prerogative. The interview took a little over an hour. The complainant didn't have a valid complaint against the trooper. In those days, no one won a one-on-one with a complaint. Today with body cameras and audio, a trooper has to be careful about what he says to a motorist. Back when I was a road trooper, if a motorist got a little testy with me, I got testy back, and if it escalated, so be it. It's much different today. Back at Newark Station, I gave my notes to my secretary, who would type up the report.

I had a secretary at Newark Station who would type my internal investigations and other work. We had another secretary for the detective's office. Of course, I found the charge of a poor attitude and demeanor against the trooper unsubstantiated. After my report went to the IAB, I received a call from them to notify the complainant that there would be no further action against the trooper. At the time, I felt this was wrong that I had to notify the complainant. I felt it was the job of IAB to notify him by letter. It would be more professional. I called the complainant and advised him of the investigation results, and he became very irate on the phone, calling it a "cover-up." I gave him the phone number and extension of IAB and told him to call them. We had a new troop commander. The previous one had retired. I called Captain Alexander Tezsla and advised him of what had happened with my phone call to the complainant and that I thought it would be more professional for IAB to notify the complainants by mail. The captain agreed and said he would bring it up at the next troop commanders' meeting. Finally, after about a month, the superintendent ordered IAB to notify all complainants of the outcome of an internal investigation in writing. Of all the requests I ever made to a supervisor, this one helped more investigators with internal investigations. Thank you again, Captain Tezsla.

There's a large hotel on US-1/9 right off the entrance to Newark Airport, but not on Port Authority property. The Newark police handle any police calls. At the time, there was a strike of phone company employees in New York City. The phone company hired additional employees and housed them in this hotel. The union employees found out and came in a bus of about forty people with signs to demonstrate against these employees, whom they called "scabs." Well, some of the union employees went into the parking lot and damaged vehicles belonging to the newly hired employees. The hotel manager called the Newark police, and no one showed up at first (The Newark police is the largest municipal police department in New Jersey, with around 1,200 members). The hotel manager called my station, and Sergeant Moe Waschmann called me at home. It was around 9 P.M. I told him to send as many troopers as possible and that I was on my way. I also told him to hold over the afternoon shift. When I arrived, I went to the hotel with my sergeant. My troopers had ended the vandalism to some of the vehicles and made two arrests for malicious damage. We now had all the forty or so demonstrators by their bus.

At this time, a Newark police sergeant showed up. He was young, and it was obvious he was just promoted to sergeant with his new shirt and stripes on. I asked him, "How long have you been a sergeant?"

He said, "Two weeks."

I asked him, "Who is in charge of your precinct?"

He said, "My lieutenant."

I asked him, "Where are your men?"

He said, "They must be tied up on other calls."

I advised the Newark sergeant to watch me and learn something (It wasn't his fault; it was his lieutenant's.) I had about fifteen troopers there already from the afternoon shift and the early men from the midnight shift. I also had some troopers coming up from the New Brunswick Station on the Turnpike. I walked up to the demonstrators, who were still a little boisterous.

I knew one of them had to be a union representative, and I was able to pick him out.

I took him aside and said, "We will not arrest all these demonstrators even though we can. I will arrest you only and let the bus return to New York with everyone except you. You will be put in the Newark police jail overnight and see a judge in the morning. Just know the jail doesn't even have a bathroom and that if you must pee, you do it in a coffee can." (This was untrue, of course).

Visibly upset, he pleaded with me, "Please let me go! I was only following orders from the union president."

I said, "Alright, if you get these people out of here right now!"

Everyone got back on the bus, and we took the names of the protesters. The bus, including the union representative, headed back to New York, where they came from.

I asked the Newark police sergeant, "Did you learn something?"

He said, "Absolutely!"

We gave the information on the people causing the damage to the hotel manager and advised him to give the information to the victims and that they could sign complaints for damage in the Newark Municipal Court if they wanted. I am not letting my men get involved with the Newark Court. It was one of the worst run courts when I was station commander of Newark Station on the Turnpike.

Speaking of the Newark Municipal Court, my troopers were getting notices to appear after the court date. Boy, was this a joke. I called the Newark Court numerous times during the day, and all I got was a busy signal. I decided to go down to the court located at 31 Green Street. I saw about six or seven desks with the phones off the hook. One woman was talking on the phone.

I met with the chief court clerk. He saw me looking at the empty desks and explained, "You have no idea what I am working with."

I told him, "I can see that. Notices are coming in late."

He said, "I will look into it. The summonses were marked not guilty and not 'lack of prosecution' where the trooper could get in trouble."

I thanked him, and back at the station, I directed all my sergeants to advise their troopers to try their best to write summonses or, while making arrests, to use the Elizabeth, Kearny, or Jersey City Courts if possible.

I had problems with the Newark Court when I was a young trooper on the TPU and working US-1/US-9 in Newark, Elizabeth, and Linden in the early 1970s. Usually, I would put my blinders on until I got into Elizabeth City. One day I came upon a car stuck on the medial curb dividing the local and express lanes in Newark. The driver was highly intoxicated, and I arrested him for drunk driving. He was a very nice older black man and told me he had a drinking problem. The problem was that this was his third offense, and he faced jail time. His breathalyzer reading was over .30 percent blood alcohol. I wrote him the summons and took him home. No bail was posted. At the time, he had a valid New Jersey driver's license. I found out shortly that contested cases for non-Newark police were handled on a Friday night (that includes State Police and Port Authority Police).

The first Friday night that I appeared on this drinking-driving case, the defendant tried to plead guilty, but the judge would not let him because it was his third offense. The judge told the defendant to get a lawyer.

I spoke to the defendant briefly and said he should have a lawyer.

A month later, we appeared again, and the same thing happened. A different judge told him to get an attorney.

On the third Friday night, as the judge tried to postpone the case again, I asked the judge, "Can I speak?"

He said, "OK."

I told the judge, "The defendant was being inconvenienced more than me. I get paid even if I'm off duty."

The judge took his plea of guilty and fined him, took his license for ten years, and sentenced him to forty-five days in the county jail to be served on weekends.

Luckily, I never had to arrest a drunk driver again in the City of Newark.

Another problem I had was with a young trooper who was a member of the US Air Force Reserves. He thought we had to give him off when he had a weekend drill. He was right, of course, but he would have to work the two scheduled days that he had off that week. He didn't know I was a New Jersey Army National Guard member. I explained to him that when I have a drill, I work here all week, go to drill on the weekend, and then work another week. I told him he would work his scheduled days off that week with another squad. He wasn't very happy, but he must have found out I was right and didn't put in a union grievance. You would think he would be satisfied getting double pay when he goes to summer camp for two weeks. Not a bad deal. I did it for twenty-three years before I retired from the New Jersey National Guard and received a military pension when I was sixty.

Another problem I had at Newark Station was steroids. Some of the troopers were using steroids to build up their muscles. One of my sergeants found a used hypodermic needle in the weight room. I started keeping an eye on certain troopers that were getting muscle-bound. One problem with steroid use is that you could lose your temper quickly if things aren't going right.

When one of the troopers I was looking at had his third internal investigation for an improper attitude and demeanor, I brought him in for questioning. I tried to explain to him the language the complainants said he was using when he stopped them, but I couldn't get through to him. It was obvious to me that he was lying. Well, on the bus he went, and he was transferred back to Troop B.

I made sure I called his new squad sergeant and advised him of his attitude. This particular squad sergeant was tough, so the trooper better be careful. I found out later that the squad sergeant found cow manure in his desk drawer. It couldn't be proven that any particular trooper did it, but the sergeant had his eye on him. Finally, he was caught writing phony summonses and even calling the court and making believe he was the defendant and entering a plea of not guilty so he could go to court and get three hours of overtime, knowing that no one was going to show up for his case.

He was brought before IAB and told he would be charged criminally unless he resigned. He resigned. I was told later that he started working for a lawn company that sprayed chemicals on lawns to feed the grass and control the weeds. He started putting water in the tank so he would buy fewer chemicals. So as the weeds grew and the grass didn't, people complained, and he was fired. Once a jerk, always a jerk. Good riddance.

I had trouble with two other troopers: Frank, "the mechanic," and "Joe." Frank liked to help people that had broken down. Frank was there, whether changing a flat or fooling around with the engine. After the patrol, he would come in with a dirty uniform and filthy hands. Helping people was OK with me, but Frank averaged about twelve to fifteen summonses a month on the New Jersey Turnpike. His sergeant and I brought him into my office for a talking to. He got very upset. We were in uniform but not armed. Frank was in full uniform and armed. When I started to mention his production output, he got very upset. He put his hand on his weapon, turned to face the rear wall of my office, and started raving on and on about us to stop telling him how to do his job. Fortunately, he didn't pull his weapon. My weapon was in my right upper drawer, and I already had it opened when he put his hand on his weapon. Frank was on the next bus back to Troop B (More on Frank when I became the Troop B commander).

Then there was "Joe." He also apparently didn't like writing summonses either and was also writing about fifteen per month. What I always liked about Joe was that he was an excellent trooper who made some nice criminal arrests but would not write a normal amount of summonses and keep up with the other troopers who had started to write more. Joe lived in Hudson County and was single. He lived about ten minutes from our station. Joe was put on the bus, also (More about Joe also when I became the Troop B commander).

To show you what can be done on the New Jersey Turnpike, the TPU trooper on the Turnpike wrote about two hundred summonses per month, concentrating on trucks and buses. They were transferred back to a station if they didn't write that much or close. Most traffic troopers had started writing about forty to fifty summons per month, or they would get on the bus back to Troop B. The power of transfer was all I needed to straighten out this station. Thanks to our major in division headquarters.

Another internal I did involved a white trooper I suspected was on steroids. It was just an attitude and demeanor complaint. The trooper stopped a Chevrolet Corvette, and the male driver had on a heavy gold necklace and a female with him. Allegedly the trooper started commenting about the driver's necklace and expensive car as if he was trying to impress his female companion. As the trooper kept talking, the female passenger recognized his voice. She looked at his name tag and realized she had gone to high school with him. The motorist complained about the trooper's poor attitude and demeanor and said he used foul language. When I interviewed the female passenger, she said the trooper "was an asshole in high school and was still an asshole." After this internal investigation, he was put on the bus back to Troop B.

One internal I did on one of my best troopers was an attitude and demeanor complaint. This trooper was, at the time, as far as I was concerned, the best all-around trooper that worked for me at Newark Station. The trooper was sent to investigate a minor car truck accident at the toll plaza. Apparently, the driver of the car didn't understand that large tractor-trailers cannot always see a car to their right front. As they attempted to enter the same toll lane, the truck struck the left front of the car with his right front fender. As the trooper was getting the information for his report, the elderly black couple in the car became very upset and thought that the truck had caused the accident. Of course, no summons were issued to either driver in this type of accident.

After the accident was investigated, the black couple made a complaint against the trooper that he used foul language against them. The internal investigation was assigned to me. I first interviewed the older couple at their Bergen County home. They were both adamant that the trooper used foul language when speaking to them during the accident investigation. When I interviewed the trooper, he denied using any improper language.

Generally, without any other proof or witness, I would find the case in favor of the trooper because he did not have any complaints against him and his impeccable record at Newark Station. But first, I had to find the truck driver and ask him if he had heard foul language. It took a while, but I finally got a hold of him at home on the phone in either Tennessee or Kentucky. The truck driver said the other driver was a pain in the neck, yelling that the accident was his fault. He added that the trooper was very professional but used some foul language at the other driver. Since the truck driver was a disinterested witness, I found that the charge was substantiated, and the trooper received a written reprimand.

The trooper filed a union grievance on the reprimand, as was his right. The Labor Relations Unit finally heard the case at a phase three hearing. They overturned the reprimand. I didn't know why but I was glad for the trooper that they did. That's their job at a phase three hearing, not mine. About a week later, one of the STFA officers stopped to use the phone like he always does. He apparently saw me in my office and first came in to say hello. Then he asked if I had heard about the phase three hearing on the internal investigation I had done. I said yes, that I had heard but didn't know why. He told me that he called the truck driver and had him change his story and that he didn't hear foul language from the trooper. Now I was pissed. I told the union rep that was witness tampering and that he should be locked up. The Labor Relations Unit should be admonished for this, as I almost physically threw the union rep out of my station. Years later, the union rep retired as a Tpr 1, and my trooper retired as a lieutenant.

All's well that ends well!

One day two new black troopers reported to me for assignment at Newark Station. Their names were Sammy Davis and Jerry Lewis. They were in my office, and I told them they could not be on the same squad (They were not going to be on the same squad anyway). I told them they might ride together on the midnight shift if they were on the same squad. I said if you stopped a drunk driver and he asked you for your names, and you told him, he would probably start a fight, and I would be doing another internal investigation. They understood.

Of the 14 black troopers, I had a couple that were prejudiced against white male troopers, but of course, with more white troopers, there were more than a couple of white male troopers that were prejudiced against black troopers. Most of this was the immaturity of young males (I never had this problem with my female troopers).

One day, while I was out doing an investigation, one of my black troopers came to work wearing some African clothes with a big hat. Of course, some of the immature white troopers didn't like it. But the black trooper was making a statement. When I got back, I called him into my office for a "chat." I told him I was more concerned with troopers coming to work in the summer with shorts with holes in them and flip-flops. I told the trooper that he could wear African clothes to work, but I requested he didn't in that he made his point. He agreed.

A week later, the same black trooper got involved in a dispute with a white trooper who was in charge of the gym at the Totowa Sub-Station in Troop B. Apparently, a black trooper didn't want to pay a gym fee because he paid one in Newark Station where he worked. Most all State Police Stations have a gym fee to buy additional equipment for their respective gyms. The black trooper from Newark Station lived much closer to Totowa Sub-Station and wanted to use that gym when he was off duty. I instructed him to pay the fee if he wanted to use that gym or ask me for a transfer to Totowa Sub-Station. He understood. I was more concerned with the other black trooper putting his nose where it didn't belong. I had him in my office alone. I asked him if the trooper thrown out of the gym at Totowa Station was white, would he have gotten involved with the problem? He didn't know what to say, so I told him. I called him a black racist right to his face, and since he only had two years in the State Police, he was out of line. I never had a problem with him after that, and he became a good trooper while working for me at Newark Station.

I had another black trooper that was very immature. I even had another black trooper on his squad sort of watch over him and make sure he didn't do anything stupid. Some of the white troopers teased him and sometimes hid his briefcase. He also was very computer-literate at the time. He was also articulate in report writing and had a good traffic program. Other than being a little immature, he was a very good trooper.

One day I got an evaluation report from the Records and Identification Section in division headquarters to fill out on this trooper for an assignment at the Records and Identification Section. I gave him an excellent recommendation since he was so good with reports and an immaculate dresser in uniform. Well, he got the assignment that he wanted. I wished him luck with his new assignment.

After about two months, he was in his unmarked State Police patrol car, sitting by the curb on a Newark street dressed like a woman. It was about 1:30 A.M. Two Newark patrolmen approached him and asked him what he was doing there. He told them that he was undercover and on a case. They checked his ID, reported to their precinct, and told their lieutenant. The lieutenant told the officers to give the information to the State Police station in Newark on the Turnpike. My sergeant on duty made a complaint form known as a "251." When I came in that morning, the sergeant told me about it and had slid the 251 form under my door. I couldn't believe what I was reading. The trooper was married and had at least one minor child. Thank God he didn't work for me anymore. I sent in the 251 form. After the IAB did the investigation, the trooper was dismissed from the State Police for lying to two Newark police officers and for misuse of troop transportation. I heard that his defense was that he was trying to locate a person in Newark that gave his friend AIDS. A while later, the trooper sued the State Police for a large amount of money in Mercer County Superior Court. This was a civil suit. I testified on this matter. After hearing all testimony, the civil jury of six members gave the trooper one dollar for his alleged problems with the State Police.

I had five squads at the station, all with 14 men on them, including the sergeant. Four sergeants were outstanding, and one was weak. I think he was burned out. His reports were always late and sometimes incorrect. I was relying more and more on his senior man. I told him I would have him transferred back to Troop B. He agreed that he had had enough of Newark Station and needed a break. At first, I thought of calling the major at division headquarters, but he would call me and not about a sergeant. I decided to call the troop commander, our captain, for the transfer request. This wasn't Captain Al Tezsla. He wasn't here yet. The captain said OK, but he wanted a request for transfer form filled out by the sergeant. I said OK (I didn't need any request forms filled out when the major and I transferred troopers). I told the sergeant to fill out a transfer request form and that he would be transferred on Friday. It was Monday. I thought the form had been filled out, and maybe my assistant sent it to the captain. Now it was Friday afternoon. The sergeant who was being transferred was coming in at 3 P.M. for the afternoon shift. I got a call from my captain wanting to know where the transfer request form was. I told him I thought it was down there already. He wasn't happy.

As the sergeant came in, I chewed him out for not doing the form yet. I told him to sit down and type the form, and I would handle the roll call with his squad. A few minutes later, the sergeant came in and asked if he should continue filling out the form since the transfer had just come out. I then yelled at him to complete the damn form. "You're even late on your own transfer." As soon as the sergeant finished the form, I relayed it to the captain.

The new troop commander was Captain Al Tezsla. He came out of Troop C central Jersey area. We were both in Troop C together in 1967 when we came in, but we were never stationed together. I had heard he was tough but fair. He came up to visit me at Newark Station one day, and we discussed the station, and I advised him that the station was running like a fine Swiss watch. After a short while, Captain Tezsla called me up and said that the administration officer had to retire due to a heart problem and asked if I would be interested in coming down to Troop D headquarters. I said sure (As I have said before, never turn down a promotion in the State Police). The next day Captain Tezsla called me again and said we had a problem; Troop B didn't have one lieutenant that wanted to go to Newark Station. So I said, why not promote my Assistant SFC Ed Phahler? He helped me get this station straightened out. The captain said, but he's been there over twenty years. So I said that's why we need him, or else I'll stay here. I then got transferred to troop headquarters as the administration officer, and SFC Ed Phahler was made a lieutenant and Newark Station commander.

I could go on and on with stories about my time at Newark Station and the 23 months I was stationed there as the station commander. When I got there, it was in bad shape, and when I left, it was running smoothly with excellent criminal work and traffic enforcement activities. Since then, the Turnpike Authority has taken over the Garden State Parkway, eliminating Troop E headquarters. The newer Troop D headquarters in Cranberry handles both toll roads. They also have built a new Newark Station, Bloomfield Station on the Parkway, and a new Moorestown Station on the Turnpike. I heard it was forty million dollars for each new station. Nice to have money.

Troop D headquarters, here I come.

12

TROOP D POST: HEADQUARTERS, NEW BRUNSWICK

I worked as the assistant operations officer at Troop B headquarters in 1987 and 1988. So I knew a little about how a Troop headquarters worked. The only problem I thought, as administration officer, I might not get out of the office much. I would be responsible for the State Police budget, evaluation reports, inspections, and internal investigations. It was the beginning of 1990, and we had a new superintendent, COL Justin Dintino. He was appointed by our new Governor, Jim Florio. COL Clinton Pagano was transferred to run the DMV. COL Dintino retired in 1985 after reaching the mandatory retirement age of 55. He retired at the rank of lieutenant colonel. The superintendent was exempt from the 55 retirement age because the governor appointed him.

First, let me explain the State Police budget. The part I had to do concerned the troopers' salaries, overtime, uniform allowance, pension payments, and any civil suits involving troopers on the Turnpike. The Turnpike took care of the buildings and transportation since it owned them. The day a trooper leaves the Turnpike, they stop paying, and the day the trooper comes to Troop D, the Turnpike starts paying. That includes all the officers and supervisors also. The first budget I did was for the fiscal year July 1, 1990, to June 30, 1991, totaling over sixteen million dollars for the 220 troopers stationed in Troop D.

Another item I found was that the Turnpike vehicles, including Turnpike officials and maintenance vehicles, gassed up at the Turnpike

maintenance yard. Still, the troopers gassed up at the gas stations at the
Turnpike rest areas. I saw the Director of Turnpike Operations and asked
him if the state of New Jersey returned the gas tax to the Turnpike. He
said no. I then asked why the troopers (including me) gas up at the commercial gas stations on the Turnpike. You might not believe this, but
he said they didn't want the troopers to get their hands dirty gassing up
their assigned vehicle. I couldn't believe it. I told him all troopers come
from troops A, B, or C, and they gassed up their vehicles, as did division
headquarters. It took about two months, and now the troopers gassed
up at the Turnpike maintenance yards, and the savings the first year was
about $125,000 in New Jersey State gas taxes.

There was still a lot of bad publicity about racial profiling on the
Turnpike. I'm sure Governor James Florio talked with the new Attorney
General Robert Del Tufo and the new State Police Superintendent COL
Justin Dintino. One of the first things COL Dintino did was eliminate
a certificate of commendation, a gold-colored ribbon worn over the left
pocket of your shirt or jacket. If you got a second one, a star was put on
the first one, similar to the military awards. He started issuing a letter of
commendation if you made a lot of criminal arrests. One trooper from
Newark Station already had a gold ribbon with a star and was looking
for his second star. He only received a letter from COL Dintino. So
what does he do? He filed a union grievance in that he only got a letter.
Fortunately, grievances come through me since I am the administration
officer. After chewing him out on the phone, he withdrew his grievance.
Also, under COL Dintino, you had to show some investigative experience to become a detective, not just criminal arrests. Word was out to
do your job right, or you may get in trouble. Criminal arrests on the
Turnpike started to go down some. For my seven years in Troop D on the
Turnpike, no trooper was ever charged with racial profiling. The charge
does not exist. It only exists if a court finds that the trooper profiled
improperly, and the criminal charges will be dismissed.

I did my share of internal investigations here, not as many as in
Newark Station but enough. I vividly remember a charge against an off-
duty trooper for aggravated assault where the complainant lost an eye.
The trooper was a black male, and everyone involved in this investigation

was black except me. The incident happened on a Sunday afternoon on an outside basketball court. The off-duty Trooper was playing with about seven other black males. The Trooper's two-year-old son sat with the trooper's wife on the bottom of the wooden stands. Another black male came around and threw a heavy-duty firecracker called an ash can onto the court. The firecracker hit a tree branch and deflected toward the trooper's two-year-old son. It went off, luckily, before the toddler picked it up.

The trooper went to check on his son, and the other players grabbed the subject who threw the firecracker and started beating him. The East Orange police were called, and two black officers arrested the subject for possession of fireworks and assault with fireworks. The off-duty trooper signed the complaints since his son was the victim. The arrested subject was first taken to a hospital, where he lost one eye. The attorney for this subject had his client sign a complaint against the trooper for aggravated assault in that his client lost an eye. Of course, I went to the basketball court on a Sunday afternoon. There were at least eight black men playing basketball. I started measuring the court with a tape measure, and naturally, the players started wondering who I was.

When they stopped playing, I went over to them and identified myself. An older gentleman about forty years old was there, and I used him as a spokesman. I asked them if they remembered the incident with the firecracker, and they stated they had heard about it, but none of them were there when it happened.

The two East Orange police officers didn't take the names of any other witnesses, only the trooper, since he signed the complaint.

I interviewed the trooper, and he stated that he didn't touch the suspect when this happened. He went right for his two-year-old to see how he was.

I called the attorney for the suspect, and I asked him why his client had signed a complaint against the trooper, and he stated that that was the only name they had.

The complaint against the trooper was dismissed at a preliminary hearing, and I completed my report with the charges against the trooper being unsubstantiated.

The information went through the deputy troop commander and the troop commander and was sent down to the IAB. They told me to get a letter from the attorney stating that he did not want me to interview his client. Of course, I protested, but I had to get a letter to no avail. I called the attorney, and he promised me a letter in a couple of days. The letter never came. I called the lawyer again, and he stated he would have it done today. Of course, the letter never came.

Now a month had gone by since the report was finished. IAB called me again about the letter, and they said I would have to get it.

The next day I went to the lawyer's office in East Orange. I entered the office, and two secretaries were typing away. I showed the girl my police ID, pulled out my handcuffs, and told the girl I was going to arrest her boss for interfering with my investigation.

She went into his office, and I heard her tell him I was there to arrest him. He laughed and said he was sorry he was late getting the letter. He then had one of his secretaries type the letter for me.

I couldn't believe that IAB would not accept my statement that the attorney would not let me interview his client and wanted a letter. I think IAB was paranoid sometimes. But the bottom line was the trooper was exonerated from this complaint.

We had a great crew at Troop D headquarters. We were insulated from the road troops. We had our own budget and drove brand-new troop cars and wanted for nothing. The state was holding back on buying cars for the road troops and division headquarters. They also stopped running new State Police classes. We had a new major in the division; the one I knew had retired. The new major couldn't replace troopers transferred off the Turnpike with new troopers. He didn't have any. So we went down from 220 to about 205. We could not fulfill our contract with the Turnpike of 220 troopers.

Finally, after nearly two years, COL Dintino got pissed and went to see the governor. Suddenly, the state road troops and division head-quarters started getting new cars, and we started running State Police classes again. COL Dintino's popularity rose with the troopers, but when Governor Florio lost his re-election bid, he resigned and didn't wait for the new governor to get into office.

We then had an acting superintendent for three months until Governor Whitman took office and appointed Major Carl Williams as superintendent.

One of the incidents affecting all police in New Jersey and the tax-paying public today was the posting of police cars at construction sites. This happened because of a fatal accident on the New Jersey Turnpike extension from Newark into Bayonne. Construction crews were always working on this bridge. One day one of the eastbound lanes was closed off with wooden dividers. A large box truck lost control and went through the wooden divider, struck a worker, and pinned his head with one of the front wheels into the metal grating of the bridge. He was killed. As this happened, a reporter for the *New York Daily News* was passing and took a picture of the dead construction worker's head being crushed into the bridge and put it in the following day's paper.

Naturally, politicians, the New Jersey Turnpike Authority, the New Jersey Department of Transportation, and the public were shocked, and all said something had to be done. So after many meetings, the politicians and the highway authorities decided that there must be a police presence at all construction sites. Don't get me wrong. I am not blaming the police, either local or State Police. They are just doing their job and getting time and one-half for these overtime jobs. The police pay for this was worked into the job bid and passed on to the public in taxes. We all drive past numerous construction sites along the roads of this state. Some of them need one or two officers or Troopers at a site, and some don't need any. I would say at least half, especially on back roads, do not need police there. There should be a State Police unit checking out a construction site and deciding if the site needs police protection. When I passed a site, the police car was parked in front of the site, sometimes even an unmarked car, and the police officer or trooper was playing with their phone. I never see one directing traffic.

I was involved in some way with the two bargaining agents, the STFA for the troopers and the NCO Association for the sergeants. I was a representative for two TPUs in Troop B, and I was the representative for all sergeants in Troop B for the NCO Asc. In 1991 the SFC salary was closing in on lieutenants. A couple of other lieutenants and I felt it was time for lieutenants and captains to organize into a bargaining unit.

In 1991 we met at the Mercer County Airport lounge in West Trenton. We had about six or seven lieutenants, one captain, and an attorney by the name of Thomas Savage III, the attorney of record for the troopers that established the STFA. He took our case before the New Jersey PERC (Public Employees Relations Commission), which recognized us in 1993 as the Superior Officers Association (SOA) as the bargaining agent for lieutenants. We still had to fight for the captains. By 1999 we were close. I was now a captain, but the superintendent, COL Carson Dunbar, did not want his captains in the SOA. He held a vote in December of 1999. There were about 27 captains there out of 29. (Two were on vacation). COL Dunbar greased the pot and offered a pay raise if the captains dropped out of trying to enter the SOA. The vote was 24 to 3 to drop out of trying to get into the SOA. The only three to vote to continue the fight were me, Captain Ken Wondrak, and Captain Joe Sarnecki. The rest sold out for a raise. It took until 2010 for the captains to enter the SOA.

Captain Tezsla agreed with me that only staff officers should have the weekend duty. I had the duty one weekend, and we had a regulation that if a trooper uncovered cash on an arrest over $20,000, the duty Lieutenant would have to respond and supervise the money count. Once on weekend duty, I got a call from Moorestown Station on the Turnpike that a trooper had just recovered about $25,000. I then drove the two-and-a-half hours to the station. When I arrived, I discovered that the subject had no contraband, just the $25,000. He had been going north on the Turnpike. He had a map that showed him a route around New Jersey through Pennsylvania, into lower New York state, and then into New York City.

I interviewed the subject and advised him since he didn't know where the money came from, it would be turned over to the county prosecutor's office. I informed him that his boss wouldn't be pleased if he didn't follow the prescribed route. I asked him if he would like to speak to a narcotics detective, and he stated he did. This poor kid was just a delivery boy. Narcotics would like to go further up the "food chain" to get a bigger fish.

This was in 1991. Still, runners of narcotics or guns would try to avoid the New Jersey Turnpike and Jersey Troopers. The State and the Federal Government kept preaching racial profiling to appease black organizations like the NAACP. But profiling was good police work if done right and not using race in your probable cause to stop a vehicle. In the early 1970s, when I was a young trooper stationed at the Somerville Station, I would park by Raritan Valley Community College, watch for longhaired young students, usually driving a van, and try to establish probable cause to stop the vehicle. I wouldn't look to stop an elderly lady at the local supermarket parking lot: just common sense and everyday police work.

Another directive that Captain Tezsla had was if you had the duty and a trooper was injured, you went to the hospital first, found out what was going on, and then called him. I had the responsibility that night, and I was getting home with my wife from a friend's house, and my cell phone went off. It was about 11 P.M. The call came from the sergeant from Moorestown Station. He advised me that an off-duty trooper was involved in a motor vehicle accident where he hit three or four parked cars and was en route to Cooper Medical Center in Camden and that he was seriously injured.

I told the sergeant I would be there in about one and a half hours and have a marked troop car out front to take me to Cooper Hospital since I didn't know where it was. I started heading down US 206 towards the Turnpike naturally at high speed (I was driving a new 1991 Chevrolet Caprice unmarked troop car with the unique Corvette engine. These were the fastest and most well-handling troop cars I ever drove in the State Police (I would know since I have owned two Corvettes in my time).

Of course, I was stopped by a local police officer in northern Somerset County. Even though I had a red light on my dashboard, he tried to stop me. I didn't want him or me to cause an accident, so I pulled over. I showed him my ID and explained where and why I was speeding.

He said, "Do you know how fast you were going?"

I said, "Yes," as I pulled out to resume my detail.

He had my name, and if he wanted to make a big deal of this, he could do it tomorrow.

He didn't follow me again. And one and a half hours later, I was at Moorestown Station and then en route to Cooper Hospital.

I spoke to the doctor, who told me the trooper was sedated and sleeping and probably would not be able to talk to me until about 7 A.M. The doctor said the trooper would probably be OK. He was a powerful young man and in good shape.

I called Captain Tezsla to advise him of the injury to the trooper. First, the captain interrupted me and asked where I was, and I said Cooper Hospital.

After I told him what was going on, he told me to go home and that he would see the trooper when he was awake.

On the way home, it was about 4 A.M. in the same area where I stopped on the way to Cooper Hospital. The same local patrolman had stopped a vehicle southbound on US-206, a one-lane roadway in this area. I stopped to back him up. I put my red dashboard light on.

After the stop, he waved and said, "thanks, trooper."

I want to mention to any young trooper or police officer reading this that you can speed to go to a call, but remember, if you crash, you don't get there. (This was just another directive I learned from Captain Tezsla that I used when I became a troop commander).

Another internal that I didn't do but worked on was when one of our black troopers accidentally left his weapon in a pouch at a McDonald's fast-food restaurant in New Brunswick. As soon as he realized it, he went back to pick it up, but a customer gave it to the manager, and the manager brought it over to the Middlesex County Courthouse and turned it over to the county sheriff's office.

Even though the trooper got his weapon back immediately, the sheriff's office had already called us to say they knew we carried a Heckler & Koch 9MM. So an internal investigation was started and assigned to a DSFC. He found out that the weapon the trooper was carrying was not the one issued to him by the State Police but the one he bought back in 1982 when troopers were allowed to purchase an exact weapon they carried at a reduced price. I also told the DSFC that this trooper was one of the best when he worked for me at Newark Station, and that's why he was still assigned to the Turnpike. The DSFC and I agreed that there should be no disciplinary action against this trooper.

We had to convince Captain Tezsla. The captain decided to take no further action, but now it was up to the IAB. There was a new captain in charge of IAB, Captain Lanny Roberson. I didn't know him then, but he agreed to look at the internal investigation himself. The result was that there was no further action against this trooper.

I learned long ago that it's bad enough to do internal investigations if you find a trooper guilty of an offense. Still, if it's close, you should find in favor of the trooper unless he has numerous complaints on the same type of violation. I put this here to remind road troopers that you will probably be road troopers for all of your careers which will probably be at least twenty-five years. If you stay on the road, you should at least reach the rank of SFC or lieutenant. So you will be doing internal investigations.

We had a great crew at Troop D headquarters. After Captain Al Tezsla, Lt. Frank Miele was deputy Troop D commander, and I was the administration officer. Eventually, Lt. Miele was made captain and became the Troop B commander in Totowa. I then became deputy Troop D commander. Lt. Ken Wondrack took my old job as the administration officer. Lt. Tom Smith was our criminal investigation officer, Lt. Bill Yodice was our traffic officer, and Lt. Joe Wattai was our operations officer. We also had some outstanding NCOs, SFC Bob Michaels, SFC Ray Chintall, and SFC Bernie Gilbert. Lt. Wondrack, Lt. Smith, and I were all in the active armed forces reserves. I was an SFC in the New Jersey Army National Guard, Lt. Wondrack was a major in the New Jersey Army National Guard, and Lt. Smith was a captain in the Air Force reserves (When Lt. Wondrack retired from the military, he was a brigadier general. Lt. Smith retired as a full colonel, and I retired as a first sergeant, E-8).

As deputy troop commander, one of my jobs was to read and correct all internal investigations and deal with the Internal Affairs Bureau (IAB). My best investigator of internal investigations was Lt. Joe Wattai. Even though we had two excellent secretaries to type the reports for us, Lt. Wattai knew I took the internals home to read. You could not read and correct the reports properly at work since there were too many distractions.

One day Lt. Wattai put a completed investigation in my inbox and asked, "Can you check this tonight?"

I liked to tease him, so I said, "Maybe, if I don't go out."

The following day he came into my office and asked, "Did you check my report last night?"

I said, "Yes, I did and found some mistakes."

He demanded to see the errors right away.

I said, "Not now; maybe later; I have some other work."

A while later, he came into my office and wanted to see the mistakes. There were only two minor typo mistakes which he immediately corrected.

Lt. Wattai never had to be corrected on content like some other investigators.

After Lt. Wattai retired from the State Police, he investigated nursing home problems for the state of New Jersey. Lt. Joe Wattai and I became close friends and continue to go to dinner and travel with our wives to this day.

Back then, a Staff Inspection Unit was under the IAB. Only a lieutenant and an SFC were in that unit. They went around doing unannounced inspections for IAB. The SFC was a military person active in the US Marine Reserves, and when large groups of troopers had to march as in a parade, he was called on to march them.

One day the SFC came to the New Brunswick Station on the Turnpike. The station was attached to Troop D headquarters and was responsible for patrolling the middle of the Turnpike. There was a hallway that divided the two areas.

The station commander called me and said, "The inspecting SFC doesn't understand our Turnpike radio log, no matter how many times I explain it to him."

I said, "I will come across the hall to see him."

When I got there, the SFC showed me a Turnpike radio log we were using, and the SFC said, "It doesn't have a number on the lower left side of the report (All State Police reports have a report number on the lower left side of the report)."

I told the SFC, "This is a Turnpike radio log because we are not yet using the new Motorola radio system used by the road troops and division headquarters. We must use the Turnpike radio log until we adopt the new Motorola system."

He continued, "But there is no number on our radio log."

I said, "Don't say there was no number again!"

I quickly explained why we use the Turnpike radio log, and the SFC again said, "There is no number on the radio log."

Knowing that the SFC was a military man and I was a lieutenant, I yelled, "Attention—right face—forward march!" I marched him right out of the building and to his car.

I returned to the station, and the station commander asked, "What about the inspection?"

I told him, "I didn't care anymore, so I marched him out."

He was an ass (I then called the inspection SFC's lieutenant and explained it to him; of course, he understood and would take care of the SFC when he came in). I guess it takes all kinds, even in the State Police.

Lt. Bill Yodice was our traffic officer and the banquet committee chairman, which ran the banquet in Atlantic City, honoring all retirees from the previous year. His nickname was "Banquet Billy." The superintendent, COL Justin Dintino, wanted Lt. Yodice closer to him to prepare for the banquet, so he promoted Lt. Yodice to captain to run the traffic bureau in division headquarters. Nice to have friends in high places. Lt. Rob Fuller replaced Lt. Yodice. Lt. Fuller was another fine officer and fit in with our present crew.

Another problem that occurred when I was administration officer was the number of black troopers at Moorestown Station. When troopers are transferred on and off the Turnpike, you can't always tell by their names if they are white, black, or Hispanic. Before you know it, the whole Station will be only black troopers. Right now, half the station was black. All the black troopers in Troop A had put in for the Turnpike and told their black friends in Troop A that the working conditions and equipment were better on the Turnpike. If the NAACP got a hold of this, they would try to make a political thing out of it against Troop A or the State Police in general. This transfer of black troopers to Moorestown

Station was stopped until the percentage of black troopers returned to the levels of other stations.

Soon Captain Al Tezsla was promoted to major and went to division headquarters. He was replaced by Captain Robert Palentchar, who came over from being the Troop C commander. He fit right in with our crew and was an excellent troop commander. One day Captain Palentchar got a phone call from a New York television news station. I happened to be in his office. The reporter was trying to discuss a trooper's problem with a motorist. The captain told the news reporter, "you seem like an intelligent man," and as soon as he said this, the reporter said you don't think I am intelligent because I am black. The captain continued this interview was over and hung up. I recognized the reporter who was an anchor for ABC News in New York. Captain Palentchar lived in south Jersey and did not get news channels from New York, only Philadelphia.

A few days later, Captain Paentchar went on vacation, and I represented him at a division staff meeting with the superintendent, troop commanders, and majors. I guess I was the only lieutenant there. COL Dintino brought up the phone call to Captain Palentchar from the ABC news anchor from New York City. I immediately raised my hand to give him the information since I was there when the phone call took place. COL Dintino didn't know me, so he looked to his left at his aid, Major Dominick Trocchia. I didn't know Major Trocchia in the State Police, but we were both active in the New Jersey Army National Guard, and when on active duty training in Fort Drum, New York, we had a couple of drinks at a local bar outside of the fort. I then explained to COL Dintino that the news anchor was out of line and Captain Palentchar had no way of knowing who he was because the captain lived in south Jersey. COL Dintino thanked me for my response. After the meeting, Major Trocchia advised me that I was on a new committee called "The Race Relations Committee," in which Major Trocchia was chairman. We went to different road stations and spoke with minority troopers, including female troopers, about how they were being treated. None of the troopers we talked to had anything derogatory about the State Police or their supervisors. I expected that since troopers fight their own battles. After a couple of months, the committee faded away.

While I was administration officer, I had surgery on my right knee for a torn meniscus on Monday of Thanksgiving week. So I was off on sick leave on Monday, Tuesday, and Wednesday and state employees were all off on Thanksgiving and the Friday after. I talked the doctor into letting me do therapy at home and work, not going to physical therapy sessions. I was back to work on Monday, and in about six weeks, I started running again.

A trooper at Newark Station had the same surgery about a month after mine. But he knew if he returned to work on light duty, he would be put on the station record and radio until he returned to full duty. We still did not have civilian dispatchers on the Turnpike. So the trooper brought a note from the doctor that put him off duty for a month while he was going to physical therapy. I was pissed, but Captain Tezsla was really pissed. So when he returned to work on full duty, we put him on the station record anyway, working 8 A.M. to 4 P.M. After about two months of this, he saw his station commander and said if he didn't return to his regular work, he would put in a grievance. We put him back with his squad. He learned a lesson. One thing that came out of it was he became pretty good on the station record and radio.

As the deputy troop commander, I dealt with the IAB extensively since I reviewed all internals from Troop D for the captain. I got to know the bureau chief, Captain Lanny Roberson. I liked his style, and apparently, he liked mine. I saw a change from the previous captain of IAB. The other troopers assigned to IAB seemed more "human" now. I had been deputy Troop D commander for about three years when Captain Roberson was promoted to major and took over field operations, which runs all the troops and other bureaus. Then, Captain Miele, the Troop B commander, retired. I thought I had a chance to go to Troop B and then be the commander, but it was not going to happen.

Another deputy troop commander who lived in deep south Jersey got the assignment. I heard that he was very friendly with superintendent COL Carl Williams. That's OK things like this happen in business and public service. I was still enjoying my position at Troop D. These things seem to happen a lot in division headquarters.

Finally, the Troop C commander retired, and Captain Palenchar advised me that he was going back to run Troop C. That left Troop D, my troop, open, and now I could get the position. I didn't know at the time that Major Roberson fought hard for me, and COL Williams agreed but decided to move the Troop B commander to Troop D headquarters since he lived so far down south and move me to command Troop B (Thank you, Major Roberson).

Other division shenanigans went on but were crushed by Major Roberson. These problems in division headquarters have been going on for a long time under many different superintendents. Troopers who may have been on the road for two or three years get an assignment in the division and then play musical chairs to get promoted. You can see why I don't like or respect division headquarters and how they operate, though there are a lot of excellent troopers there that remember where they came from, "the road." The last thing that happened before I left was that our new Troop D headquarters was almost complete and about to open soon in Cranberry on the Turnpike. With the new Troop D headquarters opening in Cranberry, all civilian dispatchers were now assigned to Troop headquarters in all five troops. No more civilian dispatchers at the stations. (Nice to have toll money.)

Troop B headquarters, here I come as the troop commander.

13

TROOP B POST: HEADQUARTERS, TOTOWA AS A CAPTAIN

Thanks to Major Lanny Roberson, he kept the captain position of Troop B commander within the section of field operations. Not just for me but all the 1800 or so troopers assigned to field operations. We didn't need some division lieutenant to come and "steal" our promotion. Major Roberson took me to meet the superintendent, COL Carl Williams, at his office in division headquarters, where COL Williams told me I would be the next Troop B commander. COL Williams told me at the meeting that I should go back to school to get a bachelor's degree since I only had an associate's degree. After we left the colonel's office, I told Major Roberson that at age 50, I didn't want to return to school. He just said screw it; you don't have to. You got the promotion. The following Friday, it came out on teletype that I was the "acting" Troop B commander. That night at home, I got a call from COL Williams congratulating me on the appointment. He added he didn't know when the promotion would come out but not soon.

I just said thanks to COL Williams. So I reported to Troop B headquarters the following Monday morning. I didn't know that two other acting captains in the division headquarters had been waiting for their promotions.

Major Roberson convinced COL Williams to add me to the promotional list, which he did. So the following Friday, four days after I arrived in Troop B, I was promoted to captain (Feb 1995).

My new staff began talking and saying, "boy, promoted already, who does he know." This was good, even though I had nothing to do with a quick promotion. It showed my staff that I had some clout.

The same happened when I was promoted to lieutenant as Newark Station commander. When you are promoted quickly, running your new command is more effortless.

I saw some problems right away. I heard some of the supervisors I had worked with years ago say, "Sal's back; we can relax." That was a misnomer. I immediately called for a station commanders' meeting at our headquarters. As I was going over things I wanted to be changed or done, I was annoyed at some of the answers to my questions or directives. The meeting consisted of my staff, station commanders, and assistant station commanders. One sergeant was the acting assistant station commander of Hope Station. Sergeant John Lennon was sitting in the back, the only person taking notes. So as the meeting continued, I was getting more annoyed at the answers from my staff. Finally, I threw my hands up and yelled, "fungool" (an Italian swear word). Sergeant Lennon, the only person taking notes, raised his hand. I said yes, John, and he asked how you spell fungool. This brought laughter into the meeting, which was good; it broke the tension. The meeting went well after that, and I think I got my points across.

I then met privately with my traffic officer, Lieutenant Robert Skok. I advised him I wanted a list of troopers not carrying their weight, especially at the three main traffic stations, Totowa Sub Station, Netcong Station, and Somerville Station. I got the list, and only about five or six were not carrying their weight. Lo and behold, on the list were "Frank the mechanic" and "Joe," both now at Netcong Station and both that I threw out of Newark Station in 1988. The Netcong Station had a new station commander, Lieutenant Joe Cannatella, whom I knew and respected as an excellent trooper and supervisor (Lt. Cannatella retired after me as a major).

We first made "Frank the mechanic" our priority. Lt. Cannatella spoke with him, and apparently, nothing was sinking in. Finally, the trooper started stopping motorists, giving them a summons for whatever, and telling them to go to court, and he would have the summons dismissed since he was being forced to write them. A couple of people came to Netcong Station to complain about their summons, and Lt. Cannatella pulled the trooper off the road and contacted me. We then set up a meeting with the trooper in my office with his lieutenant and a few staff members. The trooper was in civilian clothes and was now on sick leave. He came into my office with his briefcase. After he sat down, I saw him fiddling with something in his briefcase. I said, trooper, if you are trying to record this meeting, it's OK. Just put the recorder on my desk to get all the conversations of this meeting. He looked a little embarrassed, but he put the recorder on my desk. We advised him there was an internal investigation into what he was doing, and his case was now in division headquarters. Apparently, after seeing the division psychologist, he eventually retired on disability. When he got his first disability check, he mailed it back to the Division of Pensions. He also filed a complaint in the State Administrative Court that he wanted his job back. I did not attend the hearing, but Lt. Cannatella did. As a result of the hearing, the administrative judge did not give the trooper his job back, and he continued on disability retirement. This wasn't the first trooper I saw retired on mental disability, nor will it be the last. Disabilities can be mental as well as physical problems.

Now it was time for "Joe." He was a very good trooper but did not like writing summons. When I became the Troop B commander, I started to do this: If I had to see a trooper, especially on a minor problem, I would go to the station where the trooper worked and not have him come into headquarters. If a trooper is summoned to see the captain, rumors start at the station that the trooper may be in trouble. Nobody seemed to care when I went to a station to see a trooper.

So I went to Netcong Station to see "Joe." This single trooper was very well dressed in uniform, brass, and shoes always shined. We discussed his activities at Netcong, and he said that he writes a summons if he thinks the driver deserves one but apparently, he has a higher tolerance for a violation than I do.

I told him not to try and bring me into this, and naturally, I would not give him any numbers in that he could submit a union grievance that there was a "quota" at the station. I just told him he was evaluated along with his peers on his squad, and since he was the squad's senior man, they looked up to his work ethic. I know he knew why he was transferred out of Newark Station in 1988 when I was the station commander. I gave him the rest of the month and the next month to consider what we discussed.

Well, the month we met, he wrote about ten summonses for twenty days of work while his squad mates averaged between thrity-five and sixty summonses a month.

The following month he wrote eight, so I guess he made his mind up that he wasn't going to change his perspective on traffic activities. So I transferred him to Sussex Station. Sussex Station was the busiest general police-type station in Troop B.

There are twenty-four municipalities in Sussex County, and the Sussex Station patrols twelve of them and even helps out some of the smaller local police departments. Also, there are no dual-lane highways in the Sussex Station area, so traffic was the least of their problems.

Unfortunately, the trooper lived in Hudson County, a good hour from the Sussex Station with good traffic. Fortunately, the trooper was single. I knew he would do well up there because he was a good trooper. He didn't call in sick and did his job.

After about six months, his station commander called me and said he was tired of hitting all that commuter traffic on NJ-15 when returning home from the midnight shift.

I told the station commander to tell him to move to Sussex County if he wants to get closer to home because I am not transferring him to a traffic station.

He stayed at Sussex Station until after I retired.

Another problem I inherited when I returned to Troop B was the pistol range for the semi-annual pistol shoot. When I was on the Turnpike in Troop D, we had our range with a trailer near Interchange 8. Before I went to the Turnpike in 1988, Troop B used a range in Mansfield Township, Warren County. It was an excellent range with a building for classroom work. Troop B was now using a Boy Scout camp in Blairstown. I decided to take a look myself since the spring pistol shoot had just started. Troop B puts about six hundred troopers through the shoot, including detectives and specialist troopers from division headquarters who live in north Jersey.

I got up there and found the sergeant in charge. He showed me around. The range was OK, and the classroom was small but OK. I then asked him where the bathroom was.

He told me it was broken.

I wondered where the troopers would go if they had to go to the bathroom.

He said, "In the woods."

I said, "How about the female troopers?"

He said, "In the woods."

I told him, "Finish today, and the range was closed tomorrow; I will let you know when to start it up again."

First of all, I was not too fond of the range anyway, but it would have to do for this shoot until I found a better place. I just needed a couple of porta-potties for now. I got back to my office and called division headquarters. I told the field operations captain I needed at least two porta-potties for the range. The captain transferred me over to the administration major, who handles the budget. The major told me the budget was fixed for this year, and he could put it in next year's budget.

I didn't want to tell him he was wrong and that I did the Turnpike's sixteen-million-dollar budget and could move money around when needed.

I called the field operations captain back and told him the administration major denied me the porta-potties, so I am closing the range and sending everyone to the Troop C range at the Fort Dix Army Post.

He told me I couldn't do that because Troop C could not handle an additional 600 troopers.

I said then get me a couple of porta-potties.

Later on that day, two porta-potties were delivered to the range.

A higher headquarters supports the troops in the military, and the New Jersey State Police division headquarters only supports itself. Now you see why I am not too thrilled with division headquarters.

In time, before the fall pistol shoot, I met with the Morris County Prosecutor and the Director of the Morris County Police Academy. We worked out a deal for the State Police to rent the indoor Morris County range on weekdays after 4 P.M. so as not to interfere with the police classes or other Morris County police departments who use the range.

To this day, the Morris County Police Academy range is used by Troop B for firearms qualification.

Another problem with division headquarters was over air conditioners at the Somerville Station. Lt. Joe Cannatella somehow made a deal with the Somerset County Prosecutor to use drug money to replace five air conditioner units that didn't work at Somerville Station (Leave it to Joe). There were nine air conditioners, and five didn't work. Somerville Station did not have central air conditioning. The prosecutor wanted to do this, but he had to send the request through the Division of Criminal Justice, an arm of the attorney general. They said the State Police could request the five air conditioners through normal channels. This had been done for two years, and division headquarters never replaced them. As you would expect, I started making phone calls.

The Division of Criminal Justice has always disagreed with the State Police over "turf." I called the Division of Criminal Justice up and started making waves that they were putting their nose where it didn't belong. Well, I guess I made some waves. I got a call from LTC Mike Fedorko, the number two man behind COL Williams. LTC Fedorko advised me that he found five air conditioners at division headquarters, and they would be coming to Somerville Station in a couple of days. Of course, I thanked him for his help, but this was another bad mark on division headquarters for only taking care of themselves.

Sometime around 1984, when I was a sergeant at Washington Station, a contractor came in and offered he had a contract for replacing all the curtains at the station and wanted to measure the windows. He said he put in a bid seven years ago and just now got the OK to replace the curtains. Nice, another example of division headquarters not taking care of the road again.

I had a problem early on with a station commander at a traffic station. My traffic officer advised me the statistics at this station were slipping. I took a ride and had a "chat" with the station commander.

He defended his station and stated everyone was doing a great job.

I disagreed to a certain extent, but to no avail; he stood on his answers. I transferred him to Washington Station, which at the time was a general police-type station with no Interstate to patrol since the opening of Perryville Station on I-78.

Word got back to me that the lieutenant now at Washington Station was telling his troopers that Washington Station was a general police-type station and traffic was a secondary job. He didn't want his troopers to go on I-78 and write summonses.

I now went to Washington Station to have another "chat" with the station commander. I advised him that the last seven miles of I-78 in Warren County, accidents, aids, and traffic enforcement belong to him now. I continued, "have a nice day, lieutenant," as I left.

He came around, and the station did well with seven miles of I-78 to patrol. He eventually went back to a traffic station and did well.

An excellent happening for me, Troop B, and New Jersey was the visit by Pope John Paul II on October 6, 1995. He said mass at Giants Stadium in East Rutherford with 83,000 people attending mass. Of course, there was a little problem with the New York Police Department.

When I got to the stadium, I saw three marked and one unmarked New York City police vehicle parked by the stadium. The typical head of state detail coming from New York ends with the Port Authority police turning over the detail to the New Jersey State Police, where the Turnpike and NJ-3 meet.

I first spoke with my operations officer, who said the New York police cars kept coming to the stadium.

I then talked to the head of the New Jersey office of the Secret Service, who stated that the head man of the New York police detail was the four-star chief of patrol who wanted to meet the Pope.

I said, "OK, let's talk to him."

I told the Chief that he could stay with his unmarked car and driver, but the three marked vehicles had to leave.

He was not too happy. I guess four-star chiefs do not like taking orders from a captain. They all left, including the chief. Please don't get me wrong; I think the New York City Police Department was the best municipal police agency in the world. I don't need the press taking pictures of the New York Police vehicles, and the headline would read, "Who's in charge?"

Some of my men and I met the pope and had a picture taken with him. Pope John Paul II also gave us a set of rosary beads from the Vatican.

Because Newark Liberty International Airport was in the Troop B area, we had the privilege of assisting the US Secret Service with the security of the President of the United States. During my time on the TPU, as station commander of Newark Station and as Troop B commander, I met President Ronald Reagan, President George H.W. Bush, and President Bill Clinton three times.

The first two meetings with President Clinton were routine, and I even got my picture taken with him.

The third meeting was a little different. President Clinton was scheduled to speak at a political function in Union. The previous night, he stayed at a hotel across the street from Giants Stadium in East Rutherford. Our troop provided the motorcade security for the trip with the US Secret Service. I was downstairs in the lobby of the hotel and in uniform. It was about 7:30 A.M. on a weekday. A Secret Service Agent came off the elevator and ran up to me. He stated that the president was very upset that his visit was causing the traffic jam he saw out of the window at Interchange 16-W on the Turnpike.

Of course, the Secret Service Agent was from Washington and didn't know about Interchange 16-W every weekday morning. He asked me to tell President Clinton. So I went to the president's room with the Secret Service Agent.

I explained the traffic problem at Interchange 16-W, which only affects eastbound traffic towards New York City. I explained that we were going west toward the Parkway, and there was no backup westbound on NJ-3.

We spoke about general traffic in the New York and north Jersey metropolitan areas. It was great having a normal conversation with the President of the United States, and I will never forget it.

Of course, the detail went off without a hitch.

One of the nicest things in Troop B was the development of the Cadet Corps. I had a young black male trooper transferred to Troop B from

Troop D because he was on light duty. His name was Trooper Clayton Staton. He could not patrol since he was on light duty, but he could drive. I assigned him to the first sergeant to run errands like making the division mail run twice a week.

After a couple of weeks, Trooper Staton came to me and said he was looking into starting a Cadet Corps to help struggling students in a grammar school. I told him to go for it and report his time sheet to the first sergeant.

As time went on, Trooper Staton developed the Cadet Corps, which is still a 501-C3 (IRS) Foundation. He got the Cadet Corps started in School Four in Paterson. School Four was a grammar school with grades K through 8. Trooper Staton started alone and got another Tpr assigned by division headquarters, and he also had a college student appointed part-time. The Paterson Board of Education paid the student's salary. The principal of the school also was a great help. I also was on his board of directors along with other troopers. The incorrigible students came to Cadet Corps after school and were taught discipline, including military marching and drills. The students were kept from 3:30 P.M. to 6 P.M. It also kept them off the streets. At the end of the school year, we had a graduation, and the guest speakers were US Senator Frank Lautenberg and Paterson Mayor Bill Pascrell, now a US Congressman. All the students who graduated received diplomas. Their parents were delighted. I retired from the State Police, but the Cadet Corps went on until division headquarters wanted the program transferred to them. I tried to intercede, but the division took it over to no avail, and a division (make-believe) captain was in charge. The program was eliminated in the division in a year or so, but the Cadet Corps still exists today. Trooper Clayton Staton eventually retired as a Detective SFC and was the police chief at Tulsa University Campus Police for a time in Tulsa, Oklahoma.

One of the most critical responsibilities of a troop commander was to keep the promotions within the troop. When a lieutenant retires, you get to make three promotions, lieutenant, sergeant first class, and sergeant. You don't want division headquarters to try and steal a promotion from your troop. The only position that was shared with division headquarters was the deputy troop commander. I had seven deputies during my five years as a troop commander. Three came from Troop B, three from other troops, and one from division headquarters, a detective lieutenant, but he was a Troop B trooper when he was on the road, and he lived in the Troop B area. One of my jobs as troop commander was to watch my deputy and, when asked by the division if he was ready to be a captain, to let them know. Six of the seven deputies I had made captain.

After being there for about six months, one of my Lieutenants decided to retire. This would give me three promotions to make. I was excited. I then got a call from the field operations captain that they were sending up an SFC from the Traffic Bureau to be an acting lieutenant filling in the spot for my lieutenant who was retiring. Boy was I pissed. I wasn't going to argue with the captain since the transfer had to be approved by Major Lanny Roberson, the field operatons supervisor. I decided to go to the division headquarters the next day and complain. Before leaving, I checked on the SFC I was getting. He was promoted to SFC six months ago, was still on probation, and had been off the road for ten years. I also learned that they wanted to transfer him because the captain of the Traffic Bureau could promote one of his crony friends to SFC.

I went to division headquarters the following day and burst into the field operations office unannounced.

First, I started yelling at the captain, who was the assistant field operations officer, and then I saw the captain of the Traffic Bureau, the main culprit, and I laid into him verbally.

I also challenged him to go to the gym "and put the gloves on."

By this time, Major Roberson, I guess, heard the yelling and came out of his office. The major took me into his office and closed the door.

He let me explain my problem, that no one even told me about the transfer beforehand, and that the SFC was still on probation.

Major Roberson was fair. He told me, "You may have lost this battle but won the war. As long as I am in this division, you will never lose another promotion from the division headquarters. The SFC will not be promoted until he is off probation and until you have another promotion scheduled (Which took about ten months)."

The SFC was now running a road station in my troop. I had to watch him closely since he had been off the road for ten years.

The first thing he did to annoy me was to change his working hours. The working hours for a station commander are 8 A.M. to 4 P.M. He started working from 7 A.M. to 3 P.M.

I called him and told him the correct hours.

He told me, "I come in at 6 A.M. to speak with the midnight shift sergeant and leave at 3 P.M."

I told him, "I don't care if you come in at 4 A.M.; you work until 4 P.M."

Then he took one hour of vacation to leave at 3 P.M.

I called him and asked, "Do you have a part-time job or something?" He said, "No."

I then ordered him to stop taking a vacation hour every day (Actually, according to the contract with the NCO Association, he could do that). I also advised him, "If you have to go someplace and leave early, just call the first sergeant at headquarters and let him know. I don't care where you go. I don't want to call your station to talk to you and find out that you are gone."

He said he understood.

The next problem I had with him was attendance at the troop picnic that summer. He said he doesn't attend social functions with the State Police.

I told him if he didn't go, maybe his troopers wouldn't attend (This wasn't true, it was a great picnic, and most troopers attended if they could).

So he came alone to the picnic on a Friday in Sussex County, where we rented a picnic ground. The picnic started at about 1 P.M. and ran until dark. The SFC came at about 3:30 P.M., saw me, gave me a salute, and left. Boy, could he piss me off.

On Monday, I went to his station and spoke to him about State Police functions. I told him I was sorry for ordering him to the picnic and that it was his right not to go or go to the Christmas party we had in December.

He was promoted to lieutenant about eight months after he took over the station and became a very good station commander, just a little strange.

The only other thing that happened with him was since he was the troops' junior lieutenant, I sent him to a state-run supervision school for three days in Union. He didn't know, and neither did I, that my cousin, who worked for the Newark Board of Education as a buyer, was also sent to that school. The teacher made everyone say where they worked and their position on the first day. Naturally, the lieutenant said he was a State Police lieutenant. My cousin wondered if he knew me.

During the course, the lieutenant was asked how he got along with his supervisor (Me). He blasted me, saying I was stupid, didn't have a four-year college degree, and didn't know how to supervise.

At the end of the course, my cousin went up to him and asked if he knew me, not realizing that I was his supervisor.

My cousin could not believe it, and he almost turned pale white. He asked her not to tell me what had occurred at the school and that I wasn't that bad.

Of course, my cousin called me and told me what he had said about me. I thought this was funny.

As a troop commander, you can't expect everyone to like you. So the next business day, I called my lieutenant first to tell him I was pleased with how he ran the station, and then I asked him how he liked the state school he attended.

He said, "The school was a little boring."

I told him, "I heard you also met my cousin at the school."

He said, "Yes, I did meet her."

I said, "Thanks for your comments about me."

I hung up.

I didn't care if he liked me or not, just as long as he did a good job running the station, which he was doing. The only other thing I will say about him was as long as I was here, I would never bring him in to be on my staff because he wasn't a team player as far as I was concerned. It's a small world out there.

One of the complaints you don't want against one of your people or you is an EEOC (Equal Employment Opportunity Commission) complaint filed because of race, color, religion, sex, etc. We had an EEOC

Bureau run by a captain. I knew the captain, and he told me if I got an EEOC complaint, I could handle it myself, make a memorandum of record, send it to him and keep a copy. This will show that it was handled at one time, and now if it comes up again; it shows what you did. The first one I had involved a white sergeant complaining about his boss, a white sergeant first class, continually badgering and criticizing him on everything he did.

The sergeant had been working downstairs in the Totowa Sub Station, running a squad and working shift work. He was also getting old. His station commander recommended him for an opening in the troop traffic Office for a sergeant to check all motor vehicle accident reports, including fatal accidents for the whole troop. I then transferred the sergeant to the traffic office, which gave him a day job from 8 A.M. to 4 P.M. with an unmarked troop car. Naturally, he was delighted.

Three months later, he was in my office making a complaint against the SFC, his boss. One of the problems with the traffic office was the lieutenant. He made all three of his promotions in that office. He has seen numerous troop commanders come and go, and he didn't like me picking a sergeant for his office. So he had the SFC start to harass him. I called the Lt. and SFC into my office. I told them to stop harassing the sergeant, or one or both of you would go out of this command. Things quieted down, and the sergeant was happy with the change. I also warned the SFC that he was on thin ice because I knew of his reputation for harassing people he didn't like. I made a memorandum of record on this and forwarded a copy to the captain of the EEOC Bureau.

A few months later, I had a female trooper promoted to sergeant and assigned to the traffic office in a new position to control the federal and state overtime program. She was a white female and an excellent worker. So she worked directly for the SFC in the traffic office. On a Friday afternoon, at about 3:50 P.M., the female sergeant came into my office to see me. Our headquarters closed at 4 P.M., and most troopers were on the way out the door. The traffic lieutenant had been on vacation that week, so she was in the office with the other sergeant and the SFC. She explained the SFC continually harasses her and doesn't like women.

I got up, looked down the hall, and saw the SFC in his office. He did not leave to go home. I called him on the intercom phone and told him to stay awhile, and I was sure he wanted to.

The female sergeant gave me the information about the harassment she was getting. I asked her if she would be satisfied if the SFC didn't work in this building anymore. She said yes. I wished her a good weekend and said I would see her on Monday morning.

I then called the SFC into my office. After chewing him out, I advised him that he would never make lieutenant if I sent this down to the EEOC office for further investigation. I told him to report to his new assignment as assistant station commander at Sussex Station on Monday.

He thanked me.

It was about 4:45 P.M., so I called our office in the division since they work until 5 P.M. I got a lieutenant on the phone and told him I needed a transfer teletype sent right now.

He started to say it was almost 5 P.M., but he stopped. He knew I meant business. I had to transfer three SFCs to make this happen on Monday.

Again, I made out a memorandum of record and sent a copy to the EEOC Bureau. All's well that ends well.

This subsequent EEOC complaint was against me and the Troop E commander on the Parkway. Troopers from Bloomfield Station on the Parkway and Newark Station on the Turnpike come under the promotional jurisdiction of Troop B headquarters. I control the list with input from the other commanders. A black male sergeant was up for promotion to SFC, and he was high on the promotional list. Then he got involved in a problem with a violation of rules and regulations. He received a Summary Disciplinary Hearing, was found guilty, suspended for a short time, and lost two points toward promotion to SFC. This sergeant was a good trooper who had worked for me at Newark Station. While I was there in 1988, I recommended him for promotion to sergeant, and he got it and was transferred to Troop B, where the promotion was.

If he didn't know how the promotional system worked, he could have asked for a meeting with his troop commander, Captain Ken Wondrack.

But he didn't. He just complained to the EEOC Bureau that he wasn't promoted because he was a black male.

The case was given to an EEOC detective sergeant, a white female. She first came to my office since I controlled that promotion, even though the sergeant was stationed in Troop E at Bloomfield Station. I showed the EEOC sergeant that if he didn't lose two points due to his summary disciplinary hearing, he would have been promoted, but he lost two promotional points.

She was astonished at how we totaled promotion points and how fair it was. She explained in division headquarters; that they promote who they want.

I said that's division headquarters saying, "Do as I say, not as I do."

The sergeant was promoted on the following list to SFC. Captain Ken Wondrack and I were acquitted of violating the EEOC regulations.

I ran into this SFC at a funeral of a trooper killed on the Parkway.

I went to him and said, "Hello, how are you doing?"

He said, "OK."

I have never had any animosity towards him for filing the EEOC complaint, even though he was wrong. He was one of my better troopers at Newark Station. I still see him occasionally at a Former Troopers Association gathering. He retired as a lieutenant.

The last EEOC complaint against me was a little more complicated. The station commander from the Totowa Sub Station downstairs came to see me and wanted a certain trooper transferred out of his station. The lieutenant had the figures that this black trooper was hardly doing any traffic work and continually called in sick on the midnight shift. He was single and lived in Newark. He had been stationed at the Totowa Sub Station for six years. I have found that the transfer system was an excellent tool to get a trooper back on track. I used this tool sparingly, but it does come in handy. The only trooper that I could not transfer without their permission was the station representative of the bargaining agent of the troopers called the STFA. I had the lieutenant notify the trooper that he was being transferred to Somerville Station. Totowa Station was twenty miles from his home, and Somerville Station was twenty-two miles from

his home. I didn't want to transfer him any farther from his home. This
wasn't a disciplinary transfer, just a wake-up call. He wanted to see me
when he found out about the transfer. I have an open-door policy with
all members of Troop B.

I saw him the next day, and he was very unsettled about being transferred. He complained about learning a new area and being very happy at
Totowa Sub Station. I didn't pull any punches. I told him not only does
the station commander think he needs a change, but his squad mates also
want him gone due to him calling in sick on the midnight shift and even
other shifts. I told him if he did some work in Somerville and picked
up his activities, I would transfer him back to Totowa Sub Station in six
months. He still wasn't happy.

He went to Somerville Station, worked about ten days, and called
in sick again with a bad back. No matter how long troopers are on sick
leave, they get full pay while out until they are retired on a disability pension or come back to work. While he was now out sick again, the trooper
filed an EEOC complaint against me, stating that he was improperly
transferred because he was black and disabled with a bad back.

So now I get interviewed by a black male detective sergeant from our
EEOC Bureau. The detective sergeant interviewed all involved. About a
month later, he called me on the phone and said he was not supposed
to tell me the results of his investigation, but he thought I had a right to
know. He stated he found the charges unsubstantiated against me, but
he also noted that his report goes over to the attorney general's office for
final approval since they are the department under which the Division of
State Police works. Finally, I retired on April 1, 2000. The same trooper
was on sick leave for about eighteen months with full pay. I didn't understand why the medical bureau didn't push for his retirement on disability.

Three years later, in 2003, I received a letter from the Executive
Attorney General, the number two person in that department, that I
was found not guilty of racial discrimination but guilty of violating the
American Disabilities Act in that I transferred the trooper while he was
disabled. The letter stated that if I were still a member of the State Police,
I would have received a written reprimand. It further noted that if I
disagreed with their determination, I could file an appeal with the New

Jersey Department of Personnel. Of course, I did, and I also used my New Jersey State Supervisors training level six, in which they advocate transfer as a way to help an employee get motivated.

The trooper went on sick leave after he was transferred. I sent my appeal in, and a couple of weeks later, I was found "not guilty" of the allegation of discrimination under the American Disabilities Act. The Personnel Department also admonished the AG's office for allowing this investigation to go so long when it was supposed to be completed in ninety days. I found out later the trooper finally went back to work and then sued the State Police for discrimination that he wasn't promoted to sergeant because he was black. The court threw out the suit, and the trooper retired around 2011 as a Trooper 1.

The New Jersey State Police was a department from 1921 to 1947. When the new New Jersey State Constitution was adopted in 1947, the State Police became a division under the Department of Law and Public Safety which was run by the New Jersey Attorney General. This was a mistake. The New Jersey State Police should be a department, and the superintendent should be a department head, not a division head. I based this on all the "stupid decisions" that the AG's office has made over the years concerning the State Police. What I didn't know then, and I know now, was that while this complaint was pending (for over three years), I could not have been promoted to major even if the division wanted me to, which fortunately it didn't. A promotion should only be held up on an EEOC complaint or an internal investigation on a case-by-case basis. The trooper could always be demoted if the complaint against him was substantiated and was severe enough.

Another problem with the division headquarters was with one of my senior SFC people. When I first got to Totowa headquarters, this SFC was assigned to the operations office and was in charge of the educational unit where troopers and sergeants went out and gave safety talks to children in grammar schools. I asked him if he liked being in headquarters, and he said he would rather be an assistant station commander on the road. He was the senior man in the division.

He wasn't eligible for lieutenant because he hadn't passed the physical test in the last seven years. So at his request, I transferred him to a road station as an assistant station commander. He didn't even appear on the promotion list for lieutenant. He also had only about two years to go to the mandatory retirement age of 55. Finally, for his good fortune, division headquarters allowed troopers with a problem running to take a bike test instead of the run, which was one and a half miles long in twelve minutes and thirty seconds. Well, this SFC went down to the physical examination at the division and passed the bike test. This was the first time he had passed the physical in over seven years. He drove to my headquarters to tell me I could promote him to lieutenant. I sat him down and tried to explain the promotional system to him, but he was stuck on his seniority only. I was not going to move him to the top of the list but based on his seniority, I could probably move him to the number four spot out of fourteen SFCs on the list. The other problem I had with him was he was not good with paperwork. This came from his boss at the station he worked.

I had to find a way to hide him in headquarters until he retired. I was not going to make him a station commander. I had a very good operations officer, and I asked him if we promote the senior SFC to lieutenant; I would like to put my operations lieutenant at a station on paper only and keep the new lieutenant as the operations officer. I cannot let him run a station. My operations officer will still run the operations office, and I would let the assistant station commander at the station involved run that station. My operations officer said a defiant no to being transferred back to a station, even if only on paper. He said he would put in a grievance on what I was trying to do to appease the senior SFC. I didn't want a grievance since what I wanted to do was in a gray area (real gray).

While this was happening, the senior SFC went to see a friend of his who was a major assigned to division headquarters. That major went to see a LTC about the SFC not being promoted. I was at a meeting in the division when I got a note to visit this LTC when my meeting finished. At this meeting with the LTC, I explained why I couldn't promote him and what the operations lieutenant said about a grievance. I also told him that being an LTC, he could have the SFC transferred to division headquarters, promote him and then transfer him back to me, and I would keep him in my headquarters until he retired. Unfortunately, this didn't happen, and the SFC retired as an SFC. He still blames me for not promoting him. A mutual friend tried to set up a meeting between us years ago, but he refused. I hope if he reads this, he will understand.

Another case I had, just like the one above, involved a division headquarters DSFC, who was also very active in the NCO Association. This DSFC got friendly with the New Jersey State Treasurer. They went out drinking and visiting go-go joints along US-9 in Middlesex County. The treasurer was so happy that he wanted to know what he could do for the DSFC. The DSFC only mentioned that the Division of State Police needs new troop cars. The ones we have are getting old. The DSFC asked the State Treasurer if he could put some money in our car account. The Treasurer put about 1.1 million dollars into it. The superintendent, COL Carl Williams, was so thrilled that he moved to promote the DSFC to lieutenant. My new major, Major Anthony Sparano, called and said I must "eat" the DSFC since he lives in north Jersey. The good news was he only had six months to go before retirement. I knew I couldn't win this one since my mentor, LTC Lanny Roberson, had retired. I just told the major to send him to me, but I will put him where I want. He said OK. Here we went again with that "gray area."

The DSFC was promoted to lieutenant and took the promotion of my only acting lieutenant, who was in charge of Perryville Station. So on paper, I transferred the tactical patrol lieutenant to Perryville Station as station commander. My new lieutenant became the tactical patrol officer so that I could watch him in my headquarters. My staff wanted to know what we should call the SFC running Perryville Station, and I anointed him as "Chief of Police" of Perryville Station. He was promoted in about six months when the new lieutenant retired. This was another case in which the DSFC could have been promoted in the division headquarters where he came from, but it might have put someone's nose out of joint if they had to wait six more months for promotion. I did well and only lost two positions to division personnel in five years as Troop B commander. You can see why I don't have much respect for division headquarters.

While I was at Troop D headquarters, all staff officers and station commanders had cell phones. They were the flip-type, a little bigger than later models but fit into an inside suit or sports jacket pocket. When I took over Troop B, the present commander and I switched vehicles, and he showed me a "bag phone" in my car. It was very bulky and used only in the vehicle with a beeper. So if you get beeped in the car, you can call in. Boy, things were nicer on the Turnpike.

One day Detective Lieutenant Dave Schmelz was in my office, and a phone went off. He reached into his pocket and pulled out a flip phone like the one I carried on the Turnpike. After finishing his call, I asked him where he got the flip phone. He stated the Sussex County Prosecutor bought them for all the Troop B detectives, a total of fifteen, counting Lt. Schmelz. I told the Lt. to quickly get me a flip phone, or I would take his. I got a flip phone in a couple of days and went down to our carrier, AT&T, and had the number taken out of the bag phone and put into the flip phone. On my next trip to division, I turned in the bag phone to the field operations captain. I showed him my new flip phone and told him it was time Field Operations Section had flip phones. In a couple of months, they had flip phones. It was sure nice in Troop D on the Turnpike.

If you remember, when I was station commander of Newark Station, I had a problem with a young trooper in the Air Force Reserves and didn't think he should give up his two scheduled days off when we gave him the weekend off to attend his Air Force drills. He understood when I told him I was in the New Jersey Army National Guard, and that's how it is. Now I was advised by Detective Lt. Schmelz that one of his detectives wanted next Friday off because he was "ordered" to a three-day drill. I told the Lt. to have the detective see me. Whether in Newark Station, Troop D headquarters, or Troop B headquarters, I always kept a copy of the SOP explaining military leave on my desk.

Like me, the detective was also in the New Jersey Army National Guard but in a different unit. He showed me company orders for him to leave on Friday for a three-day drill in Fort Drum, New York.

I told him he could go, but for Friday, he has to take either a vacation day, personal leave day or compensatory time if he has any.

He still believed he should get the day off as military leave and not have to use his own time, or he would put in a grievance.

I then explained that going on the advance was "voluntary." We do not have to honor company orders, only orders from higher command. I gave him a copy of the SOP on military leave.

He didn't put in a grievance, but I am sure he checked it out. Sometimes I think some people always want something for nothing.

We had a trooper who had two internals right in a row. The IAB handled the first one. The complaint was that the trooper stole meat from a farm in Warren County. On this farm, they used the honor system. The meat was kept in a refrigerator in a barn near the farmer's house. You took your meat and put the cash in a jar near the refrigerator. An SUV-type vehicle pulled up to get some meat. The farmer's son was watching, and when the vehicle left, he checked the jar, and there was no money in it. He was unable to chase the vehicle. A couple of weeks later, the farmer's son saw the exact vehicle approach the barn. He watched the subject take some meat and leave without paying for it. The farmer's son jumped in his pickup truck and started chasing the SUV. He was unable to catch him but got his license plate number. Since the farmer lived in State Police area, he called the local State Police station and filed a theft complaint. Because the plate was registered to a trooper, IAB decided to take this case of theft. Before the IAB detective could interview the farmer's son, the trooper's father, a high-ranking state official, apparently visited the farmer and his son (IAB never found out what happened with this visit). When the IAB detective interviewed the farmer's son, he said he might have made a license plate mistake. This case became unsubstantiated.

A month or so later, a packet comes up from IAB with three internal investigations on the same trooper. IAB wanted my Troop to do all three internal investigations. I called the IAB captain up and told him his bureau should investigate. He disagreed, but I talked him into putting all the allegations into one internal investigation. I put one of my best investigators, a DSFC, on this case. After the investigation in which all charges were substantiated, I recommended a general disciplinary hearing. The trooper went to IAB and resigned from his position rather than possibly facing criminal charges from this investigation.

One day the Totowa station commander came up to see me. The Passaic County Sheriff Deputies started running radar on I-80 in Wayne, which, according to the troopers, was dangerous, and they shouldn't be on I-80 anyway. I agreed with the troopers. First of all, it's not the sheriff's responsibility. They are supposed to care for the County Court House and the County Jail. I rode to the Passaic County Sheriff's Office in Paterson. I noticed numerous personal vehicles with police union stickers parked illegally everywhere. They have a parking problem in Paterson for their employees. Then I returned to my office and tried to contact the sheriff by phone.

The sheriff had been in office for over twenty years and was a stalwart in Passaic County government. I was able to get an undersheriff. I advised him of the problem of running radar on I-80.

He stated the sheriff approved it.

I told him that if he continued to run radar, I would send my troopers down to your office and start writing parking tickets by your office. Then I will contact the AG's office about what you are doing with radar, and I will also contact the press. I advised him to tell the sheriff and get back to me in one day.

One day later, the undersheriff called me back and said his men would no longer be running radar on I-80.

In north Jersey, this problem exists with the Passaic County and Bergen County Sheriff's Offices. They have no authority to patrol even though they have police powers. But they still patrol some highways in their counties.

In 1998 there was a shooting on the Turnpike involving two troopers and a van with four people in it. I wasn't surprised that this happened. Troopers occasionally shot at vehicles against the recommendation of troop commanders and the IAB. In this van, three black males and one Hispanic male were going to North Carolina to try out for a college basketball team. They were from New York City. The driver had a suspended driver's license and knew it. When they were pulled over, the driver tried to change seats with the right front passenger. As they were doing this, the vehicle popped into reverse as the two troopers approached the van. One of the troopers thought the van was trying to hit him and fired into the vehicle, causing the other trooper to fire. There were no weapons in the van. Three of the individuals were hit, but no one died. The Hispanic male was sleeping in the rear and was not injured. The case brought uproar from the black community since two white troopers shot three unarmed black males.

The four males were represented by Mr. Johnnie Cochran, the famous attorney who represented O. J. Simpson in his acquittal of homicide. Negotiations with the New Jersey Attorney General led to a 12-million-dollar settlement. I am not going to agree or disagree with this significant settlement. I am not sure of the injuries to the three black males and what they are worth. The Hispanic male sleeping in the van's rear settled for $750,000 and was not injured. This alone was a crime. The state fired the two troopers. Unfortunately, this incident happened, but you take a chance when firing a weapon at a vehicle, not knowing who was inside. Even if someone was shooting at you from a car, you have to think and look to see who else was in the vehicle so as not to injure or kill an innocent person.

A shooting I had in Troop B as troop commander happened on I-80 in Parsippany. We had just put dash cameras in all the Totowa Sub Station patrol vehicles. Due to fiscal problems, the State was doing it one station at a time. The Turnpike and Parkway were already done. A Dover patrolman was trying to stop a vehicle in his town, and the vehicle took off, and the chase was on. It was around midnight. The Dover patrolman chased the vehicle onto I-80, and two of my troopers got involved, along with a Denville patrolman and a Parsippany patrolman. They finally got the vehicle cornered in on the berm of I-80 Westbound. A Totowa Sub-Station troop car with a dash camera recorded everything during this shooting. The two troopers and three local patrolmen, including the Dover patrolman who started the chase, left their vehicles and began approaching the subject with his girlfriend in the car.

The subject tried to run down the troopers and local officers, and they opened fire, killing the subject and wounding his girlfriend in the leg. The two troopers, the Denville patrolman and the Parsippany patrolman shot their weapons. The Dover patrolman did not fire. The dead suspect was Hispanic, and his girlfriend was white. The whole case was on the dashboard video and presented to the Morris County grand jury. The shooting was ruled justified. About a year later, the mother of the dead suspect was awarded a little over two million dollars in a wrongful death suit. I could not find out what his girlfriend got, but I'm sure it was substantial for her leg wound. The two troopers who were involved were transferred from Netcong Station. One wanted to go to Troop A, where he had just bought a home, and the other was transferred to Bloomfield Station in Troop E. The State Police has the luxury of the transfer to move a trooper away from an incident in which he was involved. The two local departments do not have that luxury.

The worst day of a troop commander's job is if he loses a trooper in the line of duty. This happened to me on October 24, 1997, when Trooper Scott Gonzalez was killed in a gunfight. I had left work around 4 P.M. with one of my traffic sergeants to play nine holes of golf at the Picatinny Army Golf Course, of which I was a member. We had just started and had played a couple of holes when my cell phone rang. It was the assistant station commander of Hope Station, SFC John Lennon. He advised me of the shoot-out with Trooper Scott Gonzalez and that Scott had expired. I ran back to the clubhouse and changed into my dress clothes. I then went to the scene.

I found out via radio that Governor Christine Whitman was coming up and would do a press conference. I directed the division to land her helicopter at the Washington National Guard Armory, next to Washington Station. The armory had a helicopter landing pad. I would meet her there. I didn't want a press conference at the Hope Station where the investigation was being handled. After leaving the scene, I went to Washington Station. My immediate supervisor, Major Lanny Roberson, was on vacation and out of state, and the superintendent, COL Carl Williams, was also out of State. With Governor Whitman was LTC Mike Ferdorko, deputy superintendent, and Captain Anthony Sparano from field operations. After settling them in, I had to leave quickly to notify Trooper Gonzalez's wife, Maureen, so she didn't see it on the news. I went to her home with the Hope Station commander, Lt. Jim Golden, my deputy, Lt. Larry Apgar, and one uniformed trooper. When she opened the door, she started crying. She just knew why we were there. She just cried. We all cried. I left the station commander and the uniformed trooper to take her to Trooper Gonzalez's mother's home to notify her.

I went back to the scene with Lt. Larry Apgar. I discovered that Tpr Gonzalez spotted the suspect's car on US-46 East and that he was wanted for a recent robbery. Tpr Gonzalez chased him into a long private driveway to a single home. The suspect, later identified as Samuel Shipps, a white male, age twenty-nine, turned around and rammed his pickup truck into the front of Trooper Gonzalez's patrol car, bending the fenders into the doors, locking Trooper Gonzalez in his vehicle. Shipps got out with a shotgun and started shooting. Trooper Gonzalez returned fire with his pistol, but the second shotgun blast fatally wounded him. Shipps then got back into his truck and started up the long driveway.

He was met by a State Police patrol car driven by SGT Stanley Rusniak and a young trooper. SGT Rusniak stopped, got out with his shotgun, and as Shipps exited his vehicle, his gun went off and blew half his head off, possibly an accidental shooting of himself. SGT Rusniak was one of my best road sergeants, and if a gunfight had happened, I do not doubt that Shipps would have lost. As I write this book, it's been twenty-five years since this incident, and I still think about it at least once a week. Every February, troopers from Pennsylvania, New York, and New Jersey gather in honor of Tpr Scott Gonzalez and all the troopers killed or injured the past year from all three states. I have been to it many times. The gathering was at a resort in eastern Pennsylvania on the Delaware River (In 2022, this gathering changed to June instead of February).

State Police Schools: Mostly, all troopers attend numerous schools during their career. A course to certify you to give a breath test for alcohol, Criminal Investigation School, Narcotics School, etc. I attended most of these schools during my career. One of the best schools I graduated from while I was a captain was the US Secret Service School for state, municipal, and county police, which helped the Secret Service with presidential visits in their area of responsibility. The school was in Washington, DC, and was nine days long. My dealings with the Secret Service started with President Ronald Reagan and ended with President Bill Clinton. It includes President George H. W. Bush. I met and shook hands with all of these presidents. Most of these details were from Newark Airport to wherever the president was going.

My mentor, Major Lanny Roberson, had been promoted to LTC and was out of my chain of command. One day LTC Roberson called me and asked if I wanted to go to this Secret Service School for nine days. Of course, I said yes. He told me to pick him up with my troop car at Moorstown Station on the Turnpike on the prescribed date. He also told me to bring my golf clubs. I had played with LTC Roberson a couple of times. He was a three-handicap, and I was a fifteen. He was an excellent golfer. I discovered the school was payback for the police departments that helped the Secret Service during the past year. There were about 35 students in the class from all over the country. The course wasn't a school but was filled with excellent guest speakers and all of what the Secret Service does in protection, counterfeiting, and credit card fraud. We also toured the Secret Service Academy in Laurel, Maryland.

We also had a private tour of the Capitol and the White House. When we were in the White House, I got to sit in President Clinton's chair in the Oval Office. At the school, we met two other students with golf clubs. One, whose first name was also Lanny, was the Deputy Chief of Police of Maui, Hawaii, and the other was a captain from the CHIPS (California Highway Patrol). After our second day, LTC Roberson told me to set up a match at some golf course after school. So I set up the match at Andrews Air Force Base outside Washington. So the four of us went to Andrews Air Force Base after school to play golf.

As I pulled up to the gate, the air policeman asked me for my ID. I gave him my military ID, and he said, "thank you, First Sergeant," and gave me directions to the golf course. LTC Roberson asked me what I showed him. I showed the LTC my military ID and said, "Boss," State Police ID means nothing here. We played eighteen holes, and LTC Roberson scored a 76. Not bad for never playing this course before (I shot a 90.) We were able to play once more, and this time we played the other course. Andrews has two 18-hole courses. The LTC shot another 76 (I shot 91). I asked the LTC if he ever shoots anything but 76, and he said sometimes 75 or 74.

In the evening, we visited some nice taverns in Georgetown. To all active troopers and police officers, do not turn it down if you ever get a chance to attend this school. You will never forget the experience.

Another problem I had with division headquarters was schools (You can see I didn't like how division headquarters was run. That's why the division was called Disneyland). During the year, traffic-related schools came through the Traffic Bureau. Nice schools in Miami and Orlando, Florida; Los Angeles and San Francisco, California would come out, and someone from the Traffic Bureau would go. I suggested at a troop commanders' meeting that a troop commander should go to a nice school once in a while. So the following year, the Traffic Bureau captain called me in February to ask if I wanted to go to a school for a week. I thought he would say a school in Florida or even Texas. He says in Minnesota. I explode and tell him he could "put that school where the sun doesn't shine." Could you imagine the weather in February in Minnesota? (No golf).

Another incident I had as a troop commander was with a very good SFC who was the assistant station commander of the Hope Station. I got a call from the station commander, who said that his SFC was now living in Pennsylvania. The LT said he was also getting a Pennsylvania driver's license.

Once the LT calls me and puts the problem in my lap, he's off the hook. So off I went to Hope Station to see the SFC. This trooper at the time was the most honest person in the State Police. He does not like to break the rules or regulations. He built a house in Pennsylvania about ten to fifteen miles into the state from New Jersey. This was a gray area as far as I was concerned. It has happened before, and the division ignored it. I told the SFC to register his New Jersey driver's license to an address in New Jersey, either a friend's or a relative's house in Warren County. I told him he could say the new house was a vacation home. I gave him a week to think about it.

A week later, he put in his retirement papers. It was his choice. I then had our retirement committee set up a date for a retirement luncheon, always on a Friday afternoon, and we gave the retiree a plaque for his service to Troop B.

The station commander called me and said the SFC wanted the plaque but would not attend his party.

I told the LT to say to him no party, no plaque.

He left on a sour note. This still bothers me. All he had to do was keep his New Jersey driver's license with a New Jersey address.

While running Troop B, I had a retirement committee that set up luncheons for retirees, usually on a Friday afternoon. Profits from our store partly subsidized the luncheons. We also gave each retiree a plaque honoring their service to the New Jersey State Police and Troop B. My committee came to me in 1999 and stated that the two remaining lieutenants wanted a Friday night retirement party together.

I said, OK, if that's what they want.

It was a fine party, which I attended, with many relatives of the two lieutenants.

The committee also said the price of the plaques was approaching $100. The committee recommended we purchase a State Police watch with the triangle logo and the trooper's badge number on the face.

I agreed with the committee. The watch was purchased through the Former Troopers Association store at division headquarters. The price was just over $100.

Speaking of plaques, I have enough plaques hanging in my recreation/bar room in my house. Since I was retiring on April 1, 2000, I was glad I was getting a watch for my retirement. All the plaques I received during my career came from some agency or association in New Jersey, except one.

Sometime in early 1999, I was advised by division headquarters that a delegation from Taiwan was stopping in to visit Troop B headquarters on their way to New York City. Two individuals arrived with their wives. One was the head of Taipei County (now called New Taipei City), and the other was the Police Chief of New Taipei City, who held the rank of colonel. I gave them a complete tour of our building, including the Totowa Sub Station and the garage. They were happy and left.

About a month later, I got a letter from the colonel requesting information on our radio system. They were having trouble with theirs. I contacted our Communications Bureau, and they sent me information on our new high-band radio system. I sent the information to the colonel in Taipei.

A couple of months later, I received a letter from the colonel stating they went to a high band system, correcting their problem. Along with the letter was a plaque in Mandarin that thanked me for my information (What a conversation piece).

One problem I had was divorce. I had some experience with it since I was divorced once in 1976. I was only married for about three and a half years with one child. So all I had to pay was child support. Still, it was a traumatic experience, and when I was served divorce papers, I spoke with my squad sergeant, who told me not to do anything stupid and that I will be a new man in about six months. It only took three months. Looking back, it was the best thing to happen to me.

On the other hand, when one of my troopers, who was married for over twenty years, was going through a divorce, he would probably have to give up half of his pension to his ex-wife. I only know of one case when a detective sergeant from the division was divorced; his wife didn't want any of his pension since he earned it. When I discovered that one of my troopers was getting divorced, I would go to their station and talk to them. I tried to convince the trooper that things would look better in six months. Usually, it did.

The worst case I remember was a sergeant married for over twenty-five years whose wife met someone on the internet. She then flew to Ohio to meet him and came back and filed for divorce so she could marry her new boyfriend. We had a very long talk, and he finally came around. I didn't want one of my troopers doing something stupid and ruining their life.

The best case I remember was with one of my classmates from South Jersey. I didn't see him much since he worked in Troop A and division headquarters. I met him at a party in Toms River. He told me he had given the ex-wife half his pension for about ten years. Then she decided to get married. His divorce decree stated that if she married again, the pension would stop, and all would return to the pensioner. I guess that's why he was celebrating.

One incident I remember vividly was assisting the Union County Sheriff, Ralph Froehlich, with an uprising at a Federal Detention Center in Port Elizabeth. About two hundred detainees were waiting for a hearing to see if they could stay in this country. A private guard service was guarding the detainees. The guards ran out of the prison as the detainees started getting unruly and lighting mattresses on fire. For some reason, the Union County sheriff's office was called, not the Elizabeth police.

I received a call at home. As usual, I contacted my duty officer and had all my tactical patrols and TEAMS troopers head down to the problem. That gave me about thirty men; of course, I also went.

When I got there, I met Sheriff Froehlich, who advised me that the Elizabeth police were not coming since it was a "Federal matter." The sheriff had about fifteen deputies, so I thought we had enough. We used tear gas to get all the subjects out of prison, marched them to a Shoprite warehouse next door, and locked them in the fenced-in lot. Then the Elizabeth fire department put out the fires. The US Customs Service sent about five large buses with customs officers, and the detainees were loaded up and taken to a detention center in South Jersey. Detail completed about 5 A.M.

Of course, I took some heat from our office in division headquarters, but I feel that "mutual aid" was essential in assisting other law enforcement agencies with a problem they might have. I could never find out why the Elizabeth police did not respond.

After this, I met with my operations lieutenant at the INS (Immigration and Naturalization) office in Newark. The head of the INS thanked us for our help and even offered us a job at the INS Detention Center, and we both declined. But it was nice that the State Police got an "atta boy" from the INS.

In the spring of 1999, the superintendent, COL Carl Williams, retired. After a search by the state, Governor Christine Whitman appointed Carson Dunbar as the new Superintendent of the State Police. COL Dunbar was a trooper in the 1970s for about four years, then left to join the FBI. He retired from the FBI to run the State Police. I first met COL Dunbar at a staff meeting. He seemed very articulate and savvy. Of course, he should have been since he was an FBI agent for twenty years.

The first incident I had with the new colonel was at a plane crash in Hasbrouck Heights, where a small plane with four aboard crashed into a private backyard killing all four people on board. The aircraft was en route to Teterboro Airport. I was returning from a meeting at Division, so I had about thirty troopers sent to the crash site via radio. When I arrived, COL Dunbar was already there. There were also about twenty-five or so local and county police there.

COL Dunbar asked, "What are all these locals doing here?"

I responded, "This is the State of Bergen. They think they own everything in the county."

He told me, "Get them out of here!"

I went to the county police chief, whom I knew, and told him, "Please take your men and leave."

He was a little upset and asked why.

I told him, "The State Police superintendent and I say so."

The chief and his men left, and the State Police handled the accident. It made me proud to make the "State of Bergen" police leave.

A couple of weeks later, COL Dunbar called me up. He said he wouldn't promote me because I had less than a year to go. But he wanted me to tell him if he was doing something wrong because he had too many "yes" men on his staff.

So I said, "OK."

The next thing I knew, he disbanded the advisory boards. The advisory boards comprised six captains on each of two advisory boards, and we would read internal investigations that had some discipline. We would meet once a month to discuss the cases and recommend punishment to the superintendent.

COL Dunbar offered he would handle all the discipline himself.

I called him up and told him he was making a big mistake and that he had a large division to run and didn't need to put so much time into discipline.

He was adamant with his answer.

So now, he made an enemy with the troopers' bargaining agent, the STFA. COL Dunbar almost eliminated the reprimand system and used the summary disciplinary hearing to get more time off for violating rules and regulations.

When Governor Jim Mc Greevey took office, the STFA went to this new administration and wanted COL Dunbar removed from being the superintendent. This was done, and COL Dunbar was relieved of his job as Superintendent of the State Police. There were probably other reasons why he was removed, like politics. This happens when a new governor takes office.

As I neared retirement, I called my new boss, Major Lee Cartwright. I asked him if my deputy, Lt. Dennis Zilinski, would take over Troop B when I left on April 1, 2000.

The major said that it looked that way.

So I started turning over the Troop to him as I did my last two months of duty.

He did an excellent job even though I was around. He didn't need my help.

I had my retirement party at the end of March 2000 on a Friday at 1 P.M. I pushed for retirement parties on Fridays at 1 P.M. for my troopers, so I would not want to be any different. I had my retirement party at a large restaurant on US-46 in Morris County. There were about two hundred people there, including my boss, Major Lee Cartwright, Retired LTC Lanny Roberson, and active LTC Vincent Modarelli, a close friend of mine. I was his coach at Somerville Station when he graduated from the academy.

After thrity-three years in the State Police, it was time. I had a great run.

I want to mention something about Troop A. Troop A in South Jersey was probably the premier troop. When I arrived in Troop B in 1968, except for an eighteen-month tour on the Parkway, until 1988, only two Troop B troopers were made troop commander. They were Captain Ray Marella and Captain Peter Hausch. All the other troop commanders were from Troop A and a couple from Troop C. That was over twenty years. Captain Hausch retired in 1991, and we had south Jersey commanders for another four years until I came along in 1995. Most of the division headquarters was loaded with south Jersey troopers and some from Troop C. The least naturally was from Troop B. A term I heard many years ago was that Troop B was the "Bastard Troop." To this day, most troopers running the State Police are from Troop A or Troop C.

For all of you road troopers and road sergeants that are still active, you never know how far you will go up the ladder on promotions. Of the 1800 Troopers assigned to Field Operations Section, someone has to make troop commander, which now holds the rank of major. At my first station, I thought retiring as a station commander would be nice. Back then, a station commander was an SFC but now a lieutenant. Some of you will leave the road and become a detective or a specialist, which is fine if that's what you want. But most of you will stay on the road. To me, the road was the best job in the State Police. So if you stay on the road, do the best you can, and with some luck, you can be a troop commander like I was.

14

LIFE AFTER THE STATE POLICE

After retiring on April 1, 2000, I decided not to work for a while and just play golf and travel. So I started playing golf four to five times a week or practicing. I also traveled with my wife. We already owned a condominium in Fort Myers, Florida, right on the Gulf. At first, the golf was good. I got my handicap down to about eleven. But golfers know that if you are an eleven, you want to be a ten or nine.

Finally, in August 2000, golf was turning into a job. I then got a phone call from retired Lt. John Pallotta, who I worked for at Somerville Station when he was a sergeant. He wanted to know if I was interested in working as a private detective for the security firm where he worked. I was ready; golf was not enough.

The company didn't have a private detective unit yet. John Pallotta was more of a salesman of guard services. I set up the service and built up a customer base. I only had to take care of myself and not the 350 troopers when I was Troop B commander.

I enjoyed the cases I handled. Insurance fraud, alimony, and divorce cases kept me busy. If I needed someone to help me on a two-man job, I used retired Sergeant Bob Higgins, who had his own license. Bob and I worked well together. We had worked together as troopers at Washington Station in the 1970s.

The only case I would like to mention occurred near the end of my career as a private detective. The case was an alimony case. My client had been paying $4,100 per month in alimony since he was divorced in 1992. In the superior court in Morris County, I could prove that my client's ex-wife was cohabitating with her male friend. Naturally, I used many days of surveillance and other means. After I testified, the superior court judge ended the alimony payments. As I still sat on the witness stand, the judge turned to me and put out his hand, which I took to shake, and he said, "Mr. Maggio, thank you for your testimony."

In all the court appearances I have made, municipal, superior, civil, and juvenile court, I have never had a judge shake my hand after I testified.

I sent my client my bill, which was about $2,000. He then invited my wife and me out to dinner.

At dinner, he told me his attorney's fee was close to $60,000, and I did most of the work (I guess I should have been an attorney).

After twelve years, in 2012, I retired from being a private detective and ultimately retired from working. I was sixty-seven years old.

Golf courses, here I come.

In 2003 John Pallotta, a past president of the New Jersey Former Troopers Association (FTA), asked me if I might be interested in becoming a director of the FTA. I was already a member joining when I retired in 2000. So he took me to a meeting of the board of directors of the FTA, and I was made a director and eventually elected to that position. The president when I became a director was Bill Townsend. He asked me if I knew anything about scholarships, and I told him that I was on the Passaic County 200 Club Scholarship Committee when I was active and now run the Warren County 200 Club Scholarship Committee. So I started getting together a scholarship committee for the FTA and our new president, George Coyle. We started giving ten $500 scholarships a year, and now it's up to twenty-five with some additional private scholarships. I was vice president under President Bill Yodice from 2010 through 2011. I became president from 2012 through 2017. As president, with my vice president, retired Captain Nick Soranno, and the board of directors, we developed the Former Troopers Heritage Foundation, a 501C-3 IRS tax-exempt foundation. Retired Captain Nick Soranno became the President of the FTA from 2018 through 2021, during which he and his vice president, retired Lt. George Wren, developed and completed the columbarium for the burial of ashes of former troopers and their spouses. George Wren took over as president on January 1, 2022. I retired as an active past president of the FTA on December 31, 2021. Retired Captain Nick Soranno was now chairman of the New Jersey Troopers Heritage Foundation.

The FTA is an excellent organization for retired troopers. Of course, not all former troopers join the FTA when they retire. Some wait a while before they join; others never join either because they left the State Police bitter for some reason or they don't want to continue with any part of the State Police. The FTA offers members a website with important information. There are two open meetings every year when after the superintendent or his designee speaks, we all go out to lunch, and the FTA pays the bill. The FTA also runs a great picnic every summer, which the FTA highly subsidizes. The FTA also offers college scholarships through the FTA Heritage Foundation to its members for children and grandchildren.

When I was president of the FTA, I was asked to address the State Police graduating class on Wednesday before they graduated on Friday. Then-superintendent COL Rick Fuentes had asked me. With me to speak to the recruits was retired Major Joseph Craparotta, an FTA director. When he was younger, Joe was a narcotics detective and spoke about the trials and tribulations of working undercover in narcotics. I talked about safety and "change" in that they will see a lot of change during their careers. I also spoke about cameras, dashboard cameras, body cameras with audio, and the public use of cameras. You have to be very careful today working in law enforcement. If you don't change with the times, you will break. I hope they realize this during their careers.

Other than playing golf, my wife and I travel a lot. We have been to Europe five times, including three riverboat trips. The riverboat trips are the best, with only about 150 passengers, and you are treated like royalty. Due to the pandemic, the riverboat company canceled our last one, scheduled for September 2021. We have been to Alaska and Hawaii twice and out west to Yellowstone and other National Parks. As the pandemic subsides, we will start traveling out of the country again. We also visit Florida twice yearly and have been doing Florida since 1989. We love visiting Florida, but I could never live there full-time; I will always be a Jersey guy.

EPILOGUE

CHANGE: The definition of change was when used as a verb, make or become different or take or use another instead of. When used as a noun, the act or instance of making or becoming different as coins as opposed to paper money. I like the definition "make or become different."

Some of the changes in benefits and pay I experienced during my career were definitely under the definition of "make or become different." Starting with salary. When I graduated from the State Police Academy on May 5, 1967, I started making about $7,200 per year. This was approximately $2,000 per year less than my last employment. But I was single and still living at home with mom and pop. There was no paid overtime; if you were lucky, you got time back for overtime, hour for hour.

Regarding health care, it was only offered to the State employee and not the family; you had to pay for any other coverage. Around 1969 Governor Richard Hughes granted free health care to the families of State employees. This was a great benefit since healthcare costs have risen dramatically. The pension benefit also changed for the good. When I entered the State Police, I was told that I had to stay until I was fifty-five years old and that I would get a 50 percent pension upon retirement. Then came the changes that affected the local police, paid firemen, and the State Police. After twenty-five years, you would get a 60 percent pension, then over the years, it was raised to sixty-five percent, and if you did thirty years, you would get seventy percent. The State Police is the only

New Jersey police agency with a twenty-year program with a 50 percent pension but no medical insurance.

A lousy change for state employees was the passing of pension law chapter 78 in 2011. This law changed the health benefits for state employees who did not have twenty years of service by July 1, 2011. They now pay up to 35 percent of their health care costs, which for a trooper was about $900 per month for the family plan. This cost follows the employee into retirement. This law ended the COLA (cost of living adjustment) for the time being. Different groups of retired state employees are fighting to get the COLA back.

Another "great" change was when we negotiated for our first union or bargaining agent, the STFA. With this came excellent raises, thanks to STFA President Thomas Iskrzycki, which eventually led to the establishment of the NCO Association and the Superior Officers Association.

Of course, there were some changes I did not like. The main one was in 1976 when we went to the eight-hour day instead of living in the barracks. I thought back then that Troops A, B, and C should have stayed in the Barracks' life. You could always get an eight-hour job on the Turnpike, Parkway, Atlantic City Expressway, or division headquarters. I went along with this change and worked rotating eight-hour shifts until I was promoted to SFC. We were told that due to the new labor laws and negotiations with the STFA, we were destined to go to the eight-hour day. Now the road troopers work a twelve-hour day with rotating shifts.

Something new, Bitcoins. Definition – Digital money that allows for secure peer-to-peer transactions on the internet. This enables the transfer of funds without the involvement of a bank, government, or other institutions. Bitcoin was created in 2008. Bitcoin was a cryptocurrency or digital money. I don't know about you young people, but I will stick with the banks and stock market. No change for me.

I'm a traditional, moderate conservative who tends to resist change as I get older. Think about yourselves; as you get older, do you fight or accept change as it comes?

This book is dedicated to the many New Jersey troopers who served and continue to serve the New Jersey State Police "on the road" in the field operations section, both active and retired. The New Jersey State

Police, today in 2023, is one of the most professional police agencies in the country and probably in the world. It far out shadows the old State Police, which I was a part of early in my career. The road trooper is highly educated, well trained, and constantly kept abreast of the continuing changes in law enforcement, now using dashboard cameras, body cameras, and audio when dealing with the public. My hat is off to the active road troopers of today, the best of the best.

As you have seen during my career as a supervisor, great leaders don't always follow the rules, whether squad sergeant or troop commander. Sometimes great leaders lead with their hearts.

ABOUT THE AUTHOR

SAL MAGGIO is a retired New Jersey State Police Captain and Troop "B" Commander. Troop "B" had eight stations in northern New Jersey with about 350 men and women assigned. He attended Fairleigh Dickinson University, graduated from Mercer County Community College, and has a level 6, Certified Public Management Certificate from Rutgers University. He worked as a private detective for a large security firm in Newark, New Jersey, for the next twelve years after retiring from the State Police. He spent the first nineteen years of his thirty-three-year State Police career as a road trooper and road sergeant. He was also a member of the board of directors of the New Jersey Former Troopers Association from 2003 to 2021 and it's President from 2012 to 2017. He lives in north west New Jersey with his wife Susan.

www.ingramcontent.com/pod-product-compliance
Lightning Source LLC
Chambersburg PA
CBHW031220090426
42740CB00038B/336